UP SOUTH

Stories, Studies, and Letters
of

African American Migrations

EDITED BY MALAIKA ADERO

The New Press   New York

Published in the United States by The New Press at CUNY,
New York
Distributed by W. W. Norton & Company, Inc.
500 Fifth Avenue, New York, NY 10110

Library of Congress Cataloging-in-Publication

Up South : stories, studies, and letters of this century's African
American migrations / edited by Malaika Adero.—1st ed.
p. cm.
Includes index.
ISBN 1-56584-168-9
1. Afro-Americans—Migrations—History—20th century.
2. Migration, Internal—United States—History—20th century.
3. Short stories, American—Afro-American authors. 4. Migration,
Internal—United States—Fiction. 5. American fiction—20th
century. I. Adero, Malaika.
E185.6.U8 1992
973′.0496073—dc20   92-53733
                                            CIP

Book design by John Morning

Established in 1990 as a major alternative to the large, commercial publishing houses, The New Press is intended to be the first full-scale nonprofit
American book publisher outside of the university presses. The Press is operated editorially in the public interest, rather than for private gain; it is
committed to publishing in innovative ways works of educational, cultural,
and community value that, despite their intellectual merits, might not nor-
mally be "commercially viable." The New Press's editorial offices are located at The City University of New York.

To my grandmothers, Eula Lee Crump and Ollie Blue,
who give me the strength for my journeys into the unknown.

ACKNOWLEDGMENT

I give thanks to all who supported my efforts to make this anthology happen: André Schiffrin, Diane Wachtell, Dawn Davis, and David Sternbach of The New Press; Howard Dodson and Sharon Howard of the Schomberg Center for Research in Black Culture; Debra Newman Ham, Ph.D., of the Library of Congress; Spencer R. Crew, curator of the wonderful exhibit *From Field to Factory,* and Marquette Folley-Regusters at the National Museum of American History, Smithsonian Institution; Barbara Summers, Joyce Dukes, Charles Harris, Irving Hamer, Dr. Robert Harris, and the Association for the Study of African American Life and History; Carole F. Hall, Paula Giddings, Ann Sandhorst, and the national offices of the National Urban League and the National Association for the Advancement of Colored People; John Morning, Marie Brown, Ted Byfield; the writers who contributed their work to this collection; and special thanks to the late John Oliver Killens, whose words of wisdom inspired the title *Up South.*

PERMISSIONS

Baldwin, George J., "The Migration: A Southern View," *Opportunity* magazine, June 1924.

Bethune, Mary Mcleod, "The Problems of the City Dweller," *Opportunity* magazine, February 1925.

Bontemps, Arna and Conroy, Jack, "The Exodus Train," from *They Seek A City* by Arna Bontemps and Jack Conroy. Copyright © 1945 by Arna Bontemps and Jack Conroy. Used by permission of Doubleday, a division of Bantam Doubleday Dell Publishing Group, Inc.

Ellison, Ralph, "Chapter Eight," from *The Invisible Man* by Ralph Ellison, pp. 124–130. Copyright © 1952 by Ralph Ellison. Reprinted by permission of Random House Inc.

Fleming, Robert, "The Ritual of Survival." Reprinted by permission of Robert Fleming.

Golden, Marita, "Naomi," from *Long Distance Life* by Marita Golden. Copyright © 1989 by Marita Golden. Used by permission of Doubleday, a division of Bantam Doubleday Dell Publishing Group, Inc.

Haynes, George E., "Negro Migration: Its Effect on Family and Community Life in the North," *Opportunity* magazine, October 1924.

Hill, Joseph A., "The Recent Northward Migration of the Negro," *Opportunity* magazine, April 1924.

Hill, T. Arnold, "Migration Again," *Opportunity* magazine, August 1932.

Holden, Arthur C., "A Northerner's View of the Negro Problem," *Opportunity* magazine, October 1929.

Hughes, Langston, "Bound No'th Blues," from *Selected Poems* by Langston Hughes. Copyright © 1927 by Alfred A. Knopf, Inc., and renewed 1955 by Langston Hughes. Reprinted by permission of the publisher.

Hughes, Langston, "One-Way Ticket," from *Selected Poems* by Langston Hughes. Copyright © 1948 by Langston Hughes. Reprinted by permission of Alfred A. Knopf, Inc.

Hurston, Zora Neale, "Backstage and the Railroad," from *Dust Tracks of a Road* by Zora Neale Hurston. Copyright © 1942 by Zora Neale Hurston. Copyright renewed 1970 by John C. Hurston. Reprinted by permission of HarperCollins Publishers.

Johnson, Charles S., "How Much Is the Migration a Flight from Persecution," *Opportunity* magazine, September 1923.

Johnson, Jacqueline Joan, "Rememory: What There Is for Us." Reprinted by permission by Jacqueline Joan Johnson.

Jones, Eugene Kinckle, "Negro Migration in New York State," *Opportunity* magazine, January 1926.

Latham, W. J., "Migration," Chicago *Defender,* August 26, 1916.

Otis, C., "Why They Come North," *Opportunity* magazine, October 1923.

Scott, Emmett J., "The Migration: A Northern View," *Opportunity* magazine, June 1924.

Shaw, Arthur G., "A Letter to the Editor," *New York Evening Globe,* 1916.

Simmons, Cynthia, "Going East." Reprinted by permission of Cynthia Simmons.

Travis, Hamilton, "A Letter to the Editor," *Newark Evening News,* November 24, 1916.

Wright, R. R., "Causes of the Migration from the Viewpoint of the Northern Negro," Chicago *Defender,* November 9, 1916.

Wright, Richard, Chapter One of *American Hunger* by Richard Wright. Copyright © 1944 by Richard Wright. Copyright © 1977 by Ellen Wright. Reprinted by permission of HarperCollins Publishers.

CONTENTS

PREFACE

The immigrants came from Europe but ultimately called themselves American, renaming themselves and the lands of the Cherokee, Chickasaw, Choctaw, Creek, and Seminole nations. They came with imperial visions and with captives—millions of men, women, and children—Africans who for generations to come would be enslaved.

Ellis Island, and indeed the United States of America itself, symbolizes mass immigration, and, for the immigrant, the promises of opportunity, entitlement, self-determination, and freedom. This promise was fulfilled for most Europeans but not for the early Africans, who had not chosen to live in America. Brought bound and chained in the hulls of ships to live as slaves, their circumstances were unique—and their descendants' circumstances remain so to the present day.

The agricultural economy of the South was built around the slave trade. So many hands were needed to keep the plantations and towns in the South running that, up until the Civil War, many areas including the Carolinas, Georgia, Tennessee, and Mississippi had more Blacks than Whites. Indeed, for decades after the slave trade ended, well into the twentieth century, roughly 90 percent of African Americans still lived in the South. Some people assumed that a mass exodus from the Confederacy would or did happen, but in fact, "Most (former slaves) stayed near if not on the land they had worked in bondage. It took the first generation born free to bring the exodus on," as Gilbert Osofsky wrote in *Harlem: The Making of a Ghetto*. Changed laws alone did not motivate Blacks to move to other regions of the country. Amiri Baraka, who also wrote about Blacks moving North, concluded that "a psychological shift . . . made Blacks go North," a shift he characterizes as "the discovery of America or its culture as would-be Americans." Now, as we approach the turn of another century, Blacks are settled in every state in the nation, with little more than half of all African Americans remaining in the South.

The subject of migration has personal meaning to most African Americans because so many of us have family who pulled up stakes in Tennessee, Georgia, South Carolina, and Mississippi—not to mention the West Indies—to resettle in New York, Philadelphia, Chicago, Kansas City, and St. Louis. Every Black family tree seems to have at least some branches reaching northward.

People often moved in stages—at first, from rural areas to cities in the South, and then on to the cities and towns of the North and the West. "Memphis developed a black community years before most Northern cities," wrote David M. Tucker in his book *Memphis Since Crump: Bossism, Blacks and Civic Reformers, 1948–1968.* "More than a hundred years ago the migration of rural Negroes made Memphis 40 percent black. It all began in the second year of the Civil War. . . ."

By the turn of the century, Ben Crump—my great grandfather and an African American—moved from Memphis, Tennessee, to Knoxville, where two of his sons were born. The youngest, Lavon, stayed and raised his family in Knoxville, but in 1920 the elder son, Kermit, at age sixteen headed for Cleveland and a factory job making airplanes. Kermit raised two children in the North while his brother raised thirteen children, supporting them with the same job as a cook in a state hospital that his father had held for fifty years. Lavon had steady work and many mouths to feed and said he "just never thought about going North." But millions of men and women of his race did. In fact, the Black exodus from the South, this country's largest internal migration ever, brought dramatic political and cultural change to the entire nation.

In the June 1924 issue of *Opportunity,* a publication of the Urban League, Charles S. Johnson summed up the primary causes of migration: the "desire for more wages and more regular wages, for better social treatment, improved cultural surroundings, the hysteria of a mass movement, simple curiosity and desire for travel and adventure, and free railroad tickets all have played their part in the divorcement of the southern Negro from the land of his birth."

Mississippi River floods in 1912 and 1913 and boll weevil epidemics at the turn of the century wiped out crops and left many workers unemployed. The combination of natural disasters that plagued farmlands and "unnatural disasters" such as lynchings contributed to the exodus "up south." Two world wars created a better job climate for Blacks in northern industry. As World War I stifled the immigration of European workers, industry actively recruited Blacks from the South. Each person or couple who left the South for an urban center in the Midwest or the Northeast paved the way for others, resulting in what historians call "link migration." One result was that many southern farms and factories were left without the workers necessary to keep them going. The enormous number of Blacks who answered the knock of opportunity meant the end of many southern Black communities.

Still, as Amiri Baraka wrote in *Blues People,* "not every Negro left the South to get a better job. Some left so they could find a greater degree of freedom, and some so they can walk the street after 10 P.M. (Many Southern towns had ordinances against 'night rambling negroes.') Some, like my father, left very suddenly after unfortunate altercations with white ushers in movies; some like my grandfather, to start a thriving business (having had two grocery stores and a funeral parlor burned out from under him in Alabama)."

Leaving the South wasn't necessarily easy, though: white southern society displayed a kind of possessiveness toward Blacks after slavery was abolished. Southern Whites didn't want their negroes to stay and live as equals, succeeding in life on their own terms, but nor did they want them to leave. As Stanley Lieberson wrote in *Black, White, and Southern,* "The etiquette of race evolved as a complicated set of rules and customs designed in part to 'place' individuals in a racial and class hierarchy that would retain its fixity regardless of the tensions and pressures swirling in and about the South. It bound whites together, though not equally and it relegated blacks to a permanent status of inferiority."

The resulting southern racial etiquette entailed—and perpetuated—great contradictions and ironies. For instance, a Black woman could prepare food for a White family but *never* could sit down at a table to dine with them. Black men were lynched or chased out of town for as much as looking "wrong" at a White woman but were relied upon to perform the most personal services for White men and women.

Yet Black people were also beaten and persecuted for quitting their jobs and trying to leave town. In 1879, General James Chalmers of Mississippi and a group of whites "threatened to sink all boats carrying Negroes"; as a result, fifteen hundred black people were stranded on the banks of the Mississippi River. The shipping companies had to be coerced by the federal government before they resumed services. During the 1880s and into the next century, eleven southern states passed laws to prohibit Black workers from moving and levied taxes on labor agents who recruited Black workers for northern industries. Some railroad stations refused to sell Blacks tickets to the North.

A great deal of speculation and blame were employed to account for the migration. Many people, White and Black, had a vested interest in damming the flood of Black folk giving up on the South, and they developed both crude and sophisticated ways to stem the tide. Rather than believe that Blacks were self-motivated to migrate, many southern whites charged that northerners were luring Blacks away from the South for partisan political reasons. Early in this century, most Blacks were Republican because that was the party of Abraham Lincoln; so Whites accused the Republicans among them of scheming to swell the ranks of their party's memberships and to influence politics in certain regions outside the deep South. At the other extreme, organizations such as Southern Negro Anti-Exodus Association of Virginia, founded in 1905, were created specifically to "preach a philosophy of contentment" to southern Blacks.

On the whole, southern Black society had much to gain and much to lose from the migration. It lost many young, energetic, talented people—churchmembers, students, teachers, crafts people, and artists. But those who remained saw a different and higher value placed on their skills and abilities. Employers in the South raised wages, sometimes even doubling them.

As Black migration became an economic, social, and political issue not just for Blacks and the South but for the nation as a whole, at least one resolution to study the "practicality" of the migration was proposed in Congress. The federal government was unwilling to take the issue on, though, and the measure died on the Senate floor.

There were vocal opponents to the migration among African Americans as well. Booker T. Washington, founder of the Tuskegee Institute, and his protégé, William James Edward (founder of the Snow Hill Institute), were among those Black leaders—preacher, politicians, businessmen—who encouraged Blacks to stay in the South, on the land. Washington built his institution and political agenda around his commitment to Black economic development, and he saw agriculture as key to this process of development. Williams and the Black Belt Improvement League urged people to "hold on the Black Belt. Develop an economic base. Proceed on the ground that was less treacherous, the economic rather than the political."

Many families shared these convictions and remained on their farms. At the same time, as Donald P. Stone writes in *Fallen Prince,* many other African Americans "boiled up out of this pot called the Black Belt and flowed into Northeastern and Midwestern industrial corridors. Coal, steel, rubber, auto and related industries captured them. . . . Without a doubt this migration weakened the conscious and material development of this Black Belt nation and underdeveloped it by removing its most valuable resource, its productive growth." However, staying on the land was made nearly impossible for some, since white supremacists harassed farm families with arson, vandalism, and murder.

Sixty-one Blacks were lynched in 1920, sixty-two in 1921, and so it went in the years before and after. Justice in law enforcement and in the courts was not the reality; it was not even an illusion. By the 1920s, more than four million whites had swelled the ranks of the Ku Klux Klan, and most of them lived and burned their crosses in the South. The North promised some relief from this racial terrorism, as well as jobs and lifestyles never available to southern rural Blacks. For many of them, the odds of economic growth in the South seemed meager in comparison to northern possibilities. Another factor was World War I, which brought not only economic opportunities for employment in the northern factories but on battlefields an opportunity for Black men to assert themselves as American citizens on the battlefields of Europe—raising the hope that when they returned home they would be treated as such.

This emphasis on job opportunities for black men is only one facet of the exodus, though. Jacqueline Jones, author of *Labor of Love, Labor of Sorrow,* has found that "the Great Migration . . . was frequently a family affair. Significantly black men mentioned the degraded status of their women folk as one of the prime incentives to migrate, along with low wages and poor educational opportunities for their children. Husbands told of sexual harassment of wives and daughters by white men and of other forms of indignities woven in the fabric of southern society." However, some women and men did come alone. Jones notes, "in general, demographic patterns of migration to different cities were determined by the nature of employment opportunities. Men almost invariably led the way North to cities like Pittsburgh and Detroit that offered industrial jobs for them but few positions outside domestic service for women. Chicago, with its more diversified female occupational structure, attracted single women and wives. . . ."

Black newspapers and magazines in general and the Chicago *Defender* in particular served as forums for Blacks to share information between the North, South, and West, as well as for airing the sentiments of those for and against migration.

"The Chicago *Defender* received thousands of letters out of the Deep South, as did the Chicago Urban League, the organization to which the paper usually referred prospective migrants inquiring about employment," write Arna Bontemps and Jack Conroy in *They Seek a City.* Many such letters were archived by Carter G. Woodson, who founded Negro History Week, which now is Black History Month. His papers are now preserved in the Library of Congress, and many of the letters are included here. The letters, editorials, and other written testimonials he collected reveal, in the words of James R. Grossman, author of *Land of Hope,* the view of migration as "an opportunity to share—as black people—the perquisites of American citizenship. What [the migrants] would eventually learn was that access defined as mere entry was not enough. Jobs did not mean promotions or economic power; votes and patronage implied neither political power nor even legitimacy as civic actors; seats in classrooms did not set their children on the road toward better jobs or places of respect in the city."

The northern, midwestern, and western cities where African Americans resettled were distinctly different from the South in many ways, but not necessarily where racial attitudes were concerned. They held forth a new cosmopolitan flavor, but with it came tradeoffs that mixed bitter in with the sweet. Many Blacks traded the gentility of the rural lifestyle for an urban one foreign in ways they had not imagined. Clifton Taulbert's memoir, *The Last Train North,* tells of one young Black man's transition from Glen Allen, Mississippi, to St. Louis. "There were no Chinaberry trees, no pecan trees. The sound of Mama's and Ma Ponks' voices could not find their way through the maze of buildings that separated us. Never again would I pick dew berries or hear the familiar laughter from the field truck. This was my world now, this strange new family and their cramped quarters over the tiny grocery store they grandly called the 'confectionery.' I had grown up and gone north, all in one day."

His "strange new family" were blood kin, but the way they went about their life at work and at home seemed foreign. There was less time and space to be friendly in a cold and crowded city. Sharing within and between families meant something different when people no longer lived off the land, instead exchanging money for food and shelter.

Although the composition of many black households changed with the migration, families did, in large part, remain intact—albeit with increasingly fractured family structures as the decades of northern urban living passed. In the first part of the century, husbands and fathers were as likely to be present as they were in the South. "Nine of ten adult women did not head either households and subfamilies," writes Herbert Gutman about early twentieth-century New York City. "Young black women heading households and subfamilies were far less important in New York City in 1905 than in Richmond [Virginia] in 1880. One of every eleven Richmond women aged twenty to twenty-nine led such a household. . . . In New York City in 1905, the proportion was one of every twenty-five similarly aged women."

Internal Black migration had a profound impact on the larger development of American culture. Such a massive movement raised pointed questions about issues as diverse as family unity, community development, electoral and grass-roots politics, and racism, among many others. It has been the subject of sociological and historical research, poems, songs, and art. And, from a historical standpoint, the subject is far from exhausted. There is still a great deal of misunderstanding, myth accepted as fact, between the South and the rest of the country—despite the fact that over the past few decades many African Americans have also been lured back to the South. Journalist Nicholas Lemann, author of *The Promised Land,* and memoirist and social scientist Dr. James P. Comer, author of *Maggie's American Dream,* are among the writers who help renew our memory.

In 1987 the Smithsonian Institution mounted an exhibit called *From Field to Factory: Afro-American Migration 1915–1940,* a moving reminder of the impact and significance of this uprooting process. It inspired me to dig deeper into an aspect of my family and community's life which I had taken for granted. As I researched *Up South,* family members such as Ben Crump became more than names in a family Bible, and I came to see their great leap from plantation slavery to modern urban life in more detail and with a new understanding.

"Problems with substandard housing, unfair employment practices, and social inequality persisted, creating an underlying sense of frustration and anger," writes Spencer R. Crew about the North in the exhibit catalog for *From Field to Factory.* "The frustrations fueled the civil rights activities and the urban rebellions of the '50s, '60s, and '70s. Building on the tactics of their predecessors, the new migrants joined with black northern residents and used boycotts, marches, litigation, and the vote to force changes in American society . . . the Afro-American community and the configuration of present-day American cities was directly influenced by the generation of Afro-Americans who moved north during the Great Migration. Their presence fundamentally changed American society."

"The Great Migration" is the label often applied to the first wave of mass movement between 1915 and 1940. The Chicago *Defender* even appointed a day—May 15, 1917—when a great "northern drive" would commence. But the phenomenon of migration began before 1915 and continued until Black America became largely urban America in the 1960s. No individual or group could claim to be its architect. It was truly a grass-roots effort that gave rise to an eclectic mix of voices, memories, and opinions of the famous, undiscovered, and anonymous, many of whom are represented in this anthology.

By and large, the voices in *Up South* echo from the past but give a new perspective on past problems of ethnicity and class, problems that linger on. It is the work not of an academician but of a lay scholar and African American who collects documents of the African American experience in order to deepen her level of understanding of how the experience is unique and what its uniqueness means.

Malaika Adero
New York, 1993

BOUND NO'TH BLUES

Goin' down de road, Lord,
Goin' down de road.
Down de road, Lord,
Way, way down de road.
Got to find somebody
To help me carry this load.
Road's in front o' me,
Nothin' to do but walk.
Road's in front o' me,
Walk . . . and walk . . . and walk.
I'd like to meet a good friend
To come along an' talk.
Road, road, road, O!
Road, road . . . road . . . road, road!
Road, road, road, O!
On de No'thern road.
These Mississippi towns ain't
Fit for a hoppin' toad.

Langston Hughes

This letter to the editor and other writings that follow express the thoughts and feelings that blacks had about the exodus from the South, why it escalated to a mass movement, and what it meant for blacks who did or did not migrate. These letters are published in their original form; no changes have been made as to style or grammar.

On "Causes of Migration"

To the Editor of the Evening Post:

Sir: The cause is complex and many-angles, not simple and categorical. Perhaps the greatest element of all is the Jim Crow car. It is worse than lynching; lynching occasionally kills one man; the Jim Crow Car perpetually tortures ten thousand.

I am writing on board a Jim Crow car from Little Rock, Ark. toward St. Louis, Mo.—a horrible night ride. The colored women have one end of a smoker, separated from smoking white men by a partition that rises only part of the way from the floor toward the ceiling of the car. All of the smoke and fumes, and some of the oaths, come over. Some of these colored people have already spent two nights in this same car-end, coming all the way from the lower side of Texas. For them the name of the train must sound very much like irony; it is the "The Sunshine Special."

Just behind us is a chair car for white people. They have paid exactly the same "first class" fares paid by these colored passengers. But in the Jim Crow car there are only straight-backed seats filled with the dust and grime of neglect. All of these colored people are wishing, and some of them giving audible expression to the wish, to reach Popular Bluff, the first stop in Missouri, so that they can go back into that chair car and out of the squalor and discomfort of this car-end. And some of these colored men are in the service of the United States, summoned from the far corners of Texas to Newport News, Va. to be trained to fight for democracy in Europe; and because they travel practically all of the way through southern territory they must sit up for three nights and days, without change of clothing or a bite of warm food—certainly a good preparation for trench warfare.

Then "Why does the negro leave the South?" indeed? You would feel a large part of the answer if you could be on this train, in this Jim Crow car, and share for one night the longing of the people to reach the line that divides Missouri from Arkansas, or any other part of "the line" that separates Dixie from the rest of creation!

William Pickens,
Morgan College
Baltimore, Maryland

DALLAS EXPRESS,   August 11, 1917

The strangest thing, the real mystery about the exodus, is that in all the southland there has not been a single meeting or promoter to start the migration. Just simultaneously all over the South about a year ago, the Negro began to cross the Mason and Dixon line. Indeed, this is a most striking case where the Negro has been doing a great deal more thinking than talking, knowing he is not give the freedom of speech. Who knows, then, what the providence of God is in this exodus. This exodus is not by any means confined to the worthless or the ignorant Negro. A large per cent of the young Negroes in this exodus are rather intelligent. Many of the business houses in Houston, Dallas, Galveston where the exodus is greatest in Texas, have lost some of their best colored help. Sanger Bros. has lost a dozen or more of its colored employees.

To tell the truth more fully, the Negroes generally throughout the South are dissatisfied with conditions and they have been for several years and there are just reasons why they should be. Every Negro newspaper and publication in this broad land, including pamphlets and books and the intelligent Negro pastor with backbone and courage are constantly protesting against the injustices done the Negro. And possibly these agents have been the greatest incentives to help create and crystallize this unrest and migration. Let it be rightly understood, however, that the Negro is quite mindful of and shows proper appreciation for every good done him by the opposite race, and that he is equally sensitive of the multiplicity of wrongs. It was never intended by the redeemers and sages of the world that one good act should be followed by one or a score of wrongs. To the contrary, as line of type, the one good act should live to another good act to infinity. And in every instance where it is a spirit of retaliation by the white aggravated by an offense or crime committed by the Negro the retaliation is vastly more brutal and far reaching in effect than the offense or crime committed by the Negro.

Too often, merely an attempt by a Negro to protect himself or to resist any discourtesy or injustice perpetrated by the whites, ex-

*cites the most atrocious crimes against him. Turn, now, from acts
of offense and crime to acts of respect and honor and good will and
the scales still show to the reverse the same inequality of weights.
That is, for every ninety nine acts of courtesy, respect and honor,
with which the Negro greets the white man, the white man shows
the Negro but one of these acts. But the Negro would prefer to remain in the South. There are undeveloped resources down here,
mills and factories are yet to be built. The geographical division is
more inviting to him than the North. And the Negro's motives for
migrating North are but natural and they are similar to those
which incite the foreigner to immigrate to America—the Negro is
simply seeking to better his condition.*

*If a baby is yelling, you can quiet him better by giving him
what he wants. The boy who is kindly treated will hardly wander
from home. A French man is seldom ever seen outside of France,
because his environments are more attractive to him than those of
the outside world. Like the Belgians' and the Russians' plea, the
Negro is pleading to the South and the American people for justice
and a square deal. Therefore let this country, the South in particular, reform its customs, practices and habits of race prejudice and
give the Negro a square deal and conform the Christian religion in
its dealings with the Negro. Let the white Christian extend to his
brother black Christian a warm, fellowship handshake, good will
and justice, remembering that God has no respect to person. Let
the white pulpit and the white press and periodicals take the initiative and fearless stand in denouncing all forms of race discrimi-
nations which are not in keeping with true culture and
Christianity. And no one but the inferior man will deny, in sum-
ming up the requisites which make a superior man or a superior
race, that courtesy, politeness, unselfishness and sympathy cannot
be left out; but they must be so regarded as the very rock bottom
upon which superiority and the Christian religion are based.*

*Many of the Negroes who are betaking their abode to the North
and the East immediately assimilate their new conditions and de-
mean themselves as good citizens such that will reflect creditably
upon the great mass of Negroes who will indefinitely remain in the
South. Too, many sentiments as a result of this exodus and the
world wide war culminate in an America that will help the Negro
to work out his destiny. No one has experienced more sharply the
pangs of American prejudice than I have. And my experience is the
common experience of all men who possess the tiniest drop of Negro blood. However, I am not inclined to become discouraged. In
the words of the poet:*

"Be strong,
We are not here to play, to dream, to drift. We have hard work to
do and loads to lift. Shun not the struggle—face it; 'tis God's gift.
Be strong.

It matters not how deep entrenched the wrong, how hard the
battle goes; the day how long; on, to-morrow come the song.

A Century of Negro Migration

THE EXODUS DURING THE WORLD WAR

Carter G. Woodson

Within the last two years there has been a steady stream of Negroes into the North in such large numbers as to overshadow in its results all other movements of the kind in the United States. These Negroes have come largely from Alabama, Tennessee, Florida, Georgia, Virginia, North Carolina, Kentucky, South Carolina, Arkansas and Mississippi. The given causes of this migration are numerous and complicated. Some untruths centering around this exodus have not been unlike those of other migrations. Again we hear that the Negroes are being brought North to fight organized labor, and to carry doubtful States for the Republicans. These numerous explanations themselves, however, give rise to doubt as to the fundamental cause.

Why then should the Negroes leave the South? It has often been spoken of as the best place for them. There, it is said, they have made unusual strides forward. The progress of the Negroes in the South, however, has in no sense been general, although the land owned by Negroes in the country and the property of thrifty persons of their race in urban communities may be extensive. In most parts of the South the Negroes are still unable to become landowners or successful business men. Conditions and customs have reserved these spheres for the whites. Generally speaking, the Negroes are still dependent on the white people for food and shelter. Although not exactly slaves, they are yet attached to the white people as tenants, servants or dependents. Accepting this as their lot, they have been content to wear their lord's cast-off clothing, and live in his ramshackled barn or cellar. In this unhappy state so many have settled down, losing all ambition to attain a higher station. The world has gone on but in their sequestered sphere progress has passed them by.

What then is the cause? There have been *bulldozing*, terrorism, maltreatment and what not of persecution; but the Negroes have not in large numbers wandered away from the land of their birth. What the migrants themselves think about it, goes to the very heart of the trouble. Some say that they left the South on account of injustice in the courts, unrest, lack of privileges, denial of the right to vote, bad treatment, oppression, segregation or lynching. Others say that they left to find employment, to secure better wages, better school facilities, and better opportunities to toil upward. Southern white newspapers unaccustomed to give the Negroes any mention but that of criminals have said that the Negroes are going North because they have not had a fair chance in the South and that if they are to be retained there, the attitude of the whites toward them must be changed. Professor William O. Scroggs, of Louisiana State University, considers as causes of this exodus "the relatively low wages paid farm labor, an unsatisfactory tenant or cropsharing system, the boll weevil, the crop failure of 1916, lynching, disfranchisement, segregation, poor schools, and the monotony, isolation and drudgery of farm life" [*American Journal of Political Economy* 30, p. 1040]. Professor Scroggs, however, is wrong in thinking that the persecution of the blacks has little to do with the migration for the reason that during these years when the treatment of the Negroes is decidedly better they are leaving the South. This does not mean that they would not have left before, if they had had economic opportunities in the North. It is highly probable that the Negroes would not be leaving the South today, if they were treated as men, although there might be numerous opportunities for economic improvement in the North.

The immediate cause of this movement was the suffering due to the floods aggravated by the depredations of the boll weevil. Although generally mindful of our welfare, the United States Government has not been as ready to build levees against a natural enemy to property as it has been to provide fortifications for warfare. It has been necessary for local communities and State governments to tax themselves to maintain them. The national government, however, has appropriated to the purpose of facilitating inland navigation certain sums which have been used in doing this work, especially in the Mississippi Valley. There are now 1,538 miles of levees on both sides of the Mississippi from Cape Girardeau to the passes. These levees, of course, are still inadequate to the security of the planters against these inundations. Carrying 406 million tons of mud a year, the river becomes a dangerous stream subject to change, abandoning its old bed to cut for itself a new channel, transferring property from one State to another, isolating cities and leaving once useful levees marooned in the landscape like old Indian mounds or overgrown intrenchments.

This valley has, therefore, been frequently visited with disasters which have often set the population in motion. The first disastrous floods came in 1858 and 1859, breaking many of the levees, the destruction of which was practically completed by the floods of 1865 and 1869. There is an annual rise in the stream, but since 1874 this river system has fourteen times devastated large areas of this section with destructive floods. The property in this district depreciated in value to the extent of about 400 millions in ten years. Farmers from this section, therefore, have at times moved west with foreigners to take up public lands.

The other disturbing factor in this situation was the boll weevil, an interloper from Mexico in 1892. The boll weevil is an insect about one fourth of an inch in length, varying from one eighth to one third of an inch with a breadth of about one third of the length. When it first emerges it is yellowish, then becomes grayish brown and finally assumes a black shade. It breeds on no other plant than cotton and feeds on the boll. This little animal, at first attacked the cotton crop in Texas. It was not thought that it would extend its work into the heart of the South so as to become of national consequence, but it has, at the rate of forty to one hundred sixty miles annually, invaded all of the cotton district except that of the Carolinas and Virginia. The damage it does, varies according to the rainfall and the harshness of the winter, increasing with the former and decreasing with the latter. At times the damage has been to the extent of a loss of 50 per cent. of the crop, estimated at 400,000 bales of cotton annually, about 4,500,000 bales since the invasion or $250,000,000 worth of cotton. The output of the South being thus cut off, the planter has less income to provide supplies for his black tenants and, the prospects for future production being dark, merchants accustomed to give them credit have to refuse. This, of course, means financial depression, for the South is a borrowing section and any limitation to credit there blocks the wheels of industry. It was fortunate for the Negro laborers in this district that there was then a demand for labor in the North when this condition began to obtain.

This demand was made possible by the cutting off of European immigration by the World War, which thereby rendered this hitherto uncongenial section an inviting field for the Negro. The Negroes have made some progress in the North during the last fifty years, but despite their achievements they have been so handicapped by race prejudice and proscribed by trades unions that the uplift of the race by economic methods has been impossible. The European immigrants have hitherto excluded the Negroes even from the menial positions. In the midst of the drudgery left for them, the blacks have often heretofore been debased to the status of dependents and paupers. Scattered through the North too in such small numbers, they have been unable to unite for social betterment and mutual improvement and naturally too weak to force the community to respect their wishes as could be done by a large group with some political or economic power. At present, however, Negro laborers, who once went from city to city, seeking such employment as trades unions left to them, can work even as skilled laborers throughout the North. Women of color formerly excluded from domestic service by foreign maids are now in demand. Many mills and factories which Negroes were prohibited from entering a few years ago are now bidding for their labor. Railroads cannot find help to keep their property in repair, contractors fall short of their plans for failure to hold mechanics drawn into the industrial boom and the United States Government has had to advertise for men to hasten the preparation for war.

Men from afar went south to tell the Negroes of a way of escape to a more congenial place. Blacks long since unaccustomed to venture a few miles from home, at once had visions of a promised land just a few hundred miles away. Some were told of the chance to amass fabulous riches, some of the opportunities for education and some of the hospitality of the places of amusement and recreation in the North. The migrants then were soon on the way. Railway stations became conspicuous with the presence of Negro tourists, and the trains were crowded to full capacity and the streets of northern cities were soon congested with black laborers seeking to realize their dreams in the land of unusual opportunity.

Employment agencies, recently multiplied to meet the demand for labor, find themselves unable to cope with the situation and agents sent into the South to induce the blacks by offers of free transportation and high wages to go north, have found it impossible to supply the demand in centers where once toiled the Poles, Italians and the Greeks formerly preferred to the Negroes. In other words, the present migration differs from others in that the Negro has opportunity awaiting him in the North whereas formerly it was necessary for him to make a place for himself upon arriving among enemies. The proportion of those returning to the South, therefore, will be inconsiderable.

Becoming alarmed at the immensity of this movement the South has undertaken to check it. To frighten Negroes from the North southern newspapers are carefully circulating reports that many of them are returning to their native land because of unexpected hardships. But having failed in this, southerners have compelled employment agents to cease operations there, arrested suspected employers and, to prevent the departure of the Negroes, imprisoned on false charges those who appear at stations to leave for the North. This procedure could not long be effective, for by the more legal and clandestine methods of railway passenger agents the work has gone forward. Some southern communities have, therefore, advocated drastic legislation against labor agents, as was suggested in Louisiana in 1914, when by operation of the Underwood Tariff Law the Negroes thrown out of employment in the sugar district migrated to the cotton plantations.

One should not, however, get the impression that the majority of the Negroes are leaving the South. Eager as these Negroes seem to go, there is no unanimity of opinion as to whether migration is the best policy. The sycophant, toady class of Negroes naturally advise the blacks to remain in the South to serve their white neighbors. The radical protagonists of the equal-rights-for-all element urge them to come North by all means. Then there are the thinking Negroes, who are still further divided. Both divisions of this element have the interests of the race at heart, but they are unable to agree as to exactly what the blacks should now do. Thinking that the present war will soon be over and that consequently the immigration of foreigners into this country will again set in and force out of employment thousands of Negroes who have migrated to the North, some of the most representative Negroes are advising their fellows to remain where they are. The most serious objection to this transplantation is that it means for the Negroes a loss of land, the rapid acquisition of which has long been pointed to as the best evidence of the ability of the blacks to rise in the economic world. So many Negroes who have by dint of energy purchased small farms yielding an increasing income from year to year, are now disposing of them at nominal prices to come north to work for wages. Looking beyond the war, however, and thinking too that the depopulation of Europe during this upheaval will render immigration from that quarter for some years an impossibility, other thinkers urge the Negroes to continue the migration to the North, where the race may be found in sufficiently large numbers to wield economic and political power.

Great as is the dearth of labor in the South, moreover, the Negro exodus has not as yet caused such a depression as to unite the whites in inducing the blacks to remain in that section. In the first place, the South has not yet felt the worst effects of this economic upheaval as that part of the country has been unusually aided by the millions which the United States Government is daily spending there. Furthermore, the poor whites are anxious to see the exodus of their competitors in the field of labor. This leaves the capitalists at their mercy, and in keeping with their domineering attitude, they will be able to handle the labor situation as they desire. As an evidence of this fact we need but note the continuation of mob rule and lynching in the South despite the preachings against it of the organs of thought which heretofore winked at it. This terrorism has gone to an unexpected extent. Negro farmers have been threatened with bodily injury, unless they leave certain parts.

The southerner of aristocratic bearing will say that only the shiftless poor whites terrorize the Negroes. This may be so, but the truth offers little consolation when we observe that most white people in the South are of this class; and the tendency of this element to put their children to work before they secure much education does not indicate that the South will soon experience that general enlightenment necessary to exterminate these survivals of barbarism. Unless the upper classes of the whites can bring the mob around to their way of thinking that the persecution of the Negro is prejudicial to the interests of all, it is not likely that mob rule will soon cease and the migration to this extent will be promoted rather than retarded.

It is unfortunate for the South that the growing consciousness of the Negroes has culminated at the very time they are most needed. Finally heeding the advice of agricultural experts to reconstruct its agricultural system, the South has learned in the school of bitter experience to depart from the plan of producing the single cotton crop. It is now raising food-stuffs to make that section self-supporting without reducing the usual output of cotton. With the increasing production in the South, therefore, more labor is needed just at the very time it is being drawn to centers in the North. The North being an industrial and commercial section has usually attracted the immigrants, who will never fit into the economic situation in the South because they will not accept the treatment given Negroes. The South, therefore, is now losing the only labor which it can ever use under present conditions.

Where these Negroes are going is still more interesting. The exodus to the west was mainly directed to Kansas and neighboring States, the migration to the Southwest centered in Oklahoma and Texas, pioneering Negro laborers drifted into the industrial district of the Appalachian highland during the [eighteen] eighties and nineties and the infiltration of the discontented talented tenth affected largely the cities of the North. But now we are told that at the very time the mining districts of the North and West are being filled with blacks the western planters are supplying their farms with them and that into some cities have gone sufficient skilled and unskilled Negro workers to increase the black population more than one hundred per cent. Places in the North, where the black population has not only not increased but even decreased in recent years, are now receiving a steady influx of Negroes. In fact, this is a nation-wide migration affecting all parts and all conditions.

Students of social problems are now wondering whether the Negro can be adjusted in the North. Many perplexing problems must arise. This movement will produce results not unlike those already mentioned in the discussion of other migrations, some of which we have evidence of today. There will be an increase in race prejudice leading in some communities to actual outbreaks as in Chester [Pennsylvania] and Youngstown [Ohio] and probably to massacres like that of East St. Louis [Illinois], in which participated not only wellknown citizens but the local officers and the State militia. The Negroes in the North are in competition with white men who consider them not only strike breakers but a sort of inferior individuals unworthy of the consideration which white men deserve. And this condition obtains even where Negroes have been admitted to the trades unions.

Negroes in seeking new homes in the North, moreover, invade residential districts hitherto exclusively white. There they encounter prejudice and persecution until most whites thus disturbed move out determined to do whatever they can to prevent their race from suffering from further depreciation of property and the disturbance of their community life. Lawlessness has followed, showing that violence may under certain conditions develop among some classes anywhere rather than reserve itself for vigilance committees of primitive communities. It has brought out too another aspect of lawlessness in that it breaks out in the North where the numbers of Negroes are still too small to serve as an excuse for the terrorism and lynching considered necessary in the South to keep the Negroes down.

The maltreatment of the Negroes will be nationalized by this exodus. The poor whites of both sections will strike at this race long stigmatized by servitude but now demanding economic equality. Race prejudice, the fatal weakness of the Americans, will not so soon abate although there will be advocates of fraternity, equality and liberty required to reconstruct our government and rebuild our civilization in conformity with the demands of modern efficiency by placing every man regardless of his color wherever he may do the greatest good for the greatest number.

The Negroes, however, are doubtless going to the North in sufficiently large numbers to make themselves felt. If this migration falls short of establishing in that section Negro colonies large enough to wield economic and political power, their state in the end will not be any better than that of the Negroes already there. It is to these large numbers alone that we must look for an agent to counteract the development of race feeling into riots. In large numbers the blacks will be able to strike for better wages or concessions due a rising laboring class and they will have enough votes to defeat for reelection those officers who wink at mob violence or treat Negroes as persons beyond the pale of the law.

The Negroes in the North, however, will get little out of the harvest if, like the blacks of Reconstruction days, they unwisely concentrate their efforts on solving all of their problems by electing men of their race as local officers or by sending a few members even to Congress as is likely in New York, Philadelphia and Chicago within the next generation. The Negroes have had representatives in Congress before but they were put out because their constituency was uneconomic and politically impossible. There was nothing but the mere letter of the law behind the Reconstruction Negro officeholder and the thus forced political recognition against public opinion could not last any longer than natural forces for some time thrown out of gear by unnatural causes could resume the usual line of procedure.

It would be of no advantage to the Negro race today to send to Congress forty Negro Representatives on the pro rata basis of numbers, especially if they happened not to be exceptionally well qualified. They would remain in Congress only so long as the American white people could devise some plan for eliminating them as they did during the Reconstruction period. Near as the world has approached real democracy, history gives no record of a permanent government conducted on this basis. Interests have always been stronger than numbers. The Negroes in the North, therefore, should not on the eve of the economic revolution follow the advice of their misguided and misleading race leaders who are diverting their attention from their actual welfare to a specialization in politics. To concentrate their efforts on electing a few Negroes to office wherever the blacks are found in the majority, would exhibit the narrowness of their oppressors. It would be as unwise as the policy of the Republican party of setting aside a few insignificant positions like that of Recorder of Deeds, Register of the Treasury and Auditor of the Navy as segregated jobs for Negroes. Such positions have furnished a nucleus for the large, worthless, office-seeking class of Negroes in Washington, who have established the going of the people of the city toward pretence and sham.

The Negroes should support representative men of any color or party, if they stand for a square deal and equal rights for all. The new Negroes in the North, therefore, will, as so many of their race in New York, Philadelphia and Chicago are now doing, ally themselves with those men who are fairminded and considerate of the man far down, and seek to embrace their many opportunities for economic progress, a foundation for political recognition, upon which the race must learn to build. Every race in the universe must aspire to becoming a factor in politics; but history shows that there is no short route to such success. Like other despised races beset with the prejudice and militant opposition of self-styled superiors, the Negroes must increase their industrial efficiency, improve their opportunities to make a living, develop the home, church and school, and contribute to art, literature, science and philosophy to clear the way to that political freedom of which they cannot be deprived.

The entire country will be benefited by this upheaval. It will be helpful even to the South. The decrease in the black population in those communities where the Negroes outnumber the whites will remove the fear of *Negro domination,* one of the causes of the backwardness of the South and its peculiar civilization. Many of the expensive precautions which the southern people have taken to keep the Negroes down, much of the terrorism incited to restrain the blacks from self-assertion will no longer be considered necessary; for, having the excess in numbers on their side, the whites will finally rest assured that the Negroes may be encouraged without any apprehension that they may develop enough power to subjugate or embarrass their former masters.

The Negroes too are very much in demand in the South and the intelligent whites will gladly give them larger opportunities to attach them to that section, knowing that the blacks, once conscious of their power to move freely throughout the country wherever they may improve their condition, will never endure hardships like those formerly inflicted upon the race. The South is already learning that the Negro is the most desirable laborer for that section, that the persecution of Negroes not only drives them out but makes the employment of labor such a problem that the South will not be an attractive section for capital. It will, therefore, be considered the duty of business men to secure protection to the Negroes lest their ill-treatment force them to migrate to the extent of bringing about a stagnation of their business.

The exodus has driven home the truth that the prosperity of the South is at the mercy of the Negro. Dependent on cheap labor, which the bulldozing whites will not readily furnish, the wealthy southerners must finally reach the position of regarding themselves and the Negroes as having a community of interests which each must promote. "Nature itself in those States," Douglass said, "came to the rescue of the Negro [*American Journal of Social Science* 9, p. 4]. He had labor, the South wanted it, and must have it or perish. Since he was free he could then give it, or withhold it; use it where he was, or take it elsewhere, as he pleased. His labor made him a slave and his labor could, if he would, make him free, comfortable and independent. It is more to him than either fire, sword, ballot boxes or bayonets. It touches the heart of the South through its pocket." Knowing that the Negro has this silent weapon to be used against his employer or the community, the South is already giving the race better educational facilities, better railway accommodations, and will eventually, if the advocacy of certain southern newspapers be heeded, grant them political privileges. Wages in the South, therefore, have risen even in the extreme southwestern States, where there is an opportunity to import Mexican labor. Reduced to this extremity, the southern aristocrats have begun to lose some of their race prejudice, which has not hitherto yielded to reason or philanthropy.

Southern men are telling their neighbors that their section must abandon the policy of treating the Negroes as a problem and construct a program for recognition rather than for repression. Meetings are, therefore, being held to find out what the Negro wants and what may be done to keep them contented. They are told that the Negro must be elevated not exploited, that to make the South what it must needs be, the cooperation of all is needed to train and equip the men of all races for efficiency. The aim of all then must be to reform or get rid of the unfair proprietors who do not give their tenants a fair division of the returns from their labor. To this end the best whites and blacks are urged to come together to find a working basis for a systematic effort in the interest of all.

To say that either the North or the South can easily become adjusted to this change is entirely too sanguine. The North will have a problem. The Negroes in the northern city will have much more to contend with than when settled in the rural districts or small urban centers. Forced by restrictions of real estate men into congested districts, there has appeared the tendency toward further segregation. They are denied social contact, are sagaciously separated from the whites in public places of amusement and are clandestinely segregated in public schools in spite of the law to the contrary. As a consequence the Negro migrant often finds himself with less friends than he formerly had. The northern man who once denounced the South on account of its maltreatment of the blacks gradually grows silent when a Negro is brought next door. There comes with the movement, therefore, the difficult problem of housing.

Where then must the migrants go. They are not wanted by the whites and are treated with contempt by the native blacks of the northern cities, who consider their brethren from the South too criminal and too vicious to be tolerated. In the average progressive city there has heretofore been a certain increase in the number of houses through natural growth, but owing to the high cost of materials, high wages, increasing taxation and the inclination to invest money in enterprises growing out of the war, fewer houses are now being built, although Negroes are pouring into these centers as a steady stream. The usual Negro quarters in northern centers of this sort have been filled up and the overflow of the black population scattered throughout the city among white people. Old warehouses, store rooms, churches, railroad cars and tents have been used to meet these demands.

A large per cent of these Negroes are located in rooming houses or tenements for several families. The majority of them cannot find individual rooms. Many are crowded into the same room, therefore, and too many into the same bed. Sometimes as many as four and five sleep in one bed, and that may be placed in the basement, dining-room or kitchen where there is neither adequate light nor air. In some cases men who work during the night sleep by day in beds used by others during the night. Some of their houses have no water inside and have toilets on the outside without sewerage connections. The cooking is often done by coal or wood stoves or kerosene lamps. Yet the rent runs high although the houses are generally out of repair and in some cases have been condemned by the municipality. The unsanitary conditions in which many of the blacks are compelled to live are in violation of municipal ordinances.

Furthermore, because of the indiscriminate employment by labor agents and the dearth of labor requiring the acceptance of almost all sorts of men, some disorderly and worthless Negroes have been brought into the North. On the whole, however, these migrants are not lazy, shiftless and desperate as some predicted that they would be. They generally attend church, save their money and send a part of their savings regularly to their families. They do not belong to the class going North in quest of whiskey. Mr. Abraham Epstein, who has written a valuable pamphlet setting forth his researches in

Pittsburgh *[The Negro Migrant in Pittsburgh]*, states that the migrants of that city do not generally imbibe and most of those who do, take beer only. Out of four hundred and seventy persons to whom he propounded this question, two hundred and ten or forty-four per cent of them were total abstainers. Seventy per cent of those families do not drink at all.

With this congestion, however, have come serious difficulties. Crowded conditions give rise to vice, crime and disease. The prevalence of vice has not been the rule but tendencies, which better conditions in the South restrained from developing, have under these undesirable conditions been given an opportunity to grow. There is, therefore, a tendency toward the crowding of dives, assembling on the corners of streets and the commission of petty offences which crowd them into the police courts. One finds also sometimes a congestion in houses of dissipation and the carrying of concealed weapons. Law abiding on the whole, however, they have not experienced a wave of crime. The chief offences are those resulting from the saloons and denizens of vice, which are furnished by the community itself.

Disease has been one of their worst enemies, but reports on their health have been exaggerated. On account of this sudden change of the Negroes from one climate to another and the hardships of more unrelenting toil, many of them have been unable to resist pneumonia, bronchitis and tuberculosis. Churches, rescue missions and the National League on Urban Conditions Among Negroes have offered relief in some of these cases. The last-named organization is serving in large cities as a sort of clearing house for such activities and as means of interpreting one race to the other. It has now eighteen branches in cities to which this migration has been directed. Through a local worker these migrants are approached, properly placed and supervised until they can adjust themselves to the community without apparent embarrassment to either race. The League has been able to handle the migrants arriving by extending the work so as to know their movements beforehand.

The occupations in which these people engage will throw further light on their situation. About ninety per cent of them do unskilled labor. Only ten per cent of them do semi-skilled or skilled labor. They serve as common laborers, puddlers, mold-setters, painters, carpenters, bricklayers, cement workers and machinists. What the Negroes need then is that sort of freedom which carries with it industrial opportunity and social justice. This they cannot attain until they be permitted to enter the higher pursuits of labor.

Two reasons are given for failure to enter these: first, the Negro labor is unstable and inefficient; and second, that white men will protest. Organized labor, however, has done nothing to help the blacks. Yet it is a fact that accustomed to the easy-going toil of the plantation, the blacks have not shown the same efficiency as that of the whites. Some employers report, however, that they are glad to have them because they are more individualistic and do not like to group. But it is not true that colored labor cannot be organized. The blacks have merely been neglected by organized labor. Wherever they have had the opportunity to do so, they have organized and stood for their rights like men. The trouble is that the trades unions are generally antagonistic to Negroes although they are now accepting the blacks in self-defense. The policy of excluding Negroes from these bodies is made effective by an evasive procedure, despite the fact that the constitutions of many of them specifically provide that there shall be no discrimination on account of race or color.

Because of this tendency some of the representatives of trades unions have asked why Negroes do not organize unions of their own. This the Negroes have generally failed to do, thinking that they would not be recognized by the American Federation of Labor, and knowing too that what their union would have to contend with in the economic world would be diametrically opposed to the wishes of the men from whom they would have to seek recognition. Organized labor, moreover, is opposed to the powerful capitalists, the only real friends the Negroes have in the North to furnish them food and shelter while their lives are often being sought by union members. Steps toward organizing Negro labor have been made in various Northern cities during 1917 and 1918. The objective of this movement for the present, however, is largely that of employment.

Eventually the Negro migrants will, no doubt, without much difficulty establish themselves among law-abiding and industrious people of the North where they will receive assistance. Many persons now see in this shifting of the Negro population the dawn of a new day, not in making the Negro numerically dominant anywhere to obtain political power, but to secure for him freedom of movement from section to section as a competitor in the industrial world. They also observe that while there may be an increase of race prejudice in the North the same will in that proportion decrease in the South, thus balancing the equation while giving the Negro his best chance in the economic world out of which he must emerge a real man with power to secure his rights as an American citizen.

CHICAGO DEFENDER   November 4, 1916

Federal Authorities Cannot Stop Northern Migration

Finds no law that prevents labor of any kind moving from one section of the country to another

Washington, D.C., Nov. 3—Migration of southern men (members of the Race) to northern labor centers, reported informally to the Department of Labor some time ago, has been brought to the attention of the department again by the recent movement of 300 from Florida to eastern cities. Such a number passed through Washington from Jacksonville Saturday night.

Meeting War Conditions

These men, it is said, were in charge of a labor agent formerly of Washington, who supplied them to a railroad, to a concern in Baltimore and to some concerns farther north. The unofficial explanation of the movement has been that these men were being taken north to meet the scarcity of immigrant labor, caused by the war.

Federal Officials Helpless

The Department of Labor is cognizant of the opposition in the south to the removal of its labor to other sections of the country, but so far as is known there is nothing the federal authorities can do about it.

In fact, it is said that the Department of Labor, through its recently organized employment service, has unwittingly been a party to some of the migration.

CHICAGO DEFENDER   September 16, 1916

The Migration of the colored workers from the South to all sections of the country is the best thing that could befall the race. When our new [white northern] friends find that there is little difference save in color of the skin between themselves and us, that demon prejudice will lose at least a few of his horns.

CHICAGO DEFENDER   November 9, 1916

Causes of the Migration from the Viewpoint of the Northern Negro

I have read with extreme interest your editorial in your issue of November 3rd upon "The Negro Exodus and What is Back of It," and since I have given considerable study to the question of Negro migration, and am only recently from the section where most of these Negroes have gone, viz. Connecticut, New York, New Jersey and Pennsylvania, I thought that you might be interested in a frank presentation of some of my observations. I may state that for 18 years I have devoted myself to the study of laboring conditions among Negroes in the North and have made publications under the United States Bureau of Labor, and Pennsylvania Bureau of Industrial statistics, the Pittsburg Survey, the University of Pennsylvania, etc., etc.

As is known, there have been several periods of migration to the North, the first from this section being of free Negroes after the Denmark Vesey plot of 1822, later after the Nat Turner insurrection of 1831. But the largest migrations have been since the Civil War, and there have been at least four of these, all of which have been because of industrial conditions.

There are to-day in the North about 1,600,000 Negroes, and three-fourths of them were born in the South. The cities of New York and Washington have three times as many Negroes as Charleston, while Philadelphia and Baltimore have about 85,000 Negroes to Charleston's 31,000. Other Northern cities having a larger population than Charleston, are Chicago, Illinois and St. Louis, while Pittsburg, Cincinnati, Columbus (Ohio), Indianapolis, Kansas City, Wilmington (Del.), and Chester (Pa.) have more than 10,000 Negroes.

Most of the Negroes have recently left for the North to work on the railroads and upon public works. They have not all remained in their first jobs, as many as 25 per cent having left during the first two months. Many of them, as your editorial stated, "went with their eyes big with wonder at the tales they have heard of the golden opportunities," and have been disappointed and have returned home. But the great majority have remained and will remain; for the same laws of migration are seen to be working with these Negroes who have gone North, as with the foreigners who have come from Europe. The vigorous Negro will remain. The inefficient Negro, the Negro who cannot stand the pace, will die out and come back South. About 20 per cent, of whom 90 per cent will be the more worthless type, will come back home. This is based upon observation in other cases of migration.

There will be a number of things which will hold the Negroes of the better type in the North; among them some of the following:

1. The Negroes do rough work, and in the competition with the foreign immigrant, the Slav and the Italian, have an advantage which has been recognized by many employers. They are not only good for that work; but ability to speak and understand English gives them an advantage, so that it is no strange thing to see a Negro foreman over a group of Italians or other immigrants. In a recent investigation made by me for the State of Pennsylvania of over 175 large and small employers of serveral thousand Negroes, 90 per cent of them declared that for rough work the Negroes were more efficient than other help.

2. The higher wages will keep the Negroes. To-day women are earning $5 to $7 a week with room and board, as maids, nurses and cooks; and $1.50 and $2 for washing and cleaning by the day. Able-bodied men are getting $1.75 to $3 a day for ordinary work, and exceptional men are making as foremen as high as $5 per day. Negroes who never earned more than $4 to $8 per week in their southern homes now receive from $2 to $3 per day.

3. Better educational opportunities will hold them. The average Negro is not awakened to the need of education until he strikes the North, when he finds it necessary. Then the superior schools are now open in some of the camps, for the employers are quick to see that intelligence is an asset to them, and they are encouraging the newly-arrived Negroes to study.

4. The opportunity to vote will also tend to hold them. Politicians are encouraging Negroes to remain; as they are very generally Republicans. Northern Negroes are encouraging them to stay because it gives them more power; and after the Negro casts his vote, takes part in the political meetings, he is just like the naturalized foreigner—he likes it, and stays. Of course, the white people rule, because superior intelligence and wealth always rule. But the black man enjoys being a part of the Governement and being called upon every year to have his "say." It has been a continual surprise to me how the Negro in the North, like the newly-arrived foreigner who has not taken any active part in voting in his native home, quickly develops a liking for politics.

5. *Better conditions of working will tend to keep the more intelligent class of Negroes. Compulsory education laws, laws of employers' liability, workmen's compensation, etc., which are for the workers' benefit, will have their influence.*

6. *The freedom of enjoyment will also hold them. While there is no more social equality in the North than there is in the South, and practically no desire for the same, the longer the Negro lives there, the opportunities to enjoy himself according to his means, appeals to him. He earns more money, can live in a better house, buy better clothes, develop more accomplishments, have more protection in his enjoyment.*

Personally I think it is good, both for the Negroes and for the whites, that a million or two million Negroes leave the South. It will make room for a larger number of foreigners to come to the South, and will tend to divorce the South's labor problem more widely from its race problem, and will give it a new perspective. It will also rob the South of the fear of "Negro domination" and will give it a new chance to give better expression to our democratic principles. On the other hand, a scattering of Negroes throughout the country will bring them in touch with the forces of organized labor in a way to give them better protection, while it will also acquaint the North with the Negro in such a way as to give it a more intelligent grasp of our general problem of racial relations.

R. R. Wright,
Editor of *Christian Recorder*

New York Evening Globe   1916

To the Editor of the Globe—

I have read with keen interest your editorial in to-day's Globe entitled "The Negro Problem, in which you say that the migration of large numbers of Negroes to the north within the past year has been due to his lack of fair treatment in the south and the effect it will have upon the country. You will concede that the Negro is an American citizen—dyed-in-the-wool, American, without even the symptoms of a hyphen. And as an American first, last and all the time he is entitled to his constitutional rights of life, liberty, and the pursuit of happiness anywhere in America he may choose to make his home, proved he is competent to work.

Because immigrants from other lands come here, cannot speak English, have no love for American Institutions and traditions, cor-

ner the labor market, and with their system of declaring strikes at
the least provocation—this has nothing to do with the rights of
Afro-Americans in this country. The Negro has just as much right
to seek higher wages as the whitest immigrant that has ever landed
here, and you can bet your sweet life if they come here in large
numbers they will be law abiding and competent, and you will
never read of a gang of "gunmen" among them.

The American white man gives the immigrant every opportunity to get up in the world because he is white. He never takes into
consideration that the immigrant is often an enemy of American
institutions regardless of the fact that a great president was assas-
sinated by one. But when war breaks out who is it that goes to the
front? Who is it that has given their lives up in Mexico willingly?
Has the Negro committed treason?

Yes, the Negro is coming north; he has a right to; his skill is on
a par with the foreigner and his claim is just. If we fight your bat-
tles we are entitled to a chance to work for a living. Feudalism,
yes, is even better than we have been getting thus far, but if there
is a God He surely will change things; all the Negro has to do is
his duty; results are the Lord's.

The Negro did not make himself black; he cannot change his
skin and he has no desire to, because if he did it might turn white
and give him a weak spine, a yellow streak, and that is what is
most despicable to every Negro.

We have the same kind of education that you have; we come
out of Columbia, New York University, College of the City of New
York, etc.; we are capable, God did not make any difference in
brains, and we are going to get justice eventually, and if you and I
live we will see it; nothing can keep us down. Just as Napoleon
said "there shall be no Alps," the Negro says "there shall be no
color line," and every man will stand on his merit as a man, be he
black or white.

(Signed) Arthur G. Shaw

OPPORTUNITY Magazine   April 1924

THE RECENT NORTHWARD MIGRATION OF THE NEGRO

Joseph A. Hill

In 1880, a little more than forty years ago, the center of the Negro population of the United States as determined by the census was located in the northwestern corner of the state of Georgia. It had traveled far since the early days of the Republic, when as shown by the census of 1790, it was near the southern boundary of the state of Virginia. It was now, in 1880, 163.1 miles farther south than it was then and 413.5 miles farther west, and the total distance it had covered in a direct line was 443 miles, representing an average advance of about 50 miles per decade. It was following the general movement of population in the Southern States. Its rate of advance was slowing down towards the close of the century but was still southwestward. In 1890 it had gone 20 miles farther in that direction, in 1900 nearly 10 miles, in 1910 another 10 miles. It was then in northeastern Alabama. That proved to be the turning point—the end, at least for the time being, of the movement southwestward, for the next census, that of 1920, revealed a complete reversal of direction. The center of Negro population was found to have moved not westward but eastward, not southward but northward, being, in fact, 9.4 miles farther east and 19.4 miles farther north than it had been in 1910. It had gone back to the northwestern corner of Georgia but was farther north than it had been in 1880, though not quite so far east.

This reversal in the movement of this sensitive index of changes in the distribution of population was by no means unexpected. It was well known before the census was taken that the Negroes had been going north in large numbers, and the movement of the center of Negro population simply registered that fact.

The immediate cause of the northward migration was the labor shortage in northern industries produced by conditions arising out of the World War. There are doubtless other contributory causes, but a discussion of them lies outside the scope of this paper, the purpose of which is simply to present some of the more significant census statistics regarding the volume and characteristics of this movement of the Negro population.

Migration After the Civil War

For a time after the Civil War there were two diverging currents of
Negro migration. One was northward from the more northern of the
southern states—Maryland, Virginia, Kentucky, Tennessee, and North
Carolina. The other was a migration southward and westward on
the part of Negroes in the lower Atlantic and Gulf States.

The northward migration from Virginia after the war was no-
tably large, and was a direct reversal of the current of migration
that prevailed under the regime of slavery, when Negroes were being
taken south in large numbers. Set free, the Virginia Negro turned
towards the North and has been facing in that direction ever since.
This northward current of migration was mostly to the states of
Pennsylvania, New Jersey, and New York. The number of Negro natives of Virginia living in these states when the war closed must
have been less than 10,000, for it was only 13,050 in 1870. But after
the war it increased rapidly, as shown by each successive census,
and in 1920 was 125,104. The southward migration practically ceased,
as is shown by the fact that the number of Virginia Negroes living
in the states of Georgia, Alabama, Mississippi, Louisiana and Texas
decreased from 107,934 in 1870 to 10,844 in 1920. Thus the Virginia-
born Negro in the cotton states of the South has almost disappeared, although no doubt his descendants there are numerous.

From the states far south there was no considerable northward
migration in this period. The North seemed too far away, and the
Negro showed no disposition to turn his back upon the cotton fields
and seek new fortunes in strange lands. He lacked the knowledge,
the means, and the initiative for such an unwise venture. Therefore
the drift of the Negro population, following the development of cotton cultivation, continued to be towards the southwest as it had been
before the war. There was no reversal of migration here such as
there had been in the case of the Virginia Negro. The voluntary migration was in the same direction as the earlier compulsory migration had been.

Mississippi as an Illustration

The effect of Negro migration upon the population of the southern
states may, perhaps, be best indicated by featuring the figures of
immigration to and emigration from a single southern state, selecting for this purpose the state of Mississippi, which apparently has
been affected to a greater degree than most other states by the recent northward migration of the colored race.

In 1870 the Negro or colored population of Mississippi included 124,377 Negroes who were born in other states. They were immigrants, and they constituted more than one-fourth of the total Negro population of the state. It is practically certain as regards most of them that their migration had not been of their own free will. Of the total number, 27,713 were natives of Virginia, 13,284 were born in Tennessee, 16,604 in South Carolina, 14,511 in North Carolina, 12,713 in Georgia, and 22,192 in Alabama.

There had been also a certain amount of Negro emigration from Mississippi as evidenced by the fact that 73,802 Negroes born in that state were living in other states, a majority of them in Louisiana (17,831) and Texas (28,639). Thus when the census of 1870 was taken, the number of Negroes who were natives of other states and had come or been brought to Mississippi exceeded the number who had been born in that state and had gone to other states by 66,944. That represented the net gain to the population of the state through the interstate migration of Negroes. In 1880 this excess, surplus, or gain had increased slightly to 68,245. It fell off to 33,764 in 1890, to 7,228 in 1900, became converted into a deficit of 26,439 in 1910, which deficit increased to 139,178 in 1920. Starting with a surplus of 67,000 we end with a deficit of 139,000. Consider what this deficit means. It means that if all the Negroes who were born in Mississippi and have gone to other states were to return and at the same time all Negroes who have come into Mississippi from other states were to leave, the number returning would exceed the number departing by 139,178, and the result would be an increase of 15 per cent in the total Negro population of the state and an increase of nearly 8 per cent in the total population, white and Negro.

There is a similar history for nearly all southern states, in that the recent censuses show either a growing deficit or a diminishing surplus in the interstate exchange of native Negroes. For another illustration take the state of Texas, which for a time seems to have been the goal of Negro migration in the lower South. In 1870 the number of Negroes in Texas who were natives of other states was 118,114, which exceeded the small number of natives of Texas who had emigrated from the state by 112,348. At the last census, 1920, the excess of Negro immigrants to the state over Negro emigrants from the state was only 3,501. In Oklahoma and in Florida the excess in 1920 was less than it was in 1910 although greater than it was at earlier censuses. In Arkansas there has been little change in the situation since 1890, the excess remaining nearly constant at about 100,000. In West Virginia alone of the southern states has the gain through Negro migration steadily increased at each successive census.

South Loses Population Through Negro Migration

The total number of southern-born Negroes in the North at the date of the last census was 727,423. There were also 43,371 in the West.* Against this total of 770,794 Negroes who, as shown by the census of 1920, had left the South and gone North or West, there was a small number of northern or western born Negroes who had gone South, the number being, in fact, 47,223, so that the net direct loss to the South by Negro migration was 680,200, which is equivalent to 7.6 per cent of the total Negro population of the South, and to a little more than 2 per cent of the total population of the South, white and colored.

The loss to any state, section, or country resulting from emigration is, however, not adequately measured either by the number emigrating within a given period or by the number of living emigrants in other states or countries on a given date. For it includes also the descendants of emigrants living in other states or countries, that is, if we may assume that the emigrants, if they had remained in their native land, would have had as many children and descendants as they have had in the states or countries to which they have gone. In the case of the Negro emigrants who have gone North there is reason to believe that they would have had larger families and more descendants if they had remained in the South than they have had in the North. So probably it is not an exaggeration, but rather the contrary, to say that the entire increase in the Negro population of the North since 1870 represents a loss in population growth to the South. In the 50 years between 1870 and 1920 the number of Negroes in the North increased by a little more than 1,000,000, i.e., from 452,818 in 1870 to 1,472,309 in 1920. One million is equivalent to about 3 per cent of the total population of the South and to about 11 per cent of the Negro population.

Percentage Negro Declining in the South

In 1870, the population of the South was more than one-third Negro. Now it is not much more than one-fourth Negro, the percentage

*The designation "North," "South," and "West" as here used corresponds with the established usage in the census reports, according to which the North extends as far west as the western boundaries of North and South Dakota, Nebraska, and Kansas; and the South extends as far west as the western boundaries of Texas and Oklahoma. The country beyond the western boundaries of these states is the West.

Negro having declined from 36 in 1870 to 27 in 1920. It is safe to say that this decrease has not been wholly due to the emigration of Negroes. For had there been no emigration the growth of Negro population in the South would apparently not have kept pace with that of the white. But the difference would not have been as great as it is now. If there had been no emigration the Negro population of the South, as I have just pointed out, would probably be at least a million larger than it is at present, and the percentage Negro would in that case be about 30 instead of 27. The difference probably represents approximately the effect which emigration has had in reducing the proportion of Negroes in the population of the southern states.

If, therefore, there had been no northward migration of Negroes in the last 50 years the total population of the South would presumably be at least 3 per cent greater than it now is, the Negro population 11 per cent greater and the percentage Negro in the total would be about 30 instead of 27.

Increase in the Northward Migration

While, as already noted, there has been a constant northward migration of Negroes since the close of the Civil War, the recent migration, that of the last census decade (1910 to 1920), differs from the previous migration in several important respects and first of all in volume or amount. Thus in the period of 40 years from 1870 to 1910 the number of southern-born Negroes in the North increased from 146,490 to 415,533, an average decennial increase of 54,000. But in the decade 1910 to 1920 there was an increase of 311,910, which was more than the aggregate increase of the preceding 40 years and six times the previous average decennial increase.

Migration From the Far South

The northward migration of Negroes in the last decade has been to a much larger extent than ever before a migration from the far South. The earlier northward migration was, as already noted, mostly from the more northern states of the South. Even as recently as 1910, 56.2 per cent, more than half, of the southern born Negroes living in northern states came from two states—Virginia and Kentucky. The migration between 1910 and 1920 reduced the proportion who were born in these two states to 37 per cent. On the other hand the proportion of northern Negroes coming from the states farther south, or from what we may term the cotton belt states, including in this class, South Carolina, Georgia, Florida, Alabama, Mississippi, Arkansas, Louisiana, and Texas, increased from 18.2 per cent of the total number of southern-born Negroes living in the North in 1910 to 40.2 per cent of the total in 1920. The absolute number of Negroes in the North who were natives of these states increased from 75,517 in 1910 to 298,739 in 1920, so there were nearly four times as many in 1920 as there were in 1910.

James Bryce, speculating in regard to the future of the American Negro in the revised edition of his "American Commonwealth," published in 1911, considered the possibility that the Negro might "more and more draw southwards into the lower and hotter regions along the coasts of the Atlantic and the Gulf of Mexico," and might thus become "a relatively smaller and probably much smaller element than at present in the whole population north of latitude 36° and a relatively larger one south of latitude 33° and east of longitude 99° W." (II, p. 536.) Bryce did not consider or suggest the possibility that the Negro might migrate northward in increasing numbers or that there might be a dispersion of the Negro race rather than a concentration of it. Yet this is precisely what has been taking place since his book was published. The region which he defines by geographic degrees as that in which the Negroes might concentrate includes the states of South Carolina, Georgia, Florida, Alabama, Mississippi, and Louisiana, and the proportion which the Negroes living in those states form of the total Negro population of the United States is at present decreasing, being 50.2 per cent in 1910 and 47.2 per cent in 1920. Within these states the percentage Negro decreased from 47.3 per cent in 1910 to 43.0 in 1920. It decreased also in the other southern states, or the rest of the South, but the decrease was not so marked, being a decrease from 20.1 per cent Negro in 1910 to 18.4 in 1920. The North is the only section in which the percentage Negro has increased in recent years.

Negroes in the North

In 1870 the total number of Negroes living in the North was 452,818, but of these 118,071 were in the state of Missouri, which had been a slave state. The northern state with the next largest number of Negroes was Pennsylvania with 65,294, next Ohio with 63,213; then New York with 52,081; New Jersey, 30,658; Illinois, 28,762; and Indiana, 24,560. No other northern state had as many as 15,000.

In 1920 there were 1,472,309 Negroes in the North as compared with 452,818 in 1870; and the northern state having the largest number of Negroes was Pennsylvania with 284,568. New York came next with 198,483, Ohio had 186,187, and Illinois 182,274. Then came

Missouri with 178,241. Indiana had 80,810, Michigan 60,082, and Kansas 57,925. No other northern state had as many as 50,000. These 8 states account for four-fifths of the total Negro population in the North. They contain only about two-fifths of the total population of the North. With the exception of Michigan and New York they are states bordering the South.

Migration to Northern Cities

In the North outside the large cities there is only a small though a rather widely distributed Negro population. Out of a total of 1,272 northern counties there are, in fact, only 83 in which there are no Negroes. But there are 671 other northern counties in which the number of Negroes is less than 100, making 754 counties—about 60 per cent of the total number—in which there are either no Negroes or less than 100 Negroes; and there are only 183 counties in which there are more than 1,000 Negroes. If for purposes of comparison we make a similar classification of counties for the preceding census, we obtain no indication that any dispersion of the Negroes in the North is in progress. They go to the large cities mostly and remain there.

Of the 182,274 Negroes in the state of Illinois 60 per cent are in the city of Chicago, which city includes only 42 per cent of the total population of the state.

Detroit, in which there are 40,858 Negroes, accounts for 66 per cent or two-thirds of the total Negro population of Michigan.

Of the 198.483 Negroes in New York state 152,467 or 75 per cent are in New York City.

Three cities in Ohio, Cleveland (34,451), Cincinnati (30,079), and Columbus (22,181) account for 46 per cent of the Negro population of that state although these cities comprise only about 22 per cent of the total population of the state.

Philadelphia contains 47 per cent of the total number of Negroes in Pennsylvania as compared with 21 of the total population of the state. Add Pittsburgh and we have accounted for 60 per cent of the Negro population of that state and 28 per cent of the total population.

The above 10 cities contain 45.8 per cent of the total Negro population of the North. The same cities contain 22.5 per cent of the total population of the North. Three of these cities—New York, Chicago, and Philadelphia—contain 26.9 per cent of the total Negro, as compared with 15.9 per cent of the total population.

Percentage Negro in the
Population of the North

The total population of the North is now a little more than 2 per cent Negro, or to be more exact it was 2.3 per cent Negro in 1920. From 1870 to 1910 the percentage had been nearly constant, being either 1.8 or 1.9; but the last census, 1920, showed a slight but significant increase. The percentage, however, is still small, equivalent to about one-fiftieth of the total population. So only one person in fifty in the northern states is a Negro. If, therefore, the Negroes were evenly distributed over the northern states, to correspond with the distribution of the white population, their numbers would not be large enough to constitute a disturbing factor in the social organism or arouse racial antagonism or introduce a race problem. But as already pointed out they are concentrated largely in certain cities, where they form a considerable and an increasing proportion of the total population. Over 4 per cent of the population of Chicago, Cleveland, Detroit, New Bedford, and Newark is Negro; about 5 per cent of the population of Youngstown and of Cambridge, Mass.; over 6 per cent of the population of Pittsburgh; over 7 per cent of the population of Cincinnati and Philadelphia; not less than 9 per cent of the population of Columbus, St. Louis, and Kansas City, Mo.; 11 per cent of the population of Indianapolis; and 14.2 per cent of the population of Kansas City, Kan. These are all cities of over 100,000 population. Some of the smaller northern cities have still larger percentages of Negroes. Atlantic City is 21.6 per cent Negro.

Within each city there is usually a local segregation, or concentration of Negroes in certain sections or localities—a Negro quarter. In New York City 42.3 per cent of the total Negro population are located in two assembly districts and within these districts Negroes form, respectively, 35 per cent and 49 per cent of the total population. In Chicago there is one ward which contains 44 per cent of the total Negro population of the city and within which Negroes form 69 per cent of the total population. In Detroit the concentration is not so marked, although there is one ward in which Negroes constitute about 25 per cent of the total population, and another in which the percentage is nearly 20.

Per Cent Negro Decreasing in Southern Cities, Increasing in Northern

In almost every southern city the percentage Negro, as indicated by the last census, is decreasing. Thus in Atlanta it decreased from 33.5

in 1910 to 31.3 in 1920; in Savannah from 51.1 to 47.1; in Charleston from 52.8 to 47.6; in Columbia from 43.9 to 38.5; in Memphis from 40.0 to 37.7; in Nashville from 33.1 to 30.1; in Dallas from 19.6 to 15.1; in Fort Worth from 18.1 to 14.1; in Houston from 30.4 to 24.6; in San Antonio from 11.1 to 8.9; in Richmond from 36.6 to 31.5; in Washington from 28.5 to 25.1. There are, however, three important cities of the South in which the decrease is hardly appreciable, namely Birmingham (39.4 to 39.3), Baltimore (15.2 to 14.8), and New Orleans (26.3 to 26.1).

In northern cities, on the other hand, the percentage Negro is increasing. In Chicago it increased from 2.0 to 4.1; in Philadelphia from 5.5 to 7.4; in Pittsburgh from 4.8 to 6.4; in New York City from 1.9 to 2.7; in Cincinnati from 5.4 to 7.5; in Cleveland from 1.5 to 4.3; in Detroit from 1.2 to 4.1; in St. Louis from 6.4 to 9.0; and so in many other northern cities.

Occupations of Negroes in the North

What are the Negroes doing in the North? In the South a majority of them—57.7 per cent of the total number of Negro male workers—are employed in growing cotton or other farm crops either as laborers or tenants or owners. In 1920 there were 628,029 Negro farm laborers in the southern states and 834,686 Negro farmers of whom probably about 200,000 were farm owners, the others being tenants or croppers. Leaving out West Virginia, in which only 5.1 per cent of the male Negro workers are engaged in agriculture, the percentage in the other southern states ranges from 29.9 in Maryland to 78.2 in Mississippi.

The fact that most of the Negroes in the North have gone to the cities indicates at once that not many of them are on farms. As a matter of fact less than 6 per cent (5.7) of Negro male workers in the North were reported in the census of 1920 as engaged in agricultural pursuits.

In Chicago Negroes are represented by larger or smaller numbers in nearly all the principal occupations or occupational groups. There is one notable exception. No Negroes are employed as motormen or as street car conductors. But these appear to be the only numerically important occupations from which they are entirely excluded.

In the professions they are represented by 215 clergymen, 95 lawyers, 254 musicians or music teachers, 195 physicians and there are at least a few Negroes in most of the other professions.

They are represented also in the skilled trades. There were in 1920, 126 brick and stone masons who were Negroes; 275 carpenters; 113 compositors and typesetters; 148 coopers, 431 machinists; 286 house painters; 105 plumbers; and 371 tailors.

But the great majority of Negro workers in the cities of the North are employed either in domestic or personal service or as unskilled or semi-skilled laborers. In the stockyards of Chicago, there were 5,300 Negro laborers in 1920 and in the iron and steel industries, 3,201. In the slaughter and packing houses 1,242 Negroes were returned as laborers and 1,490 as semi-skilled operatives. There were 1,835 Negroes returned as building or general laborers, 1,210 as laborers, porters, and helpers in stores, 2,139 as porters in domestic or personal service, besides 2,540 railway porters, which means doubtless Pullman porters. There were 1,822 Negro janitors, 2,315 Negro waiters and 1,942 Negro male servants. Then there were 1,659 Negro male clerks outside of clerks in stores. These occupations include 55 per cent of the total number of male Negro workers in the City of Chicago, as compared with less than 10 per cent of the white male bread-winners.

That the extensive employment of Negroes as laborers or semi-skilled operatives in the stockyards, slaughter houses, steel mills, and building trades, and as general laborers is a recent development, is shown by the fact that the percentage of Negroes in the total number of males employed in these occupations in Chicago increased from 3.5 in 1910 to 20.7 in 1920. Of the laborers in the automobile plants of Detroit, 13.5 per cent were Negroes in 1920, as compared with less than one-half of 1 per cent in 1910. The proportion of Negroes among building and general laborers in that city increased from 3.2 per cent in 1910 to 19.4 per cent in 1920, the number of Negroes so employed increasing from 149 to 1,261.

In New York the percentage of Negroes in the total number of longshoremen and stevedores increased from 6.4 in 1910 to 14.5 in 1920; and in Philadelphia it increased from 44.7 per cent in 1910 to 59.2 in 1920. It is of interest to note that while in each of these cities there was a large increase in the number of Negroes employed as chauffeurs, the increase no more than kept pace with the growth of the occupation, so that the percentage of Negroes was no larger in 1920 than it was in 1910. But the absolute number of Negro chauffeurs in New York increased from 490 to 2,373, and in Philadelphia from 312 to 2,195.

In contrast to the increasing extent to which Negroes are being employed as laborers in the manufacturing plants or industries of the North is the very slight increase in the employment of male Negroes in domestic and personal service. Of the total number of janitors, porters, male servants, and waiters in Chicago 33.9 per cent were Negroes in 1910, and in 1920 this percentage had increased only to 34.8.

All this goes to show that the male Negroes who have recently been migrating northward in such large numbers have most of them become industrial laborers, finding employment in mills, factories, and stockyards, rather than in hotels, restaurants, office buildings, and dwelling houses. I am sure that if we could distinguish in the census occupational statistics those who have emigrated recently from the earlier emigrants, this fact would be brought out very strikingly. It is another distinctive feature of the new immigration.

Negro Women in Domestic Service

The statistics relating to male Negro workers indicate that new fields of employment have been opened to them in the North, which doubtless invite immigration by the lure of high money wages. This does not appear to be true to the same extent of the female Negro workers. Their field of employment in the North continues to be largely restricted to personal and domestic service.

In the case of the Negro male workers in Chicago, the percentage employed in personal and domestic service fell off from 52.5 per cent to 28.1, and in the case of female workers from 84.5 to 64.2.

Of the Negro women who have migrated to northern cities a large proportion are domestic servants. About 30 per cent of the Negro female breadwinners in Chicago were reported as servants and 47 per cent of those in New York. For Philadelphia the percentage is 54, for Detroit 35, and for Pittsburgh 50. In general from one-third to one-half of the total number of Negro women workers in northern cities are servants.

It may be noted in this connection that the total number of female servants of all classes, white and colored, as reported by the census decreased materially in the last decade, the number being 1,012,133 in 1920 as compared with 1,309,549 in 1910, a decrease of about 23 per cent or nearly one-fourth. In New York City the number of female servants fell off from 113,409 in 1910 to 84,615 in 1920; in Chicago the decrease was from 34,472 in 1910 to 26,184 in 1920; in Philadelphia it was nearly the same—from 37,050 to 28,290. Evidently people are learning to do without domestic servants. I shall not stop to inquire how. But doubtless the increasing resort to the

simplified housekeeping of the apartment furnishes a partial explanation of this phenomenon. In the meantime, white female servants
in northern cities are to a large extent being supplanted or replaced
by Negroes. For while the number of white female servants, foreign
born as well as native, has decreased, the number of Negro female
servants has materially increased, so that they form an increasing
proportion or percentage of the diminishing total. Thus in Chicago
in 1920, 24 per cent or about one-fourth of the female servants were
Negroes as compared with 10 per cent in 1910. In New York the
percentage Negro in the total number of female servants increased
from 12.4 in 1910 to 22.4 in 1920; in Detroit from 6.1 to 23.1; in
Cleveland from 8.7 to 30.1; in Philadelphia from 38.5 to 53.8 per
cent. And there are similar increases in the percentages for all the
northern cities to which Negroes have migrated in considerable
numbers.

Thus it becomes evident that in the North the southern Negro
is to a certain extent supplying the places of the foreign-born immigrant as a source of labor supply for both industrial plants and
domestic kitchens, but only to a limited extent. The falling off in
the flow of foreign immigration caused by restrictive laws can never
be offset or made good by immigration from the South. For consider: In the last 10 years of unrestricted immigration, by which I
mean the years 1905 to 1914, inclusive, more than 10,000,000 foreign immigrants came to these shores. That exceeds the entire Negro
population of the South by about 1,000,000. At present the restriction law limits the annual immigration to 357,000. So the maximum
possible immigration of the foreign born in a decade is 3,570,000.
The difference between this number and the 10,000,000 that came
in when immigration was unrestricted would absorb 72 per cent of
the entire Negro population of the southern states (8,912,231).

Natural Increase of Negro Population in the North

Will the colored people in the North multiply by natural increase or
are they dependent upon continuous immigration from the South?
In other words, if immigration were to cease would the Negro race
in the North gradually die out? This is a very fundamental question.
If the race can not maintain itself in the North save by continuous
recruiting from the South, then immigration acts as a drain upon
the Negro population and if it were to continue in large volume it
might in the distant future even prove to be the destruction of the
Negro race. I do not suggest this, however, as a catastrophe that is

likely to be realized. It may be a possibility, but if so it lies beyond the range of any predictable future.

Whether the Negro race can maintain itself in the North by natural increase remains to be seen. We can inquire only as to present tendencies. Professor Willcox in a recently published article on the "Increase and Distribution of Negroes in the United States" pointed out that in those states in the North for which statistics were available there had been within a period of five years 114 deaths of Negroes to 100 births. The area included the New England states, New York, Pennsylvania, Michigan, Minnesota, and the period covered the years 1914 to 1919 inclusive. Conditions within that period could hardly be called normal. It was the period of the World War, of the influenza epidemic, and the period within which the first northward rush of Negroes took place.

The statistics of more recent years show a different relationship. For within these same states, the number of deaths of Negroes to 100 births in the three years, 1920 to 1922, inclusive, was 83. The birth rate for the Negro, however, remains lower in the North than it is in the South and the death rate continues to be higher in the North, and that means, of course, that the natural increase in the North is less than it is in the South; and it seems fairly evident that the northward migration of the Negroes has retarded the increase of the Negro population and constitutes one reason, and perhaps the main reason, why the increase recorded at the last census was smaller than ever before, being, in fact, only 6.5 per cent as compared with 11.2 per cent in the preceding decade and with 13.8 per cent (corrected figure) in the decade before that. But these conditions may be only temporary. The death rate in the North may decline with improvement in living conditions, sanitation, and personal hygiene—and with adaptation to climate. The birth rate might increase if conditions among Negroes in the North become more settled and family life better established. And the northward migration itself may be only temporary. These are questions the answer to which the future alone will reveal.

Resumé

I am aware that the statistics presented within the brief limits of this paper can serve only as an introduction to the subject of Negro migration. They indicate the recent great increase of migration, the fact that this recent migration comes largely from the cotton states of the far South, that it is a migration to the cities of the North and to the industrial plants in these cities, that it is replacing to a limited extent the immigration from Europe, and that it is probably retarding the growth of the Negro population. But as to what the effects of this movement are going to be upon the Negro, or upon the North or upon the South—these are profoundly interesting and more or less speculative questions which I could not undertake to discuss within the limits of this paper, whatever my qualifications for that task might be.

THE RITUAL OF SURVIVAL

Robert Fleming

The door of hope might have remained closed so far as the progress the Negro was to make for himself was concerned. He has never created for himself any civilization. He has never risen above the government of club. He has never written a language. His achievements in architecture are limited to the thatched-roofed hut or a hole in the ground. No monuments have been builded by him to body forth and perpetuate in the memory posterity the virtues of his ancestors. For countless ages he has looked upon the rolling sea and never dreamed of a sail. In truth, he has never progressed, save and except when under the influence and absolute control of a superior race.

—U.S. Senator for Mississippi
James K. Vardaman, 1910

Mississippi, the cradle of segregation and the staunchest bastion of Jim Crow, was the place that awaited Will Fleming, my grandfather, who worked for several years as a laborer on a merchant ship before coming to America. When this tall light-skinned man arrived in New Orleans, he understood very little about Mississippi, Vardaman, Jim Crow, or the Ku Klux Klan, but he learned very quickly. It was 1915. If a black man was to survive, he had to know his place, to step off the curb when a white person approached, and to lower his eyes whenever he spoke to a white woman. It seemed that daily lynchings of blacks were the meat-and-potatoes stories for the various Southern newspapers in those days, complete with graphic details of the grisly deed and the alleged crime for which the person of color lost his or her life. Fleming knocked around in the Crescent City for awhile, doing odd jobs on the wharves and listening to the cotton merchants haggle over prices for the countless bales of the white gold. What he learned here would serve him well later when he journeyed north to the Mississippi Delta.

Somehow Will Fleming raised enough money to buy a large block of land in Alligator, Mississippi, a small town in the Delta, divided it up into sizable parcels, and hired on black families to sharecrop for him. Writer Eudora Welty immortalized Alligator as one of the locales in her story, "Powerhouse," the tale of a great black jazz pianist who lives life to the fullest. The difference between the farm Fleming ran and the surrounding white plantations was how he treated his workers—everyone as an equal, and the operation was managed in many ways like a commune. The profits were shared by the families and a doctor was often summoned to attend to tenant farmers and their clans.

"My father was a Jamaican, quiet and sharp as a tack," Robert Fleming, my father, recalls of Will. "He was one of maybe four black men who owned big plantations back then. It was unusual for a black man to own a place in those days, believe that. He never talked much but people respected him. He was a fair, honest man who believed in doing what he said. He once told me that he had a brother and that they worked on boats. I knew nothing about my father's parents. He didn't like to talk about the past. I asked him about how he got the place, but he never said anything."

Operating a full-scale plantation required a keen business sense, a large measure of bravado in dealing with the white cotton merchants, and nerves of steel to confront the nightriders or the Ku Klux Klan. The Klan often worked in cooperation with the local white sheriff and clergy in the small Delta towns. Will Fleming, a foreigner, didn't act like the rest of the niggers. His plantation produced ample crops of cotton, cane, corn, and soybeans. He brought in modern equipment, including the latest tractors, and the local whites started paying closer attention to this "uppity nigger."

"He was real smart," my father says, thinking back. "He seemed to know everything. I wish I had the head he had on him. He knew all about the Stock Market, how to buy supplies and equipment, and how to sell and get the best price. For the most part, the white folks were good to him, but you know how those peckerwoods are. A lot of black folk can't take low and tom for the white man. I couldn't do it and my father couldn't do it.

"The peckerwoods wanted my father to sell his cotton to one group of white people, a clique, but he wouldn't. He would wait and find out if the cotton had gone up in price. He wanted to sell it to whoever would buy it at the highest price. The white people would buy it from him at a certain amount a bale and put it in a warehouse. When it would go up, they would sell it. My father started doing like they were doing, hold the cotton, then sell it for top dollar. So he had trouble with the nightriders."

Late one night, there was the sound of a crowd and the glow of several torches outside Will Fleming's house. It was not his first visit from the hooded white men, all of whom he knew from business dealings in town.

"The Klan was real bad in the Delta," my father says. "They were very active. The white folks used them to keep black people scared, in their place. The nightriders came at night. You could see the lights from inside the house. My father went out, by himself, unafraid, and they talked. He didn't back down. He was different from most black men in that way. He never worried about them. Well, the white men were shouting and he was talking in a low voice. I don't know what he said but they left and nobody got hurt. But they promised to come back."

The families on the plantation rallied around my grandfather, offering to arm themselves to fight if that was called for. In other Delta towns such as Louise, Drew, and Midnight, times were especially bad for blacks. One black man was burned alive for allegedly fondling a white woman's leg. Another was hung and parts of his body sliced away for souvenirs, while white women and children looked on. A father and two sons were dragged from their shack, beaten, mutilated and shot after it was alleged that he had shot and wounded a white man who had forced himself on the black farmer's wife. The woman became pregnant and later had the child.

"The peckerwoods would kill someone for what they called reckless eyeballing, some black man supposedly letting his eyes linger too long on a white woman's body," my father notes. "Often, the black person wasn't even paying the woman no mind, but he would lose his life anyway. A lot of black men lost their life that way. My mother told me about a boy in Shelby who they put a noose around his neck and tied him behind a horse. They told him to run. He ran until he got tired. When he fell, they dragged him around and around the town until the skin peeled off him and he died."

Life at the plantation went as usual. The shacks were poorly constructed, drafty, with newspapers stuck in the cracks. A morning meal consisted of oatmeal and molasses. Dinner was collard greens, pan bread, rice, chicken backs or necks and pump water. The blacks were careful to stay out of town where signs of FOR COLORED ONLY and FOR WHITES ONLY governed daily life. One day, Will Fleming noticed a tall, red-skinned young woman picking cotton in the fields. Her name was Mary Taylor; she had been born in New Orleans of mixed black and Creole parentage. She had come to Mississippi with her family in search of work. The other workers watched as Will wooed the willowy woman whose fiery temper and long black hair brought her quite a lot of attention among the workers.

"My father treated everyone nice," my father remembers. "No one went hungry and everyone got their fair share, unlike blacks working for white bosses. So he met my mother, who became his girlfriend. She was just a farmhand and she had his child. I have no full brothers and sisters. I have only half brothers and sisters. I'm a Fleming and the others are Dunns. I was Will's only child with my mother. Just me."

That relationship was cut short by the nightriders, who returned to give Fleming an ultimatum: Leave or be killed. A picture of Will Fleming taken around this time, the only surviving photo of my grandfather, shows a stout man, with a Panama hat on his head and a patch over one eye, standing next to a Model-T Ford, with his foot on the running board. The car is parked on a levee. He is dressed in an all-white suit.

There was some debate about how he lost his eye. Some say it was an industrial accident. Others say the white folks held him down and put the eye out with a sizzling-hot iron rod. My grandmother always said the latter explanation was the truth. When the Klan returned the last time, they were not going to be denied. They wanted him out or dead. He was a bad example for other niggers in the area.

"Things got real rough," my father says bitterly. "You know how it was, down there in the twenties. Those peckerwoods were crazy. They were the Law. They ran him out from Alligator and he settled in a small town in Arkansas. He started all over again. Sometimes you cannot deal with certain of those bastards. That hate is embedded in them like ants."

Another man took control of the plantation and most of the families stayed because work was hard to find. Mary Taylor was never to be with her man again and my father, then in his teens, worked in the fields like the other children. He dreamed of the day when he could leave the fields and go North. Most of the other workers laughed at him, saying the Devil you knowed was better than the one you didn't.

"I was fifteen when I left," my father recalls, going back to his great escape from those hard days. "I lived with my mother in Mississippi and she didn't want me seeing my father much, only now and then. When I would go and see my father, I'd go on weekends, then I had to be back home. He'd give me money and I had to share with my other brothers and sisters. They didn't have any money, you know. I drove a tractor. I had trouble with my boss. I stopped and kissed a girl once on the road so he took half my pay. I was making $3 a week working from six to six."

The girl he kissed was a black girl—he would have been killed otherwise. Still, it was not uncommon for white bosses on some of the Delta plantations to decide which man and woman would be best suited. Pairings outside of their approval were frowned on and often forcibly separated. If a young black woman was exceptionally pretty, the white boss would keep her for himself.

There is a glint of anger in my father's eyes as he recalls what happened after the kiss at the roadside. "Some nigger there, Benny Banks, told the boss that I kissed this black girl. He was a tom. My boss took part of my money so I got mad. I told him to take all of the damn money. I had $25 buried somewhere in a tree so I took the money and headed North. I never cared for picking cotton anyway. I stayed as I could to help out my family."

My father, who physically looked like a mix of both parents, hiked to Memphis, where he found work as a laborer in an ice house. Sometimes he'd go to Arkansas and drive a tractor for his father on weekends. He did his work and stayed out of the way of the bigoted whites who were eager to find a reason to harass or kill a young black man.

"Jim Crow didn't bother me," he says. "I'd go around Memphis and it was not as bad as Mississippi. Nothing in the South was that bad. The Delta was the worst place in the world. I knew I would never do anything with my life living in Alligator. I picked up my education on the road. That's one of my biggest regrets. I regret that I never got a good education. Young people don't know how lucky they are. We were needed in the field, so the white folks gave us only two months of schooling a year. Then they'd close it and put us to work. So when I left home, I had no intentions of going back. I wanted to make it on my own. I didn't want my parents helping me."

As a young teen, he remembers listening to the Mississippi Governor Theodore Bilbo, soon to be a U.S. senator, speak over the radio. A group of white man, chewing tobacco and dipping snuff, stood around it, cheering on their hero. "Don't let a single nigger vote," Bilbo said in his best fire-and-brimstone voice. "If you let a few register and vote this year, next year there will be twice as many, and the first thing you know the whole thing will be out of hand." Bilbo died of cancer of the mouth a few years later, and very few blacks grieved his passing.

In those days, Memphis, immortalized by jazz master W. C. Handy, had a population that was nearly one-third black. It was one of the industrial centers of the South—a city of 200,000 people—and it lured a sizable number of blacks yearly. My father says he stayed away from the tawdry pleasures of the infamous Beale Street and worked hard and saved his dollars. On his eighteenth birthday, he went into the army and off to boot camp. The Second World War was winding down. He was only in the uniform for a year and a half before he was wounded in the leg. He was sent home. By the age of 21, he found his way to Cleveland, Ohio, and a steel plant job. It was in Cleveland that he would meet Dorothy Jean Smith, an attractive brown-skinned woman who would later become his wife and my mother.

My mother's family came from a small town in central Georgia. Her mother, Rose Smith and her parents arrived in Cleveland in 1916. Like most blacks, they faced the uncertainties and fears of being second-class citizens with a sense of style, strength, and grace. At age 97, my great-grandmother, Ida Hollingshead was still very active, able to read fairly complex books and get around. Her memory about black life in America during the Victorian era was incredible and full of rich detail.

"My father was a slave but he took nothing off the white people," she recalls. "He would sass them and fight back. That brother of mine was quiet but he'd fight you to the finish. I worked for a white woman who trusted me so I never had no trouble. But a lot of colored people didn't have it so good. There was a code you had to obey."

Getting an education for their children was the main reason for my great-grandparents migrating to the North; they saw book learning as the sole channel to gaining a life of opportunity.

"When we went to school, colored couldn't mix with white," Rose, my grandmother, says. "Daddy wanted something different for us. I went to school partly here and partly down South. When we first came to Cleveland, the schools were almost all white. There weren't hardly any colored in Cleveland. The president was Woodrow Wilson. Teddy Roosevelt had died. My daddy had worked and saved up some money. He bought the house where we live now for the high price of $1400. It was just a cottage then with lots of woods around it. Lots of trees. There were no street lights, just dirt roads. It was the country then."

My great-grandmother became angry when she remembered how she had allowed my grandmother to work as a young girl to help make ends meet. Money was tight and my great-grandfather sometimes barely made enough to cover the bills and save. "Rose used to work," my great-grandmother says. "I had to hide her when the school authorities came around. I was young. I didn't have any sense then. If I knew what I know now, I'd made her go to school."

Rose had a different slant on the issue. "I was a young girl. I worked in a bag-making factory in town. I worked on a machine. They would come around to see if I was in school. It wasn't bad work. Young kids got good opportunities now. In the South, a lot of colored valued education then, but the white folks didn't want you to have it. In the old days, in my mother's time, I heard colored people had to pray in secret and learn to read in secret. The white man didn't want us to learn. My mother went to school with Uncle Moses. Colored taught each other then. A book was a precious thing. If they knew something, then they passed it on to someone else. We got a good foundation.

"We had land. My father had a good spread. He had a house, land and a store. The South was still segregated. You couldn't eat at certain places. You couldn't sit anywhere you wanted. A lot of things colored couldn't do. The Klan was raging down there when I was young. Colored was scared of them. I never saw them but I heard my father talk about them."

"It wasn't paradise," my great-grandmother adds.

In the South at the turn of the century, riots and lynchings were commonplace. Thousands of blacks lost their lives during this period. Even though Georgia was not as violent as Mississippi or other parts of the region, it had its share of racial conflict.

"Some colored had guns back then and wasn't afraid to use them," Rose says. "They had a big riot in Atlanta when I was a girl. Colored tore the town up. It was something. Like a war. It seemed after that time that the white folks respected the colored there a little more. They had a bad riot in Macon too. A lot of colored were killed by the white people. Just for being colored. When I was 15, they had one. One woman brought her son to our house in the middle of the night, all scared, said the white men were looking for him to kill him. We sent him on away from there that night. Whenever they had a riot, the colored would give them what for. Colored men were strong back then. They would give as good as they got. They weren't afraid. You never read that in the history books."

Armed resistance occurred much more often than traditional history books would have us believe. The years before my great-grandparents came North were filled with strife as blacks fought back in the bigger cities and small towns. "We were still in Georgia," my great-grandmother notes, her eyes narrowing. "It was just before we came up here. I don't remember the year. They used to pass word where we was that the nightriders were going to come through the colored part that night. The men would get guns and lay in ditches waiting. We women would wait inside with the babies. If the whites caught you off by yourself, they would hurt you, kill you."

Upon arriving in Cleveland, the Hollingsheads settled into their new home. My grandmother, Rose, met a young man, Allen Clinton Smith, who had just left the navy. He was a strong, muscular man from Branch, Tennessee, a small town just outside of Nashville. Like Will Fleming, my great-grandfather owned a farm but he traded in horses and cattle. He traded his stock through a white agent in Alabama and Georgia. He had a big family, no one knows exactly how many offspring he had. Rose Hollingshead became Mrs. Smith and the couple moved in with her parents after my great-grandfather became seriously ill.

"My husband bought the house just before he passed," my great-grandmother says. "He had a few strokes and I think he knew he was going to die. He sent for my daughter and her husband to come here and take care of me. They did just that."

Then the Depression hit. If the hard times caught whites by surprise, devastating them financially, then its effect were even more severe for blacks who had just arrived in the North. However, black families had learned the art of survival while enduring the social difficulties of the vicious Jim Crow South. In a way, they were ready for the Depression.

"Depression times were real bad, real bad," Rose says. "Your mama was just a little girl. All my children were small at that time. They used to call my husband 'Walkin' and Talkin'. They used to say he was a God-sent man. We sold hamburgers. This was before McDonald's. He started out with a little steam-wagon and drove it all over town. He sold them so cheap, five and ten cents. Since he had been in the navy on the USS *Utah* in the First World War, he got a bonus. All of the soldiers got them. He was a laborer, just like a lot of the colored they let serve back then. They did the work the white folks didn't want to do. When he got a bonus, he got a better wagon.

"I made pies. He used to get beef and chop it up himself. He'd seasoned it and the people loved it. We'd put them on biscuits and sell them. He was nice to the poor, the people who didn't have as much as we did. Sometimes he'd take scissors, tie clips and things from them if they didn't have any money. He hated to see anyone go hungry. That was his way. He had a big heart. One time, some people went to rob him and the people drove them off. They wouldn't let them rob him."

With their street smarts and hustle, they fed their growing brood of ten children and kept a roof over their heads. Finally times became easier, but a war came as Hitler tried to assert Aryan superiority over the world. My uncle, Russell, one of the older children, followed in his father's footsteps by joining the navy.

"Russell was on a destroyer," Rose explains. "He got all banged up in the war. He went all around the world, even to North Africa. When he got back, they put him in the hospital. I was glad he got back. A lot of them didn't come back."

She went to visit him with her magic bag of herbs and roots, something she would do years later with me when I was laid low with a severe bout of pneumonia. In my case, her herbs and potions did the trick after the doctor had walked from my room, shaking his head and saying it was in the hands of a Higher Power now.

"I treated Russell with some Jimson weed and herbs," she says. "They drained the poison out of his legs. The doctors saw the herbs and asked him what was that. He said, 'Something my mother put on me.' I believe in natural cures. The natural remedies are the best. And a little prayer doesn't hurt. There's only so much a doctor can do sometimes. The Earth has everything we need for the body."

A funny incident when my grandfather won the grand prize in a contest. It was another example of how deeply racism was embedded in American society. As Rose describes it, it was both a painful and humorous experience. "If your grandfather had been born a white man, he'd gone far. You know a colored man could only go so far back then. The white man had his thumb on him. In some ways, the white man ain't changed much. He still can't stand the colored and never will. We colored go through so much. I remember there was a contest and my husband entered it. He sold so much product that his name was high on the list for the prize. But the white man didn't want to give it to a colored man, so they snooped around to find out what he was. When they came out to the house, he said to me not to answer the door so they wouldn't know. He could speak Polish real good, so the Polish people liked him. He got a lot of them. When the white people found out what he was, he didn't get the prize."

My mother, Dorothy, and my father, Robert, met some time in 1948. The city girl, still in her teens, was intrigued with the cocky, ambitious country boy. My father was living with an uncle up the street from where my mother lived with her parents. Despite some objections from my mother's family, they married and I was born a short time later.

"You were your granddaddy's favorite," Rose says. "He loved you so. He used to take care of you when you were a baby. What lungs. You'd scream, then they would pick you up and you'd laugh like crazy. Your mother loved sweets. She'd make your formula so sweet that you'd get a stomach ache."

And my great-grandmother adds: "You were just a baby when you came to us. You were always into something. I remember I got stung by a wasp and you went out and found the nest and destroyed it. You brought it back and showed me, so proud. You were so proud."

I remember the stubble of my grandfather's beard and how later I discovered how much he looked like Hemingway or vice versa. I remember being a little boy waiting in the snow with my grandmother for my mother to come on the bus and get me. Often she never did. I remember the family farm, the animals and the ditches along the sides of the road. It was through my great-grandmother that I discovered the world of books and writing. She gave me books by Dickens, Twain, Wright, and H. G. Wells to read. My vision of the world swelled and I would never be same. The other new element in my life that altered my world was the arrival of father's mother from Mississippi. Ornery and full of tales of the Old South, Mary Taylor could be both a delight and a holy terror. My grandparents treated her as an alien, someone from another world—polite yet reserved. This was largely due to Mama Taylor's love of voodoo.

"She was Creole and wasn't to be messed with," Rose says. "I didn't mess with anyone's business. I stayed away from her. Those Louisiana people believe in all that Hoodoo mess. I don't mess with that."

There were conflicts between Mama Taylor and my mother, so she moved out to a small house near a grocery store. I was sent to live with her. I became the sorcerer's apprentice. She did spells. She read futures for people or gave them numbers to play. She burned white or black candles, split eggs in her wrinkled palms to reveal all-red yolks, and burned a purple powder that gave off a yellow smoke. One of the neighborhood boys once threatened her, and she smiled slyly, telling him that he would not live to see his seventeenth birthday. He was sixteen. Five weeks later, the boy drowned in a gravel pit near a factory. Mama Taylor was not to be toyed with.

Sometimes on quiet evenings, she would talk about Old New Orleans, the Creoles and Cajuns she knew as a girl or my father as a boy. Talk would often shift to Mardi Gras, the "foolishness" in the French Quarter or "the Quarter" as she called it. When she wasn't looking, I would go through her things and handle dark bottles with such names as Come To Me Powder, Mexican Luck, Goofer Dust, Mind Oil, Snake Root, Black Cat Oil, and Mad Water. She sprinkled two handfuls of powder brick on our doorstep as a barrier to evil spells. In a strange way, she was very religious, seeing a link between God and the spirits who were her friends. She hated rhythm and blues records or "reels."

Suddenly, Mama Taylor became ill. At night, she would hear voices and see things. I sat with her and watched for hants and devils. I was 12. One day, I went to school and returned home to find she had been taken to the hospital. At the hospital, she refused to take any medicine, throwing pills under her bed and spitting up elixirs. She died the next day. It was a terrible time because my grandfather had died that summer and my Uncle Russell was killed in a car accident shortly before Mama Taylor's death. A sadness crept over me that lasted for almost a year because I knew that these links to my past were gone and that the harsh reality of adulthood in an often insensitive white world lay ahead.

Robert Fleming *(b. 1950) was born in Cleveland, Ohio; he was formerly a reporter for the* New York Daily News *and is the recipient of the New York Press Club Award and the Revson Fellowship. He lives in New York City.*

HOW MUCH IS THE MIGRATION A FLIGHT FROM PERSECUTION?

Charles S. Johnson

Desire for more wages and more regular wages, for better social treatment, improved cultural surroundings; the hysteria of a mass movement; simple curiosity and desire for travel and adventure, and free railroad tickets, all have played their part in the divorcement of the southern Negro from the land of his birth.

Reasons are one thing; motives another. The former with all persons are likely to be merely a rationalization of behavior, while the latter usually play first role in inspiring the behavior. All Negroes (no more than all whites) are not uniformly sensitive to their social environment. And altho emphasis upon the pernicious nature of the social environment of southern Negroes should and doubtless will have the effect of improving it, such emphasis is apt to obscure what seem to be even more vital issues and more substantial elements of Negro character. After all, it means more that the Negroes who left the South were motivated more by the desire to improve their economic status than by fear of being man-handled by unfriendly whites. The one is a symptom of wholesome and substantial life purpose; the other, the symptom of a fugitive incourageous opportunism. Persecution plays its part—a considerable one. But when the whole of the migration of southern Negroes is considered; this part seems to be limited. It is indeed more likely that Negroes, like all others with a spark of ambition and self-interest, have been deserting soil which cannot yield returns in proportion to their population increase. The Census of 1920 indicated that the rate of Negro increase declined from 18.0 for the decade 1890–1900, to 11.2 for the next, and to 6.5 for the last. This does not mean that fewer children are being born, for actually more Negro than white babies per family are being born, but that more of them are dying. This desertion of the soil has taken three distinct directions: (a) urbanization—a species of migration; (b) quest for more productive lands; (c) transplantation to industrial communities, practically all of which are in the North. During the past thirty years, 1890–1920, there has been an increase in the rural population of 896,124 Negroes as compared with 2,078,331 for cities. The urban increase has been just about 100 per cent as rapid as the rural. In 1890, 19.8 per cent of the Negro population lived in cities; in 1920, this proportion grew to about 40 per cent. In the Southern States, between 1890–1900, the rural population increased 13.6 per cent, and between 1910 and 1920 it actually decreased 3.3 per cent. The Negro population increase in southern cities, considered as a whole, has been greater than the increase in the North, considered as a whole, despite the half-million added during the last decade. Here, of course, is the economic factor at work, hand in hand, with greater mobility, increased transportation, restlessness and the monotony and uncertainty of agricultural life ever against the allurements of the city.

The greatest inter-state movements of southern Negroes have been further South and West. In 1910, 52.3 per cent of the migration from Southern States was to the area west of the Mississippi; while in 1920, after the tremendous migration to the North, 42.9 per cent were living in the Southwestern States as compared with 42.2 per cent living in the North and West. For 130 years the center of the Negro population moved steadily some 478 miles toward the southwest—from Dinwiddie county, Va., to northern Alabama.

This shifting is further evident in the instability of Negro population in southern counties. Between 1900 and 1910, for example, 33.5 per cent of the counties increased rapidly, 31.1 increased at a rate above the average, while only 3.4 per cent showed an actual decrease, and 9.8 per cent an average increase equivalent to the total increase of the section. In 1879 there was a migration, similar to the one which we now experience, to Kansas. This followed a depression in 1878. Some 60,000 Negroes left. In 1888–1889, there was a similar movement to Arkansas, which carried 35,000 Negroes. Arkansas, for example, gained, between 1900–1910, 105,516 Negroes, the largest net gain of any state north or south; Oklahoma gained 85,062; and Texas, 19,821; while all the eastern, southern and central states suffered a loss. The counties of most rapid increase in the South between 1910 and 1920 were those south of the region of maximum Negro population density in 1910.

It is further significant here that the white populations have been showing in general outline the same trend of mobility as the Negroes. For example, their rate of mobility was 20 per cent as compared with 16 per cent for the Negroes and they also have left the counties deserted by Negroes, taking the same direction of migration.

Had persecution been the dominant and original stimulus, the direction of Negroes during the sixty years following emancipation would have been north instead of further south.

As a working test, a rough correlation was made between counties of the South in which lynchings had occurred during the thirty year period 1888–1918 and the migration from and to these counties.

Of ten Georgia counties, in which five or more lynchings occurred, the Negro population increased in five. Of the other five, in which the Negro population decreased, there was a corresponding decrease in the white population in three, and an increase in the other two considerably less than the average. To use one example,— in Montgomery County, in which five lynchings occurred, the Negro population decreased from 7,310 to 4,348 and the white population from 12,328 to 4,768. If this were a measure of persecution, the whites are the greater victims.

In Jasper County, Ga., there were nine lynchings, the largest number for any county of the state in thirty years. The Negro population actually increased in this county between 1890 to 1920, while the white population during 1900 and 1910 actually decreased.

Or to take the State of Texas. Of the six counties with five or more lynchings, the Negro population increased in four and decreased in two. Of the two in which there was a Negro decrease, there was a corresponding but more serious decrease in the white population. In Waller County, the Negro population decreased from 6,712 in 1910 to 4,967 in 1920; the white population decreased from 6,375 in 1900 to 5,426 in 1910 and to 4,082 in 1920. In Harrison County, with the largest number of lynchings (16), the Negro population showed a similar increase from 13,544 to 15,639.

In the State of Alabama, Jefferson County, with ten lynchings, increased from 90,617 in 1910 to 130,211 in 1920—the largest recorded increase in any county; Dallas County, with the largest number of lynchings (19), lost only 1,246 Negroes, while Sumter, with no lynchings at all, lost 3,491.

In spite of a considerable progress by Negroes, the great bulk of this population is in an almost hopeless struggle against feudalism. In four of the most congested Southern States: Georgia, Alabama, Mississippi, Louisiana, containing 37,405,760 Negroes or over 36 per cent of all the Negroes in the country, 83.3 per cent of them are landless. The per cent of tenant farmers instead of changing over into owners actually increased in practically every Southern State during the past decade, while the per cent of owners decreased. Altho this was to some extent true of white farmers, the proportion among Negroes was just twice as great. The large plantation owners it seems are gradually taking over the land, thus reducing tenants, white and colored, to a state of unrelieved and helpless peasantry.

Cotton is a peculiar crop. Its nurture requires about seven times as many hands as other crops and only then for certain periods of the year. It does not yield readily to labor saving devices. It can be grown profitably only with cheap labor, and plenty of it, and Negroes have been the South's cheap labor. Immigrants are not welcomed because of their tendency and frequent ability in time to purchase their own plots of ground. As a matter of fact, small white tenants are not as desirable in the plantation scheme as Negroes; and if Negroes persist in leaving, the plantation system itself, an anomaly in this country and notoriously unstable, is doomed

Knowing just why Negroes left the South and what they were looking for will carry one further toward making their adjustment easier. The thought of flight from persecution excites little sympathy either from the practical employer or the northern white population among whom these Negroes will hereafter live. Every man who runs is not a good worker and from the point of view of the Negroes who have come, they cannot sustain themselves long on sympathy. It is indeed not unthinkable that the high mortality so conspicuous in the abnormally reduced rate of Negro increase will be strikingly affected by the migration. The relief of over-population in certain counties of the South will undoubtedly give each Negro child born a better chance for survival, while, on the other hand, the presence of Negroes in cities exposes them to health education and sanitary regulations. The death rate of Negroes in northern cities, in spite of the fact that migrations there are principally of adults to whom death is more imminent, is not as great as in most of the Negro counties of the South.

Charles S. Johnson *(1893–1956), born in Bristol, Virginia, was named director of the Department of Research and Investigation of the National Urban League in 1921. Two years later he became editor of* Opportunity *magazine, where he remained until 1928. He was a social scientist and became the first black president of Fisk University.*

OPPORTUNITY Magazine   October 1923

Why They Come North

As to Negro migration, the Negro realizes that wages in the North are higher, but he also realizes that living conditions are equally high, which offsets any profit to himself. Can we conscientiously

say that it is the dollar which makes him crave for the North? Emphatically no. The wages of the North have always been higher.

The Negro of today is a new Negro. He has been taught new ideas and his white brethren are responsible. He fought for his country. He was carried with his pack and gun into a foreign country; he came into contact with dark-skinned brethren, citizens of foreign countries, especially France, who told him of their rights as citizens and how their country protected them as citizens. Even the French populace were surprised to learn of the southern Negro's treatment in this country and lauded him as being extremely loyal under such conditions.

The Negro has played well his part, and is it not fair that he should expect better pay, better working and living conditions, and the full rights of loyal citizens?

Here is why he leaves the South: Unjust treatment, failure to secure a square deal in the courts, taxation without representation, denial of the right to vote thru the subterfuge of the white primary, no representation in any form of government, poor schools, unjust pay for and division of crops, insulting of women without any redress, and public torture.

The Negro longs for free air, happiness and all that goes to make for a full and free citizenship—and that brings him North.

—C. Otis of Ithaca, N. Y.
in the N. Y. Tribune.

OPPORTUNITY Magazine   October 1923

Housing the Migrants

Eight northern cities with a combined Negro population of 709,630, report as a result of the recent movement northward of southern Negroes an unparalleled shortage of houses and living accommodations. New York, for example, has about 40,000 more Negroes than present buildings can comfortably or even decently accommodate. This situation was given point when to the existing congestion there was added, a short while ago, several thousand delegates to the convention of a fraternal organization. Those whose relations with the residents would not permit the intimacy of further doubling up found it necessary to sleep in the parks.

In Pittsburgh the Negro home seekers have been forced to retreat to the uninhabitable cliffs, isolated from the city's gas and water supply. Rents have been rapidly and consistently rising. Families here report paying $6.00 a night for one room, lodging in houses that should not even be allowed to remain standing.

A report from Detroit indicates that "Landlords have no trouble in getting $45.00 and $50.00 a month for four rooms without electric light and frequently without bath." In Chicago practically no building is going on in the neighborhoods of Negro residence as newcomers continue to pour in but, on the other hand, several squares of good buildings, occupied almost exclusively by Negroes, have been torn down by the city in its plan to widen the boulevard and provide school playgrounds.

The housing of Negroes, unfortunately, is bound doubly by the housing for the whites. The former have less capital for building and can borrow less. The homes they get are most often those abandoned by the whites and so long as there is nothing better in sight no one, however strong his antipathy to contact with Negroes as neighbors, actual or potential, is likely to abandon what he has. Speculations, thus, concerning relief for the Negro population are conditioned very largely upon the actual state of housing among the whole population.

This is anything but cheerful. The National Association of Real Estate Boards has sent out questionnaires to 475 local real estate boards throughout the United States seeking light on this question. To date they have received 225 returns. In 61 per cent of the cities an actual shortage exists; in 53 per cent of the cities rents are still on the increase; in 36 per cent they are given as stationary. The most interesting feature of the inquiry is the reported tendency of many families to move into the suburbs.

This is after all perhaps the most hopeful sign for the relief of the Negroes. This movement to the suburbs is most noticeable in the larger northern cities, where the greatest problems of Negro housing have been encountered. Once an appreciable outlet is provided, an opening will be made in the iron ring which now with such uncompromising rigor holds the Negroes within prescribed residential areas too crowded for further building, and in buildings too old to keep up.

CHICAGO DEFENDER   September 2, 1916

The exodus of labor from the South has caused much alarm among the Southern whites, who have failed to treat them decent. The men, tired of being kicked and cursed, are leaving by the thousands. . . .

CHICAGO DEFENDER   August 26, 1916

Migration

I have read several articles recently from the pen of Race leaders advising the Negroes against going to the north for employment. I am thoroughly convinced that this advice is wrong, however honestly and well intended it is being given. These leaders give reasons why the Negro should stay in the south, but none of them give any good reason why our people should not go to the Chinaman, the Japanese, the Italian, the Pole, the Scandinavian and other foreigners to come to America for work, why should it be not profitable for the Negro to go to the same field for employment?

In the first place, there is but little work at the present for us in the south, except growing cotton, and cotton growing is so unprofitable under present conditions, that those who stick to it do so under starvation conditions. There is more cotton raised than the world has ready use for. The cotton grower is unable to hold his crop and make his own prices, therefore the speculator fixes the prices and the grower is the loser. Why then keep our people raising cotton for which there is no profitable market when he is needed in the mines and factories and farms of the north and west, producing the things which the world most needs?

Through this migration to the north and west, he has a golden opportunity to learn. We will get new ideas of life, new ideas of agriculture and manufacturing, new ideas of civilization, new ideas of a larger world. Many will return home when the weather gets cold but they will bring back with them these ideas and impart them to the folds at home. Others will come and go, and in this manner develop themselves as they could not otherwise do.

This man who travels is the man who learns most. The sons of Ham got into the jungles of Africa and were satisfied with the native products and hence remained in the dense ignorance. But the Caucasian roamed from place to place, followed the sun in its westward course, and are the enlightened people of the globe.

In the early days of our American civilization Horace Greeley said to the young man, "Go west!" The white man has gone westward until he has reached the east. I say to the young men of my race: "Go west!" Go east! Go north! Go south! Go everywhere the sun shines! Go everywhere there is found an opportunity to make a living and develop this wonderful world of ours.

W. J. Latham, Jackson, Mississippi

"The Chicago Defender" named the exodus "The Great Northern Drive," and set the date May 15th [1917], announced the arrivals and took responsibility for inducing "the poor brethren" from the south. It was accused of ruining Hattiesburg, Mississippi by promoting this rush to the North. The sale of this paper was, therefore, forbidden in several towns in the South."

"The labor agents were a very important factor in stimulating the movement. The number at work in the South appears to have been greatly exaggerated."

> Negro Migration During the War.
> Emmett J. Scott

Montgomery, Alabama   May 7, 1917

My dear Sir:
I am writing to solicit your aid and advice as to how I may best obtain employment at my trade in your city. I shall be coming that way on the 15th of May and I wish to find immediate employment if possible.

I have varied experience as a compositor and printer. Job composition is my hobby. I have not experience as linotype operator, but can fill any other place in a printing office. Please communicate with me at the above address at once. Thanking you in advance for any assistance and information in the matter, I am

Rome, Georgia   May 13, 1917

Dear Sir:
I am writing you in regards to present conditions in Chicago in getting employment. I am an experienced hotel man—in all departments, such as bellman, waiter, bus boy, or any other work pertaining to hotel and would like to know in return could you furnish me transportation to Chicago as you advertise in the Chicago Defender. Am good honest and sober worker, can furnish recermendations if necessary. Have worked at the Palmer House during year 1911 as bus boy in Cafe. But returned south for awhile and since the Northern Drive has begun I have decided to return to Chicago as I am well acquainted with the city. Hope to hear from you soon on this matter as it is of great importance to me.

New Orleans, Louisiana   April 25, 1917

Dear Editor:
I am a reader of the Defender and I am ask so much about the
great Northern drive on the 15th of May. We want more under-
standing about it for there is a great many wants to get ready for
that day & the depot agents never gives us any satisfaction when
we ask them they dont want us to leave here, I want to ask you to
please publish in your next Saturdays paper just what the fair will
be that day so we all will know & can be ready. So many women
here plan to go that day. They are all working women and we cant
get work here so much now, the white women tells us we just want
to make money to go North and we do so please kindly ans[wer].
this in your next paper if you do I will read it for I read every
word in the Defender, had rather read it then to eat when Satur-
day comes, it is my hearts delight & hope your paper will continue
on in the south until every one reads it for it is a God sent blessing
to the Race. Will close with best wishes,

Yours for success.

New Orleans, Louisiana   May 2, 1917

Dear Sir:
Please Sir will you kindly tell me what is meant by the great
Northern Drive to take place May the 15th on tuesday. It is a ru-
mor all over town to be ready for the 15th of May to go in the
drive. the Defender first spoke of the drive the 10th of February.
My husband is in the north already preparing for our family but I
hear that the excursion will be $6.00 from here north on the 15 and
having a large family, I would profit by if it is really true. Do
please write at once and say is there an excoursion to leave the
south. Nearly the whole of the south is getting ready for the drive
or excoursion as it is termed. Please write at once. We are sick to
get out of the solid south.

Resp[ectfully] yours.

1916

Dear Editor:
As I was reading the Defender to some male members of the Race
Sunday afternoon as I returned from a short service, they say the
Defender is all bull and it is only some white man putting you all
up to that.

THE PREACHER OF THE BIG ZION CHURCH is in the pulpit preaching in the members of the Race telling them not to come North, that they cannot work for those people up there and they'd better stay here. He is telling them when the train puts you off in the North you all have got no place to put us and nothing for us to eat till we can get something, are part of them that are gone there have frozen to death for the want of fire. He said he saw it in the paper. He says if the white man goes and doesnt like it, we have got to keep our nose down the grind stone will we can get money enough to come back.

I heard some talk of the prejudices saying that all the members of the Race should not come North. Before they would stand for it they would have blood.

Well, that shows no freedom and if they are going to do that, it shows that we are still under the bonds of slavery.

I take the Defender and I think it is the only paper in this whole world. I used to take plenty of southern papers, but now give me the Defender. For my sake and for the sake of others, please put it in the paper explaining to the nuts that the train that's taking members of the race from the South is not carrying them away to starve and freeze. But I have been talking to some of them and they say just as soon as the train hits old Pensacola, they are gone. These prejudices are telling us that we better study ourselves and stay away from the North; that we will be glad enough to get back here if we can make the money to get back with. Try to give the nuts the understanding in the paper if you all can.

(Signed) From an unknown party,
but a member of the Race.

CHICAGO DEFENDER   August 26, 1916

Laborers Going North

CHICAGO DEFENDER NEWS SERVICE

Ensley, Ala., Aug. 25.—The men on the railroad here are thinking seriously of going north to work. The railroads are paying white men 90 cents per day more than they pay members of the Race. Such a discrimination is being felt and the time has come for them to leave and go north, where labor pay is higher and no discrimination in salary. The northern agents for labor will find this a splendid field to find workmen.

Taken From Train

CHICAGO DEFENDER NEWS SERVICE

Americus, Ga., Aug. 25—Fifty members of the Race were arrested last week when they attempted to leave for cities in the north and east. Several policemen were sent to the depot when the chief heard that many were leaving. Armed with John Doe warrants, they boarded the train when it began to speed toward Leslie. The arrested men were brought back and held pending investigation and legal operations to stop the wholesale immigration north.

New Orleans, Louisiana   February 26, 1917

Dear Sir this is to let you know that i read your advertisement in the Chicago Defender. i am a subscriber to the Chicago Defender. I would like to get a good occupation on codition that you could send me a pass I am a truck driver competant bar tender or any inside job that you see fit to give me. If you do not send passes recomend me to a place that sends the passes so that I could get a good job at once. I am very anxious to obtain a good position as soon as possible.

Yours respect.

NEWARK EVENING NEWS   November 24, 1916

To the Editor of the News:

Sir—It may be of interest to you to know that we are deeply grateful because of the encouraging tone of your editorial comments with respect to the recent influx of colored people from the South. Admittedly, unless we have the sympathy and cooperation of our white neighbors, their coming in such large numbers will create a problem of considerable moment. They come not as paupers, many indeed being possessed of fair financial resources, and, since they are not shiftless, they are not apt to become a weight upon the community if the avenues of employment are kept open to them.

The environment they have abandoned, however, is essentially different from that in which they now find themselves. It is for us to carry to them the lesson of sanitary living, they must be acquainted with the economic problem that confronts our people here, and they must be taught to avoid the many pitfalls afforded by the glamour of surroundings the more attractive in that they are new and strange.

Our churches, the respective branches of the National Association for the Advancement of Colored People, this organization and the many others among us have set themselves to this task. Religious meetings are being held to which these people are invited that they may be encouraged to maintain the religious standards that are always a part of the lives of our people. Efforts are being made to secure for them suitable living accommodations, and, with the settling of each family, our men and women speak to them of the health and economic conditions that obtain here.

Coming out of a section that affords but the remotest semblance of social and civil liberty, it is to expected that they will at time lose sight of the fact that even this, to them the Land of Promise, does not accept the black man at all times and in all places, so that we are acquainting them with conditions in this respect against the time when these barriers are removed. They have left the land of their nativity in search of greater freedom and increased opportunity, prime factors in the migrating of any people. The land they have abandoned has, to be generous, treated them unkindly, the lynchings and other injustices have made life there unbearable. Again the small wage to be earned in their former homes in no wise compares with that offered here, and perhaps the latter as much as the former is a factor in the present pilgrimage.

The Negro has never been a wanderer. Fixed ties have ever held for him attractions that have outshone opportunities that lie elsewhere. It is a sad commentary upon the splendid traditions of the American people that the patient black should feel called upon to thus abandon a land that is so intimately associated with his history. The South will not be the gainer. We of his common blood are concerned that the North may not be the loser. To that end we urge the co-operation of our white neighbors with whom we have lived on terms that have given to the progress of both races, that we who, perhaps more than any, are to be the gainers or losers, may assimilate our brothers who have come to us from the Southland.

Hamilton Travis
President of Colored
Organizations of New Jersey.

THE MIGRATION: A NORTHERN VIEW

Emmett J. Scott

*(From an address delivered before the Annual Conference of the National
Urban League)*

The effect of the migration has been to bring to the North new and
difficult problems. In some sections there has been much exploitation. At the same time many of these untutored people have found
themselves suddenly intoxicated with the freedom of northern, eastern and western centers and in some instances have seemed to mistake liberty and freedom for license. It is well to state, however, that
general observation bears out the statement that, in the main, these
migrants have proved law-abiding, industrious citizens who are
anxious to improve their general social condition.

In undertaking to fill the places in northern industry formerly
occupied by skilled and unskilled European labor, it was to be expected that the Negro would meet with difficulties. These difficulties were experienced not only in his work but in connection with
his social position as well.

Discussing this subject recently Mr. E. V. Wilcox, one of the
editors of *The Country Gentleman,* in a broadcast message, said:

"The mecca of this great Negro pilgrimage is found in the industrial cities, especially in Pittsburgh, Akron, Detroit, Chicago,
Cincinnati, St. Louis, Indianapolis, Philadelphia, Buffalo, Bridge-
port, etc. These people are going mostly into mining, packing, steel
and rubber industries, the building trades, and highway construction. What happens to the Negro when he comes North? Within two
months he is apparently just as much at home in the steel mill as he
previously had been in the cotton field. Perhaps the first thing the
newcomer learns is thrift. He realizes that it costs more to live in
Detroit than down in the Yazoo Delta. He at once begins to save
money. About 80 percent of the colored people in Detroit have bank
accounts, and 50 per cent of them carry life insurance. In many
northern cities Negroes are rapidly buying homes. More than 50 per
cent of the colored homes in Boston have been bought since 1918.
How does the Negro fit into northern cities? Big employers say that
they like him better than alien laborers. The Negro is tractable,
adaptable, sometimes shiftless, but becoming more thrifty, and is

always in good humour. The fact that he speaks English is a big point in his favor."

Following the close of the great World War, agitation was made for national legislation to restrict alien immigration. This was said to have been a reaction growing out of the experiences of this country during the war when it found that there was such a large alien population which could not be counted upon as substantial defenders of our country in time of war. The legislation enacted by the Congress of the United States, according to Honorable Elbert H. Gary, Chairman of the Board of Directors of the U.S. Steel Corporation, closed up the avenues of labor supply for American industries. A statement to this effect was issued by Mr. Gary early in 1923, following his return from Europe, when he said that the operation of the new regulations regarding immigration were bringing about a serious labor shortage in American industries. In a telegram at that time, I called Mr. Gary's attention to the fact that there are in this country twelve million colored people; that eight million of these twelve million are in the South; that they are citizens of the Republic; that they are tied to a one crop system and oppressed by economic conditions that hinder and prevent their fullest development and the enjoyment of the guaranteed privilege of American citizenship. I also pointed out that they possess strong bodies and have a genuine patriotic attachment to American institutions; that they are in a position to supply the labor shortage to which he referred if plans be undertaken, on a large and important scale, to transfer them to centers where their services are needed. I also added that it seems unnecessary to look to foreign shores to supply any labor shortage that may exist in American industries when there is this large and sympathetic group so easily within reach. These colored Americans are not aliens; they have never sought to disrupt the Government nor do they harbor bolshevistic or anarchistic ideals. They are ready and willing to help develop the resources of their country.

This telegram was broadcast by the Associated Press and evoked both favorable and unfavorable criticism on the part of northern and southern editors and hundreds of others. One of the criticisms came from a Mr. John M. Gibbs, Secretary-Treasurer of the North Carolina Pine Association, Norfolk, Virginia, in which he objected to the suggestion that southern Negro labor be used in northern industries, on the ground that the Negro is needed in the South.

It is not necessary for me to quote in detail the answer sent to Mr. Gibbs aside from calling his attention to the fact that I advised him that the Negro is no longer content to accept the intolerable conditions to which he has been subjected in the past and a lowered wage at the same time. I also called his attention to the vagrancy laws of the South which are invoked to intimidate Negro laborers and force them to work under oppressive conditions. I felt compelled to say to him that if unwillingness to work under these restrictive and dehumanizing conditions is to be interpreted as a shortage of labor, then, if there is not a shortage of labor in the lumber camps and the other industries of the South, there should be such a shortage. Finally, I felt compelled to add that it is the duty of colored people, wherever opportunity offers, to leave those sections where lynchings and peonage are practiced upon them with impunity.

The bulk of the colored people of the South will not be transferred to the North. The problem of the races in America will not be wholly settled by the present migration movement. Undoubtedly, however, barriers are being broken down, the race is being liberated industrially, and the Negro has given evidence of his willingness as a patriotic American to serve the nation industrially as he has served it upon so many other occasions during its periods of stress and storm.

Emmett Jay Scott *(1873–1957), born in Houston, Texas, was best known as Booker T. Washington's private secretary, a post he held from 1897 to 1915. He was also a university administrator, an active Republican, and author of* Negro Migrations During the War.

Augusta, Georgia   May 12, 1917

Dear Sir:
Just for a little information from you i would like to know
wheather or not i could get in tuch with some good people to work
for with a firm because things is afful hear in the south let me here
from you soon as possible what ever you do dont publish my name
in your paper but i think peple as a race ought to look out for one
another as Christians friends i am a schuffur and i can't make a
living for my family with small pay and the peple is getting so bad
with us black peple down south hear. now if you ever help your
race now is the time to help me to get my family away. food stuf is
so high. i will look for answer by return mail. dont publish my
name in your paper but let me her from you at once.

(Signed) *ONE OF THE NEGRO RACE.*

New Orleans, Louisiana   May 1, 1917

Dear sir
I am a reader of the Chicago defender I seen in the defender that
you are interested in the well fair of the colored people those of the
class that is interested in them selves and coming to the north for a
better chance so i pake [speak?] about conditions of geting work as
i see that you are in turch with the foundrys warehouses and the
manufacturing concerns that is in need of laborers and i thought it
was best to rite you and get some understanding as it is 4 of us
expecting to leave hear in a few days to come north but we are not
coming for pleasure we are looking for wirj abd [work and] better
and more money and i ask you aid in helping us to secure good
position of work as we are men of familys and we canot aford to
loaf and i will be very glad to hear from you and on my arrival i
will call at your place to see you.

Yours truly.

Memphis, Tennessee   April 23, 1917

Gentlemen
I want to get in tuch with you in regard of good location & a job i
am for race elevation every way. I want a job in a small town some
where in north where I can recieve verry good wages and where I
can educate my 3 little girls and demand respect of intelegence. I
prefer a job as cabinet maker or any kind of furniture mfg. if pos-
sible.

Let me hear from you all at once please. State minimum wages
and kind of work.

Yours truly.

BACKSTAGE AND THE RAILROAD

Zora Neale Hurston

There is something about poverty that smells like death. Dead dreams dropping off the heart like leaves in a dry season and rotting around the feet; impulses smothered too long in the fetid air of underground caves. The soul lives in a sickly air. People can be slaveships in shoes.

This wordless feeling went with me from the time I was ten years old until I achieved a sort of competence around twenty. Naturally, the first five years were the worst. Things and circumstances gave life a most depressing odor.

The five years following my leaving the school at Jacksonville were haunted. I was shifted from house to house of relatives and friends and found comfort nowhere. I was without books to read most of the time, except where I could get hold of them by mere chance. That left no room for selection. I was miserable, and no doubt made others miserable around me, because they could not see what was the matter with me, and I had no part in what interested them.

I was in school off and on, which gave me vagrant peeps into the light, but these intervals lacked peace because I had no guarantee that they would last. I was growing and the general thought was that I could bring in something. This book-reading business was a hold-back and an unrelieved evil. I could not do very much, but look at so-and-so. She was nursing for some good white people. A dollar a week and most of her clothes. People who had no parents could not afford to sit around on school benches wearing out what clothes they had.

One of the most serious objections to me was that having nothing, I still did not know how to be humble. A child in my place ought to realize I was lucky to have a roof over my head and anything to eat at all. And from their point of view, they were right. From mine, my stomach pains were the least of my sufferings. I wanted what they could not conceive of. I could not reveal myself for lack of expression, and then for lack of hope of understanding, even if I could have found the words. I was not comfortable to have around. Strange things must have looked out of my eyes like Lazarus after his resurrection.

So I was forever shifting. I walked by my corpse. I smelt it and felt it. I smelt the corpses of those among whom I must live, though they did not. They were as much at home with theirs as death in a tomb.

Gradually, I came to the point of attempting self-support. It was a glorious feeling when it came to me. But the actual working out of the thing was not so simple as the concept. I was about fourteen then.

For one thing, I really was young for the try. Then my growth was retarded somewhat so that I looked younger than I really was. Housewives would open the door at my ring and look me over. No, they wanted someone old enough to be responsible. No, they wanted someone strong enough to do the work, and so on like that. Did my mother know I was out looking for work? Sometimes in bed at night I would ask myself that very question and wonder.

But now and then someone would like my looks and give me a try. I did very badly because I was interested in the front of the house, not the back. No matter how I resolved, I'd get tangled up with their reading matter, and lose my job. It was not that I was lazy, I just was not interested in dusting and dishwashing. But I always made friends with the children if there were any. That was not intentional. We just got together somehow. That would be fun, but going out to play did not help much on jobs.

One woman liked me for it. She had two little girls, seven and five. I was hired as an upstairs maid. For two or three days things went on very well. The president of the kitchen was a fat, black old woman who had nursed the master of the house and was a fixture. Nobody is so powerful in a Southern family as one of these family fixtures. No matter who hires you, the fixture can fire you. They roam all over the house bossing everybody from the boss on down. Nobody must upset Cynthia or Rhoda or Beckey. If you can't get along with the house president you can't keep the job.

And Miz Cally was President in Full in this house. She looked at me cut-eye first thing because the madam had hired me without asking her about it. She went into her grumble just as soon as I stuck my head in the kitchen door. She looked at me for a moment with her hands on her hips and burst out, "Lawd a'mercy! Miz Alice must done took you to raise! She don't need no more young'uns round de place. Dis house needs a woman to give aid and assistance."

She showed her further disapproval by vetoing every move I made. She was to show me where to find the aprons, and she did. Just as soon as I pulled open the drawer, she bustled me right away from it with her hips.

"Don't you go pulling and hauling through *my* drawers! I keeps things in they place. You take de apron I give you and git on up dem stairs."

I didn't get mad with her. I took the apron and put it on with quite a bit of editing by Sister Cally, and went on up the back stairs. As I emerged on the upper floor, two pairs of gray-blue eyes were ranged on me.

"Hello!" said the two little girls in chorus.

"Hello!" I answered back.

"You going to work for us?" the taller one asked, and fell in beside me.

"Yeah." Maybe I cracked a smile or something, for both of them took a hand on either side and we went on into the room where Mrs. Alice was waiting for me to show me what to do and how to do it.

She was a very beautiful woman in her middle twenties, and she was combing out her magnificent hair. She looked at me through the looking-glass, and we both started to grin for some reason or another.

She showed me how to make beds and clean up. There were three rooms up there, but she told me not to try to do too much at a time. Just keep things looking sort of neat. Then she dressed and left the house. I got things straightened out with Helen and Genevieve acting as convoy at every step. Things went all right till I got to the bathroom, then somehow or other we three found ourselves in a tussle. Screaming, laughing, splashing water and tussling, when a dark shadow filled up the door. Heinz could have wrung enough vinegar out of Cally's look to run his pickle works.

"You going 'way from here!" she prophesied, and shook her head so vigorously that her head rag wagged. She was going to get me gone from there!

"No!" screamed Helen, the littlest girl, and held on to me.

"No! No! No!" Genevieve shrieked.

"Humph! You just wait till yo' daddy come home!" Cally gloomed. "I ain't never seen no sich caper like dis since I been borned in dis world." Then she stumped on back downstairs.

"Don't you go," Genevieve begged. "I like you."

"Me too, I like you too," Helen chorused. "If you go home, we'll go with you."

I had to wait on the table at dinner that night, with my apron too long for me. Mrs. Alice and the children were giving a glowing account of me. The boss glanced at me tolerantly a time or two. Helen would grab hold of my clothes every time I passed her chair, and play in the vegetable dishes when I offered them to her, until her father threatened to spank her hands, but he looked up at me and smiled a little. He looked to me like an aged old soul of thirty-five or so.

Cally kept on cracking the kitchen door to see how I was getting along in there, and I suspect to give the boss a view of her disapproving face.

Things rocked on for a week or two. Mrs. Alice went out more and more to bridge clubs and things like that. She didn't care whether I made up the rooms or not so long as the children were entertained. She would come in late in the afternoon and tell Cally to run upstairs and straighten up a bit.

"What's dat gal been doing?" Cally would growl. Dat gal she was talking about had been off to the park with the children, or stretched out on the floor telling stories or reading aloud from some of their story books. Their mother had been free to go about her business, and a good time was had by all—except Cally.

Before a month passed, things came to a head: Cally burst into the dining-room one night and flew all over the place. The boss had to get somebody to do his cooking. She was tired of doing all the work. She just wasn't going to cook and look after things downstairs and then troop upstairs and do the work somebody else was getting paid for. She was old. Her joints hurt her so bad till she couldn't rest of nights. They really needed to get somebody to help.

Mrs. Alice sat there stark, still and quiet. The boss looked at her, then at old Cally, and then at me.

Finally, he said, "I never meant for you to work yourself down like that, Aunt Cally. You've done more than your share."

" 'Deed, Gawd knows I is!" Cally agreed belligerently, rolling her white eyeballs in my direction.

"'Isn't Zora taking care of the upstairs? I thought that was what she was hired for," the boss asked, and looked at his wife.

"Taking care of what?" Cally snorted. " 'Deed, I ain't lying, Mr. Ed. I wouldn't tell a lie on nobody—"

"I know you wouldn't, Auntie," he soothed.

"Dat gal don't do a living thing round dis house but play all day long wid these young'uns. Den I has to scuffle up dem stairs and do round, cause effen I didn't, dis here place would be like a hawg-pen. Dat's what it would. I *has* to go and do it, Mr. Ed, else it wouldn't never git done. And I'm sick and *tired*. I'm gwine 'way from here!"

"Naw, Cally, you can't do it. You been with me all my life, and I don't aim to let you go. Zora will have to go. These children are too big now to need a nurse."

What did he say that for? My public went into sound and action. Mrs. Alice was letting a tear or two slip. Otherwise she was as still as stone. But Helen scrambled out of her chair with her jaws latched back to the last notch. She stumbled up against me and swung on. Genevieve screamed "No!" in a regular chant like a cheer leader, and ran to me, too. Their mother never raised her head. The boss turned to her.

"Darling, why don't you quiet these children?" he asked gently.

"No! No! No! Zora can't go!" my cheering squad yelled, slinging tears right and left.

"Shut up!" the boss grated at the children and put his hand on the table and scuffled his feet as if he meant to rush off for the hairbrush. "I'll be on you in one more minute! Hush!"

It was easy to see that his heart was not in any spanking. His frown was not right for it. The yelling kept right on. Cally flounced on back to the kitchen, and he got up and hauled the children upstairs. In a minute he called his wife and shut the bedroom door.

Well, then, I didn't have a job any more. I didn't have money either, but I had bought a pair of shoes.

But I was lucky in a way. Somebody told the woman I was staying with about another job, so I went to see about it, and the lady took me. She was sick in the bed, and she had a little girl three years old, but this child did not shine like Helen and Genevieve. She was sort of old-looking in the face.

I didn't like that house. It frowned at me just as soon as I crossed the doorsill. It was a big house with plenty of things in it but the rooms just sat across the hall from each other and made gloomy faces back and forth.

I was soon out of a job again. I got out of many more. Sometimes I didn't suit the people. Sometimes the people didn't suit me. Sometimes my insides tortured me so that I was restless and unstable. I just was not the type. I was doing none of the things I wanted to do. I had to do numerous uninteresting things I did not want to do, and it was tearing me to pieces.

I wanted family love and peace and a resting place. I wanted books and school. When I saw more fortunate people of my own age on their way to and from school, I would cry inside and be depressed for days, until I learned how to mash down on my feelings and numb them for a spell. I felt crowded in on, and hope was beginning to waver.

The third vision of aimless wandering was on me as I had seen it. My brother Dick had married and sent for me to come to Sanford and stay with him. I got hopeful for school again. He sent me a ticket, and I went. I didn't want to go, though. As soon as I got back to Sanford, my father ordered me to stay at his house.

It was no more than a month after I got there before my stepmother and I had our fight.

I found my father a changed person. The bounce was gone from the man. The wreck of his home and the public reaction to it was telling on him. In spite of all, I was sorry for him and that added to my resentment towards his wife.

In all fairness to her, she probably did the best she could, according to her lights. It was just tragic that her light was so poor. A little more sense would have told her that the time and manner of her marriage to my father had killed any hope of success from the start. No warning bell inside of her caused her to question the wisdom of an arrangement made over so many fundamental stumbling stones. My father certainly could not see the consequences, for he had never had to consider them too seriously. Mama had always been there to do that. Suddenly he must have realized with inward terror that Lucy was not there any more. This was not just another escapade which Mama would knot his head for in private and smooth out publicly. It had rushed him along to where he did not want to go already and the end was not in sight. This new wife had wormed her way out of her little crack in the world to become what looked to her like a great lady, and the big river was too much for her craft. Instead of the world dipping the knee to the new-made Mrs. Reverend, they were spitting on her intentions and calling her a storm-buzzard. Certainly if my father had not built up a strong following years before, he could not have lasted three months. As it was, his foundations rotted from under him, and seven years saw him wrecked. He did not defend her and establish her. It might have been because he was not the kind of a man who could live without his friends, and his old friends, male and female, were the very ones who were leading the attack to disestablish her. Then, too, a certain amount of the prestige every wife enjoys arises out of where the man got her from and how. She lacked the comfort of these bulwarks too. She must have decided that if she could destroy his children she would be safe, but the opposite course would have been the only extenuating circumstance in the eyes of the public. The failure of the project would have been obvious in a few months or even weeks if Papa had been the kind of man to meet the conflict with courage. As it was, the misery of the situation continued for years. He was dragging around like a stepped-on worm. My brief appearance on the scene acted like a catalyzer. A few more months and the thing fell to pieces for good.

I could not bear the air for miles around. It was too personal and pressing, and humid with memories of what used to be.

So I went off to another town to find work. It was the same as at home so far as the dreariness and lack of hope and blunted impulses were concerned. But one thing did happen that lifted me up. In a pile of rubbish I found a copy of Milton's complete works. The back was gone and the book was yellowed. But it was all there. So I read Paradise Lost and luxuriated in Milton's syllables and rhythms without ever having heard that Milton was one of the greatest poets of the world. I read it because I liked it.

I worked through the whole volume and then I put it among my things. When I was supposed to be looking for work, I would be stretched out somewhere in the woods reading slowly so that I could understand the words. Some of them I did not. But I had read so many books that my reading vocabulary at least was not too meager.

A young woman who wanted to go off on a trip asked me to hold down her job for two months. She worked in a doctor's office and all I had to do was to answer the telephone and do around a little.

The doctor thought that I would not be suitable at first, but he had to have somebody right away so he took a deep breath and said he'd try me. We got along very well indeed after the first day. I became so interested and useful that he said if his old girl did not come back when she promised, he was going to see to it that I was trained for a practical nurse when I was a bit older.

But just at that time I received a letter from Bob, my oldest brother. He had just graduated from Medicine and said that he wanted to help me to go to school. He was sending for me to come to him right away. His wife sent love. He knew that I was going to love his children. He had married in his Freshman year in college and had three of them.

Nothing can describe my joy. I was going to have a home again. I was going to school. I was going to be with my brother! He had remembered me at last. My five haunted years were over!

I shall never forget the exaltation of my hurried packing. When I got on the train, I said goodbye—not to anybody in particular, but to the town, to loneliness, to defeat and frustration, to shabby living, to sterile houses and numbed pangs, to the kind of people I had no wish to know; to an era. I waved it goodbye and sank back into the cushions of the seat.

It was near night. I shall never forget how the red ball of the sun hung on the horizon and raced along with the train for a short space, and then plunged below the belly-band of the earth. There have been other suns that set in significance for me, but *that* sun! It was a book-mark in the pages of a life. I remember the long, strung-out cloud that measured it for the fall.

But I was due for more frustration. There was to be no school for me right away. I was needed around the house. My brother took me for a walk and explained to me that it would cause trouble if he put me in school at once. His wife would feel that he was pampering me. Just work along and be useful around the house and he would work things out in time.

This did not make me happy at all. I wanted to get through high school. I had a way of life inside me and I wanted it with a want that was twisting me. And now, it seemed I was just as far off as before. I was not even going to get paid for working this time, and no time off. But on the other hand, I was with my beloved brother, and the children were adorable! I was soon wrapped up in them head over heels.

It was get up early in the morning and make a fire in the kitchen range. Don't make too much noise and wake up my sister-in-law. I must remember that she was a mother and needed the rest. She had borne my brother's children and deserved the best that he could do for her, and so on. It didn't sound just right. I was not the father of those children, and several months later I found out what was wrong. It came to me in a flash. She had never borne a child for me, so I did not owe her a thing. Maybe somebody did, but it certainly wasn't I. My brother was acting as if I were the father of those children, instead of himself. There was much more, but my brother is dead and I do not wish even to risk being unjust to his memory, or unkind to the living. My sister-in-law is one of the most devoted mothers in the world. She was brave and loyal to my brother when it took courage to be that way. After all she was married to him, not I.

But I made an unexpected friend. She was a white woman and poor. She had children of my own age. Her husband was an electrician. She began to take an interest in me and to put ideas in my head. I will not go so far as to say that I was poorly dressed, for that would be bragging. The best I can say is that I could not be arrested for indecent exposure. I remember wanting gloves. I had never had a pair, and one of my friends told me that I ought to have on gloves when I went anywhere. I could not have them and I was most unhappy. But then, I was not in a position to buy a handkerchief.

This friend slipped me a message one day to come to her house. We had a code. Her son would pass and whistle until I showed myself to let him know I heard. Then he would go on and as soon as I could I would follow. This particular day, she told me that she had a job for me. I was delighted beyond words.

"It's a swell job if you can get it, Zora. I think you can. I told my husband to do all he can, and he thinks he's got it hemmed up for you."

"Oooh! What is it?"

"It is a lady's maid job. She is a singer down at the theater where he is electrician. She brought a maid with her from up North, but the maid met up with a lot of colored people and looks like she's going to get married right off. She don't want the job no more. The lady asked the men around the theater to get her somebody, and my husband thought about you and I told him to tell the rest of the men he had just the right girl for a maid. It seems like she is a mighty nice person."

I was too excited to sit still. I was frightened too, because I did not know the first thing about being a lady's maid. All I hoped was that the lady would overlook that part and give me a chance to catch on.

"You got to look nice for that. So I sent Valena down to buy you a little dress." Valena was her daughter. "It's cheap, but it's neat and stylish. Go inside Valena's room and try it on."

The dress was a navy blue poplin with a box-pleated skirt and a little round, white collar. To my own self, I never did look so pretty before. I put on the dress, and Valena's dark blue felt hat with a rolled brim. She saw to it that I shined my shoes, and then gave me car-fare and sent me off with every bit of advice she could think of.

My feet mounted up the golden stairs as I entered the stage door of that theater. The sounds, the smells, the backstage jumble of things were all things to bear me up into a sweeter atmosphere. I felt like dancing towards the dressing-room when it was pointed out to me. But my friend was walking with me, coaching me how to act, and I had to be as quiet and sober as could be.

The matinee performance of H.M.S. Pinafore was on, so I was told to wait. In a little while a tenor and a soprano voice quit singing a duet and a beautiful blond girl of about twenty-two came hurrying into the dressing-room. I waited until she went inside and closed the door, then I knocked and was told to come in.

She looked at me and smiled so hard till she almost laughed.

"Hello, little girl," she chanted. "Where did you come from?"

"Home. I come to see you."

"Oh, you did? That's fine. What did you come to see me about?"

"I come to work for you."

"Work for me?" She threw back her head and laughed. That frightened me a great deal. Maybe it was all a joke and there was no job after all. "Doing what?" she caroled on.

"Be your lady's maid."

"You? Why, how old are you?"

"Twenty," I said, and tried to look serious as I had been told. But she laughed so hard at that, till I forgot and laughed too.

"Oh, no, you are not twenty." She laughed some more, but it was not scornful laughter. Just bubbling fun.

"Well, eighteen, then," I compromised.

"No, not eighteen, either."

"Well, then, how about sixteen?"

She laughed at that. Instead of frowning in a sedate way as I had been told, here I was laughing like a fool myself.

"I don't believe you are sixteen, but I'll let it go at that," she said.

"Next birthday. Honest."

"It's all right; you're hired. But let's don't bring this age business up again. I think I'm going to like you. What is your name?"

I told her, fearing all the time she was going to ask questions about my family; but she didn't.

"Well, Zora, I pay ten dollars a week and expenses. You think that will do?"

I almost fell over. Ten dollars each and every week! Was there that much money in the world sure enough? Com-press-ti-bility!! It wouldn't take long for me to own a bank at that rate.

"Yes, ma'am!" I shouted.

"Well, change my shoes for me."

She stuck out her foot, and pointed at the pair she wanted to put on. I got them on with her tickling me in the back. She showed me a white dress she wanted to change into and I jumped to get it and hook it up. She touched up her face laughing at me in the mirror and dashed out. I was crazy about her right then. I washed out her shoelaces from a pair of white shoes and her stockings, which were on the back of a chair, and wrung them out in a bath towel for quick drying, and sat down before the mirror to look at myself. It was truly wonderful!

So I had to examine all the curious cosmetics on the table. I was sort of trying them out when she came in.

That night, she let me stand in the wings and hear her sing her duet with the tenor, "Farewell, my own! Light of my life, farewell!" It was so beautiful to me that she seemed more than human. Everything was pleasing and exciting. If there was any more to Heaven than this, I didn't want to see it.

I did not go back home, that is to my brother's house, at all. I was afraid he would try to keep me. I slept on a cot in the room with Valena. She was almost as excited as I was, had come down to see me every night and had met the cast. We were important people, she and I. Her mother had to make us shut up talking and go to sleep every night.

The end of the enchanted week came and the company was to move on. Miss M——— whom I was serving asked me about my clothes and luggage. She told me not to come down to the train with an old dilapidated suitcase for that would make her ashamed. So the upshot of it was that she advanced me the money to buy one, and then paid me for the week. I paid my friend the six dollars which she had spent for my new dress. Valena gave me the hat, an extra pair of panties and stockings. I bought a comb and brush and toothbrush, paste, and two handkerchiefs. Miss M——— did not know when I came down to the station that morning that my new suitcase was stuffed with newspapers to keep my things from rattling.

The company, a Gilbert and Sullivan repertoire, had its own coach. That was another glory to dazzle my eyes. The leading man had a valet, and the contralto had an English maid, both white. I was the only Negro around. But that did not worry me in the least. I had no chance to be lonesome, because the company welcomed me like, or as, a new play-pretty. It did not strike me as curious then. I never even thought about it. Now, I can see the reason for it.

In the first place, I was a Southerner, and had the map of Dixie on my tongue. They were all Northerners except the orchestra leader, who came from Pensacola. It was not that my grammar was bad, it was the idioms. They did not know of the way an average Southern child, white or black, is raised on simile and invective. They know how to call names. It is an everyday affair to hear somebody called a mullet-headed, mule-eared, wall-eyed, hog-nosed, 'gator-faced, shad-mouthed, screw-necked, goat-bellied, puzzle-gutted, camel-backed, butt-sprung, battle-hammed, knock-kneed, razor-legged, box-ankled, shovel-footed, unmated so-and-so! Eyes looking like skint-ginny nuts, and mouth looking like a dish-pan full of broke-up crockery! They can tell you in simile exactly how you walk and smell. They can furnish a picture gallery of your ancestors, and a notion of what your children will be like. What ought to happen to you is full of images and flavor. Since that stratum of the Southern population is not given to book-reading, they take their comparisons right out of the barnyard and the woods. When they get through with you, you and your whole family look like an acre of totem-poles.

First thing, I was young and green, so the baritone started out teasing me the first day. I jumped up and told him to stop trying to run the hog over me! That set everybody off. They teased me all the time just to hear me talk. But there was no malice in it. If I got mad and spoke my piece, they liked it even better. I was stuffed with ice-cream sodas and Coca-cola.

Another reason was that it was fun to them to get hold of somebody whom they could shock. I was hurt to my heart because the company manager called me into his dressing-room and asked me how I liked my job. After I got through telling him how pleased I was, he rushed out with his face half-made up screaming, "Stop, oh, Zora! Please stop! Shame on you! Telling me a dirty story like that. Oh! I have never been so shocked in all my life!"

Heads popped out of dressing-rooms all over. Groans, sad head-shakings and murmurs of outrage. Sad! Sad! They were glad I had not told them such a thing. Too bad! Too bad! Not a smile in the crowd. The more I tried to explain the worse it got. Some locked their doors to shield their ears from such contamination. Finally Miss M—— broke down and laughed and told me what the gag was. For a long while nobody could get me inside a dressing-room outside of Miss M——'s. But that didn't stop the teasing. They would think up more, like having one of the men contrive to walk down the aisle with me and then everybody lift shocked eyebrows, pretend to blush and wink at each other and sigh, "Zora! Zora! What would your mother say?" I would be so upset that I wouldn't know what to do. Maybe they really believed I wasn't nice!

Another sly trick they played on my ignorance was that some of the men would call me and with a very serious face send me to some of the girls to ask about the welfare and condition of cherries and spangles. They would give me a tip and tell me to hurry back with the answer. Some of the girls would send back word that the men need not worry their heads at all. They would never know the first thing about the condition of their cherries and spangles. Some of the girls sent answers full of double talk which went over my head. The soubrette spoke her mind to the men about that practice and it stopped.

But none of this had malice in it. Just their idea of good back-stage gags. By the time they stopped, it seemed that I was necessary to everybody. I was continually stuffed with sweets, nut meats, and soft-drinks. I was welcome in everybody's coach seat and the girls used to pitch pennies to see who carried me off to their hotel rooms. We played games and told stories. They often ordered beer and pretzels, but nobody offered me a drink. I heard all about their love affairs and troubles. They were all looking forward to playing or singing leads some day. Some great personage had raved about all of their performances. The dirty producers and casting directors just hadn't given them their chance. Miss M——— finally put a stop to my going off with the others as soon as she was ready for bed. I had to stay wherever she stayed after that. She had her own affairs to talk about.

She paid for a course for me in manicuring and I practiced on everybody until I became very efficient at it. That course came in handy to me later on.

With all this petting, I became as cocky as a sparrow on Fifth Avenue. I got a scrapbook, and everybody gave me a picture to put in it. I pasted each one on a separate page and wrote comments under each picture. This created a great deal of interest, because some of the comments were quite pert. They egged me on to elaborate. Then I got another idea. I would comment on daily doings and post the sheets on the call-board. This took on right away. The result stayed strictly mine less than a week because members of the cast began to call me aside and tell me things to put in about others. It got to be so general that everybody was writing it. It was just my handwriting, mostly. Then it got beyond that. Most of the cast ceased to wait for me. They would take a pencil to the board and set down their own item. Answers to the wisecracks would appear promptly and often cause uproarious laughter. They always started off with either "Zora says" or "The observant reporter of the Call-board asserts"—Lord, Zora said more *things!* I was continually astonished, but always amused. There were, of course, some sly digs at supposedly secret love affairs at times, but no vicious thrusts. Everybody enjoyed it, even the victims.

When the run came to an end, Miss M——— had a part in another show all set, but rehearsals would not start for two weeks, so she took me to her home in Boston and I found out some things which I did not want to know, particularly.

At times she had been as playful as a kitten. At others, she would be solemn and moody. She loved her mother excessively, but when she received those long, wordy letters from her, she read them with a still face, and tore them up carefully. Then she would be gloomy, and keep me beside her every minute. Sometimes she would become excessively playful. It was puzzling to see a person cry awhile and then commence to romp like a puppy and keep it up for hours. Sometimes she had to have sherry before she went to bed after a hard romp with me. She invented a game for us to play in our hotel room. It was known as "Jake." She would take rouge and paint her face all over a most startling red. Then I must take eye-shadow and paint myself blue. Blue Jake and Red Jake would then chase each other into closets, across beds, into bathrooms, with our sheet-robes trailing around us and tripping us up at odd moments. We crouched and growled and ambushed each other and laughed and yelled until we were exhausted.

Then maybe next day she hardly said a word.

While I was with her, she met a wealthy business man of Newark, and I could tell that she was sunk. It all happened very suddenly, but gloriously. She told me that now that she was going to be married and leave the stage, she did not want me to work for anyone else in the business. In fact, she thought that I should not be working at all. I ought to be in school. She said she thought I had a mind, and that it would be a shame for me not to have any further training. She wished that she herself could go abroad to study, but that was definitely out of the question, now. The deep reservoir of things inside her gave off a sigh.

We were in northern Virginia then, and moving towards Baltimore. When we got there, she inquired about schools, gave me a big bearful hug, and what little money she could spare and told me to keep in touch with her. She would do whatever she could to help me out.

That was the way we parted. I had been with her for eighteen months and though neither of us realized it, I had been in school all that time. I had loosened up in every joint and expanded in every direction.

I had done some reading. Not as much as before, but more discriminate reading. The tenor was a Harvard man who had traveled on the Continent. He always had books along with him, and offered them to me more and more. The first time I asked to borrow one, he looked at me in a way that said "What for?" But when he found that I really read it and enjoyed it, he relaxed and began to hand them to me gruffly. He never acted as if he liked it, but I knew better. That was just the Harvard in him.

Then there was the music side. They broke me in to good music, that is, the classics, if you want to put it that way. There was no conscious attempt to do this. Just from being around, I became familiar with Gilbert and Sullivan, and the best parts of the light-opera field. Grand opera too, for all of the leads had backgrounds of private classical instruction as well as conservatory training. Even the bit performers and the chorus had some kind of formal training in voice, and most of them played the piano. It was not unusual for some of the principals to drop down at the piano after a matinee performance and begin to sing arias from grand opera. Sing them with a wistfulness. The arias which they would sing at the Metropolitan or La Scala as they had once hoped actively, and still hoped passively even as the hair got thinner and the hips got heavier. Others, dressed for the street, would drift over and ease into the singing. Thus I would hear solos, duets, quartets and sextets from the best-known operas. They would eagerly explain to me what they were when I asked. They would go on to say how Caruso, Farrar, Mary Garden, Trentini, Schumann-Heink, Matzenauer and so forth had interpreted this or that piece, and demonstrate it by singing. Perhaps that was their trouble. They were not originators, but followers of originators. Anyway, it was perfectly glorious for me, though I am sure nobody thought of it that way. I just happened to be there while they released their inside dreams.

The experience had matured me in other ways. I had seen, I had been privileged to see folks substituting love for failure of career. I would listen to one and another pour out their feelings sitting on a stool backstage between acts and scenes. Then too, I had seen careers filling up the empty holes left by love, and covering up the wreck of things internal. Those experiences, though vicarious, made me see things and think.

And now, at last it was all over. It was not at all clear to me how I was going to do it, but I was going back to school.

One minute I felt brave and fine about it all. The wish to be back in school had never left me. But alone by myself and feeling it over, I was scared. Before this job I had been lonely; I had been bare and bony of comfort and love. Working with these people I had been sitting by a warm fire for a year and a half and gotten used to the feel of peace. Now, I was to take up my pilgrim's stick and go outside again. Maybe it would be different now. Six of my unhappy visions had passed me and bowed. The seventh one, the house that needed paint, that had threatened me with so much suffering that I used to sit up in bed sodden with agony, had passed. I had fled from it to put on the blue poplin dress. At least that was not before me any more. I took a firm grip on the only weapon I had—hope—and set my feet. Maybe everything would be all right from now on. Maybe. Well, I put on my shoes and I started.

Zora Neale Hurston *has written four novels, including her acclaimed* Their Eyes Were Watching God. *She has published two books of folklore,* Mules and Men *and* Tell My Horse, *as well as her autobiography,* Dust Tracks on a Road.

OPPORTUNITY Magazine   October 1924

NEGRO MIGRATION: ITS EFFECT ON FAMILY AND COMMUNITY LIFE IN THE NORTH

George E. Haynes

Types of Migrants

The types of Negro migrants are interesting. In 1916 and 1917, the earlier years of the present migration, the majority of the newcomers were men—particularly detached men—either men without families or men who would not venture to bring their families with them into an unknown country. Included among them were a great many younger men, with the "floaters" and ne'er do wells, who had been easily attracted away from southern towns and cities by the stories of easy work at high wages and by free transportation offered promiscuously by labor agents and railroad companies. A second class was made up of a large number of single women, detached from their families, who came because of the large opportunities for remunerative work, particularly in domestic service.

These gradually were accompanied and followed by the third type, the substantial laboring man of unskilled or semi-skilled abilities. For the most part these men either brought their families, soon married, or sent for their families as soon as they could find remunerative employment. Fourth, with parts of such families as fathers and sons had left behind came a great many broken families—widows with children, attracted by the opportunities for an education for the children in public schools and wages in domestic service. There came also the aged relatives of the wage earning men and women of families. As those in the larger southern cities and towns moved on to the North, others moved in from the hamlets and rural districts to fill their places and to swell the proportions. Thus much of the movement was by successive stages.

Beginning about 1919 those who had come in the two or three years preceding had gained a substantial economic footing and knowledge of being able to stand the climate and other living conditions. Consequently a general assurance spread throughout cities, towns and rural districts of the South. Frequently whole families or neighborhoods, sometimes with previous arrangements for employment in some of the industrial communities, migrated in a group. A

few cases have been recorded of whole church congregations bringing their pastors with them.

As the types described above settled, they furnished a field for
the small tradesmen and the professional class who either came along
with the crowd or followed closely after. In many cases, of course,
the more enterprising wage earners, finding themselves in the midst
of a large Negro population with considerable wages to spend, ventured into business. Along with this host of mixed humanity, there
came a vicious and criminal element. It is the testimony, however,
of social workers, railroad officials, law officers and other observers,
that to an unusual degree these people are law-abiding, unoffending
folk who are seeking larger opportunities in a new environment.

Effects of Migration on Negroes

The foregoing facts lead the way to our consideration of effects on
families and communities in the North.

Some of the outstanding effects of migration on the average Negro family are better standards of food and clothing due to higher
wages. The children have better school buildings with teaching
equipment and higher paid, better trained teachers. The permanent
effects on health and mortality can only be surmised. Statistics of
the births and deaths are as yet meager but they seem to indicate a
trend toward improvement. A survey made by Forrester B. Washington, under the auspices of the Inter-racial Committee of Toledo,
Ohio, showed a Negro death rate for 1922 of 15.2 per cent as compared with the general death rate of 11.7 per cent—a difference of
3.5 per cent; but in 1912, before the 200 per cent increase of Negro
population due to migration, the Negro death rate was 20.5 per cent
while the general death rate was 13.8 per cent—a difference of 6.7
per cent. In Cincinnati, the Negro death rate was 34.9 per cent for
the decade 1902–1912 and declined to 27.4 per cent for the decade
1913–1923. Dr. Dublin, of the Metropolitan Life Insurance Company, states that in nearly two million Negro industrial policyholders, including men, women and children, the "mortality rate was
17.5 per 1000" in 1911 and 14.5 in 1923, a decrease of more than
one-sixth; death from tuberculosis, "the outstanding cause of death
among colored people," was 41 per cent less in 1923 than in 1911.
. . . "Nothing indicates so well the general health condition of a
race as the incidence of tuberculosis and nothing reflects so well an
improvement in its mode of life as does a big drop in the tuberculosis death rate. . . . The improvement in typhoid fever is especially
noteworthy," declining 77.5 per cent between 1911 and 1923. There

has been a "marked increase in the number of colored policyholders" in Illinois and Michigan, mainly concentrated in Chicago and Detroit.

In most northern cities the housing condition shows a majority of the Negro families coming North are grievously overcrowded and in practically all of the cities the rents for them have been far in excess of those for residents who are residing at the same time in similar localities. A survey made by the Federation of Churches of Buffalo in 1922 disclosed the fact that about 75 per cent of the colored families occupied a section of that city which contained the poorest houses, some of which had formerly been condemned as not habitable. A similar survey made by the Federated Churches of Cleveland showed that while a substantial part of the colored people have secured good houses, inadequate and unsanitary conditions still exist in one of the principal Negro communities of the city.

In Philadelphia, the Philadelphia Housing Association found in a recent survey that only 10.5 per cent of the houses occupied by Negro families were equipped for sanitation, convenience and comfort, while 28.6 of the houses occupied by whites were so equipped. There was no room overcrowding, however. In New York, Pittsburgh, Chicago and other cities, while there are many good houses, the majority of the people are overcrowded in houses lacking in facilities for sanitation, convenience and comfort. A striking development of their settlement has been their effort to improve their housing condition. This is evinced in their increased striving to purchase the homes they occupy. In the survey of Toledo, previously referred to, about 27.6 per cent of the families investigated owned or were purchasing their homes, nearly half of these having their homes free and clear. In 1910, in thirteen northern cities and two boroughs of New York City, from ten to over twenty-five per cent of Negro families owned or were buying the houses they occupied, and in seven additional cities and two boroughs of New York, from four to ten per cent owned or were buying the houses they occupied. During the past ten years there has been a great eagerness of Negro migrants to buy houses and in some cities real estate manipulators have forced many to buy or move. We may conclude then that in northern cities from ten to twenty-five per cent of the Negro families own or are buying their homes.

Negroes believe that the Negro community in the North, although considerably segregated, has advantages over their former homes in the South, such as theatres, public libraries, parks, playgrounds, museums and non–"Jim Crow" railroad and street cars.

Negroes are taking part more and more in the civic and political affairs of the community. Newspapers and magazines, especially Negro newspapers and magazines, are being read as never before. Negro newspapers and magazines with the largest circulation are published in Chicago and New York. The headquarters of nearly every one of the Negro betterment organizations are now in northern cities and many of the general officers of the Negro churches have moved North. Small Negro business enterprises are increasing rapidly. A study of "The Negro at Work in New York," in 1910, before the present migration, listed about 475 enterprises in Manhattan; in 1921, a similar survey showed at least 584 such business enterprises in the Harlem district alone—a larger number than in the three Negro neighborhoods of Manhattan in 1910. General observations in Philadelphia, Chicago, Detroit and Cleveland give a similar impression of increase.

Effects on Negro Church

What has been the effect of migration on the Negro church, which we saw was the most influential institution in Negro life in the South? In the northern cities it has increased greatly in membership, although many small mushroom store-front churches have sprung up and often become a hindrance to progress. There have developed some strong organizations in every one of these cities. Their great need is better trained leadership. In a few cities Negro congregations have bought or built institutional plants and are employing trained social workers. Abyssinia Baptist Church, St. Philip's P. E. Church, Williams Institutional C. M. E. Church, and Mother Zion A. M. E. Church in New York City; St. John's Congregational Church in Springfield, Mass.; Mount Zion Congregational Church and St. John's A. M. E. Church in Cleveland; Olivet Baptist Church and two community churches in Chicago; and Sharpe Street M. E. Church in Baltimore, are prophecies of great community service and show the possibilities.

I realize the serious shortcomings of the church in community service and I respect the opinion of many social workers who think that the church is not able to function with technical efficiency in case work. Yet I am moved to maintain that the Negro church is by far the most substantial institution we have for reaching the Negro rank and file with our social programs. Trying to look at the matter without bias, it seems to me that many of our efforts have not carried over to the masses of the Negro people because we have not sold our social programs through the Negro churches which have already a hold upon the thousands who had developed the churches for more than a hundred years and now find them their social agency. If we get our plans accepted in the programs of those churches, much of our efforts would not need to go into building social service programs and trying to force Negroes into them. It is true that there are great obstacles in the way of getting scientific technique in this field. There are other dangers involved. There are baffling difficulties of leadership and restricted vision. These Negro church organizations, however, have a willingness and zeal for service which has brought results wherever skilled social workers have been able to link them up to the scientific methods and directions needed. In Wichita, Kansas; in Kansas City, Mo.; St. Louis, Chicago, Toledo, Cincinnati, Brooklyn and other cities, the white and Negro social workers and the white and Negro church leaders have begun inter-racial committees through Urban Leagues and Y. M. and Y. W. C. A. cooperative community planning which has already achieved results and promises larger things for the future. Perhaps the most fully worked out and best piece of social engineering in race relations in a northern community has been developed during the past six years in Cincinnati, Ohio, in the inter-racial work of the Council of Social Agencies, with James H. Robinson as executive secretary. They have coordinated the Negro churches, fraternal bodies, women's clubs, Y.M.C.A. and Y.W.C.A. with the white social agencies and organizations. The Negro population increased from about 20,000 to 35,000 in ten years, largely during the 1916–18 migration. These people have been integrated into the city's life through their leaders and organizations to an extent which hardly seemed workable ten years ago. In Philadelphia the Armstrong Association, with Forrester B. Washington as secretary, has successfully started somewhat similar plans and policies. Other cities, with the cooperation of Urban Leagues, are beginning such policies.

Effects on Northern White Community

This leads us logically to the effect of Negro migration on the white community in northern cities. In such communities the reaction of public opinion seems to have become one of our foremost problems. For instance, anyone would have been considered an alarmist twenty years ago had he predicted that public opinion would allow 58 Negro homes in Chicago to be bombed with impunity as increasing numbers forced Negro residents to spread beyond the areas where they had formerly lived. Race riots and outrages in East St. Louis, Omaha, Chicago and Washington paralyzed these cities for days and shocked the Nation. In public schools in more than a dozen northern cities Negro children are being directly or indirectly segregated. In one small city recently a company of leading white citizens spent a whole evening deliberating how they might control the adjustment of Negroes in the community with some fairness and yet not make it favorable enough to attract additional numbers. In some cities the former Negro residents have felt an unfriendly reaction toward their former free participation in community life.

This reaction of white public opinion has shown itself decidedly in the housing situation. These newcomers meet tremendous racial friction which grows out of their efforts to improve their housing conditions. It is very important that northern public opinion should not regard Negroes as things, nor as serfs, nor as half-men and half-women. Many of them are handicapped by ignorance, previous conditions and poverty, yet they possess all the rights and needs of whole men and women and are seeking the opportunities of free citizens.

The newspapers, the pulpits and other community channels of information may influence public opinion toward friendly racial attitudes. The Inter-racial Committee of Youngstown, Ohio, recently had an educational campaign which included a pageant produced by five hundred of the Negro people of the community on two nights at the leading theatre in the city. It received the praise of the leading newspapers and over two thousand white citizens who packed the theatre. The music and dramatic ability were a revelation to the performers as well as to the community. During the Sunday that preceded the performance, the ministers of the leading churches gave strong addresses or sermons on the problems of inter-racial adjustment and on two days following in the elementary and high schools through songs and addresses information was given to the pupils about the achievements of Negroes along lines of art, literature, science, and invention. The newspapers gave liberal space to reports of these events.

The effect upon political life in northern communities when large numbers of Negro voters come in is too extensive a subject to be considered here.

The dramatic and musical contributions of Negroes have greatly changed the comedy, the song and the dance of the North where opportunity the past fifteen years has brought ragtime, jazz, comic acting and art songs of high quality which have influenced the whole community.

The effects of increasing thousands of Negro workers in northern industries is of great importance, for in this field the masses meet face to face. In the past Negroes often got chances to work when white workers went on strike. They were then taunted as scabs by white workmen who had previously objected to their being on the job and had excluded them from their unions. Gradually, however, Negro workers are winning their way into the ranks of labor. The Negro worker is not militant-minded. He is drawn more to persons than to property. He often considers the interest of the other group as a part of his own. Is not this spirit of conciliation the ethical value that must more and more control both white capitalist and white worker before we shall have democracy in industry or industrial peace? The Negro worker needs help that his preference for persons above property may not make him a tool in the hands of employers who may wish to use him to fight the unions. As the Negro worker gets into labor ranks he may bring a spirit of cooperation that the new day in industry requires.

There is a special call to social workers for types of service in addition to the usual case work for dependents, defectives, and delinquents. What is needed by the large majority of the Negro migrants is friendly integration fully into the economic, educational, civic, and religious life of the community. These people by their brain and brawn are seeking to pay their way by their labor in the expanding industries of northern communities. They are not a group of economic dependents or social delinquents. Many are ignorant and unused to the complex life about them, but they are very teachable and most adaptable. They need help, for instance, against the exploitation of real estate sharks, white and Negro, who exploit them for the houses and shacks they buy or rent; from the shameless profiteers who sell them goods on the installment plan; from commercialized vice which flourishes unmolested by public authorities in their tenements and neighborhoods. They need the liberal interest of white citizens such as prompted the Americanization efforts for the foreign-born. The Negro, however, only needs help in securing the opportunity to embrace American advantages. He does not have to forget foreign customs and foreign loyalties for he is not a naturalized but a natural-born American citizen.

These Negro migrants are a part of a great body of American citizens who are permeated with a deep community and group consciousness and who have shown their ability for team work with other racial and national groups in America by unselfish cooperation on their part in communities, North and South. They have demonstrated their undying loyalty to American ideals of democracy by offering their life blood upon every battlefield of Liberty, from Bunker Hill to the Fields of Flanders. What greater loyalty has any people shown than the Negroes who, during the Civil War, remained behind on the plantations and took care of the helpless wives and children of the very masters who were away fighting to keep them in slavery, and later remained to provide support for many of those same families when the masters did not return from the battlefield? Thousands of them during the World War fought and died to make America safe for democracy, although fully conscious that they and theirs would not be allowed to enjoy the full measure of the very blessings of liberty for which they were pouring out their life's blood. These people, seeking opportunity for self-development and self-determination, have moved by thousands to the North. If we help them to integrate their lives into the community and to make their contribution to the common life as the years come and go, there will grow increasingly in America, our America, a realization of that democracy which is to be in "the land of the free and the home of the brave."

Charleston, South Carolina   February 10, 1917

Gentlemen:
Upon reading the N.Y. age, have seen where there are need of employees in some sugar concern in New York. Kindly answer this letter, and tell me the nature of the work.

As I am from the south and it is an average difficulty for a southerner to endure the cold without being climatize. If it is possable for you to get any other job for me regardless to its nature just since the work is indoor I'll appreciate the same.

As it is understood the times in the south is very hard and one cans scarcely live. Kindly take the matters into consideration, and reply to my request at your earliest convenience.

Yours respectfully.

OPPORTUNITY Magazine   January 1926

NEGRO MIGRATION IN NEW YORK STATE

Eugene Kinckle Jones

(Delivered at the New York State Conference of Charities and Corrections, Hotel Roosevelt, New York City, Friday, December 11, 1925)

The Negro population in northern United States increased in the ten years between 1910 and 1920 from 1,000,000 to more than 1,500,000. Since the larger part of this half million increase occurred in the few years prior to 1920 and the increase since 1920 has been at about the same rate, it is fair to estimate that there are now close to two million Negroes north of the Mason and Dixon line. The increase was due in the main to the migration of Negroes from the South and to the relatively small West Indian immigration.

The increase in the Negro population of New York State from 1910 to 1920 was 64,292. In 1910 the Negro population was 134,191; in 1920, 198,483. Estimated on the basis of an annual increment of 9,363, the 1925 Negro population of this State can conservatively be estimated at 245,296. This is on the assumption that the annual increase from 1910 to 1915 was the same as between 1900 and 1910, and the 1915 to 1920 annual increment continued through to 1925. Of the State's Negro population of 198,483 in 1920, 31,425 were born in Virginia; 26,428 in the Carolinas (about an equal number from North and from South Carolina); Georgia furnished 8,650; Maryland, 4,272; Florida, 3,657, and the Northern States of Pennsylvania and New Jersey, 3,537 and 3,611 each. There were 25,454 from the West Indies outside of the United States' possessions and 1,431 from the Virgin Islands. It is estimated that there was a net increase of about 24,000 foreign born Negroes in the United States between 1920 and 1923. New York City's Negro population in 1920 was 152,467, leaving a total of 46,016 in other sections of the State. The Negro population in New York City at present is in excess of 200,000.

Before discussing in detail the situation in regard to the factors which led to the Negro migration to this State and the social complexion of the Negro population here, it might be well to discuss a little the general Negro question from the standpoint of the Negro in the North, which will have a direct bearing on the situation in this State.

Although the migration from the South has been largely from rural and small town districts, the population in the North is almost entirely centered in urban communities, where death and birth rates are about equal, thereby providing practically no natural increase. The majority of the million Negro new-comers mentioned above came to the North preceding and following the participation of the United States in the World War. The causes of this migration are well known—the industrial labor vacuum caused in the North by the departure of foreign reservists for service in Europe, drafting of many men from the North's industrial centers, the speeding up of industry incident to the war, and the push from the South caused by the withholding of personal, civic and educational rights from the Negro, and especially the persistent persecution of Negroes by the lawless white element, against which no protection was afforded. Though it is true that in the South the Negro has not been denied industrial opportunity as a skilled or unskilled worker, his wages there have been relatively low and his treatment at the hands of white men in authority, both on the job and in connection with his civic and home affairs, has made him feel constantly restricted and oppressed.

A discussion ten years ago on the Negro in the North would have consisted primarily of a consideration of the housing conditions and the general wage scale of Negroes employed here and there in responsible positions where their work was in the main associated with white people. But a discussion of this subject today would embrace a study of these masses of Negroes who have recently come to the North, the successes or failures with which they have met in seeking social adjustment, the development of larger industrial opportunities individually and as a group and the material progress made thus far in business and professional life. Negro cities, as it were, within the already established cities, may be seen in New York, in Pittsburgh, in Boston, in Chicago, in Cleveland, in Detroit, in Philadelphia and in many other Northern and border communities. Here Negro banks, theatres, hotels, restaurants, stores of all kinds, real estate offices and modern churches with social service facilities are in evidence, and Negro doctors, lawyers, architects, social workers and other professional men and women are kept constantly busy ministering to the needs of their own people.

Of course, Negroes have been migrating to the North in large numbers during the period between the Civil War and the World War. But this migration has only been in answer to the demand, in the main, for personal servants, and such social problems among Negroes as arose in Northern cities were of such gradual growth that, though existent, they did not alter to any great extent the condition of the communities. When the war period set in, however, communities to which Negroes went began to realize that they had a new problem of their own.

The economic urge has probably been the strongest force at work in inducing Negroes to seek new abodes. Records show that even from many counties in Georgia, Alabama and Texas where lynchings have been most numerous, Negroes have left in smaller proportionate numbers than from those counties where no lynchings have occurred, provided the economic conditions were not unfavorable in the former sections. In fact, in several counties where lynchings have been frequent, the whites have left in larger proportionate numbers than have the Negroes.

Therefore, in moving North, the Negroes have sought those communities giving them the most promising industrial and economic outlook. These communities in an overwhelming majority of cases have been those where basic industries thrived. Thus Pittsburgh and Detroit, Cleveland and Chicago, and the satellite towns of Gary, Duquesne, Homestead and Steelton have received large Negro accretions. Between 1910 and 1920 Negro population of Akron increased 749.3%; Detroit, 611.3%; Chicago, 148.2%; Cleveland, 307.8%; Toledo, 203.2%.

New York State has but few cities of the type sought by Negroes in the recent migration. Thus with the exception of New York City and Buffalo few cities in the State have received very great additional Negro citizens. Buffalo's Negro population increased 154.4 per cent between 1910 and 1920 and New York City's 66.3 per cent.

Withal, life among the Negroes in New York City is approaching a normal state. The cosmopolitanism of the city attracts the Negro. The heterogeneity of the population has generated an atmosphere of freedom and democracy. The city's reputation has been broadcasted to every nook and corner of the Southland, and when Negroes decide to move it is natural for those along the Atlantic Seaboard to think of New York and act accordingly.

The present British West Indian immigration of the Negro is now very small due to the recent interpretation of the British quota understanding which links the British West Indian citizen with those of the British Isles in determining the number of West Indians who are eligible to enter our port. The custom has been for those who have come in the past to remain in New York with but few going on to other cities.

Buffalo's increase in Negro population from 1,773 to 4,511 between 1910 and 1920 and to 9,058 by 1923 was due principally to the activities of the Lackawanna Steel Company, which at one time had as many as 1,000 Negro employees. It brought 6,000 Negroes into Buffalo, but its wages were so much lower than those maintained by other industries in that community that it was able to retain less than one thousand of this number, the excess being employed by six other industries which used Negroes in considerable numbers. The brick-yards along the west shore of the Hudson River, centering at Haverstraw, employ Negroes in considerable numbers during the brick-making season and there are several industries in Syracuse and Rochester that use them in some numbers.

The largest majority of the Negro migrants have settled in New York City and the adjacent counties of Westchester and Nassau. One has to seek a variety of occupations to locate the attraction, and it is found that Negroes are employed in numbers in New York in 316 of the 321 occupations listed in the Federal Census for New York City. In each of 175 of these occupations over 50 Negroes are employed. It is interesting to note the preponderance of women over men in the Negro population of New York City, the ratio being 92.6 Negro men to 100 Negro women. This is because of the fact that there have been more jobs available for women than for men—domestic service claiming, as in years past, the largest number of Negro women employees.

In recent years some significant changes have taken place. Last year there were over 3,000 women workers in the garment trades. They are also employed as milliners and as novelty makers. Although there has been an increase in the actual number of colored women employed as domestic servants, the proportion of colored women to the total number of domestic servants has decreased. This is a reflection of the increase in men's wages and improvement in the types of jobs available to Negro men. There has been an actual reduction in the number of married colored women at work. There are over 6,000 Negro longshoremen in New York City. Men are also employed as chauffeurs, porters in mercantile establishments and in railroad terminals and on the subway and elevated lines. There is a great increase in the number of Civil Service employees—Municipal, State and Federal. Negroes are entering business and engaging more largely in the professions. Their physicians, lawyers, clergymen, school teachers, real estate operators and social workers are increasing rapidly as capable persons are acquiring the necessary training.

Mrs. G. E. McDougald, in a study of advancement of former Negro public school pupils cites several interesting typical cases of individual achievement of Negroes. The first and the last positions of the individuals are listed:

First Position	Promoted to
Prescription clerk	Assistant manager of store of large drug syndicate
Junior clerk	Superintendent of P. O. Station
Laborer	Clerk in the U.S. Customs
Watchman	Inspector of Immigration
Errand boy	Machine operator on furs
Stenographer	Editor-in-chief, New York Branch of a Rome publishing house.
Helper	Mechanic
Draftsman (electric)	Designer in charge
Letterer	Combination man—oil picture signs
Waiter	Steward
Carpenter	Foreman
Baker	Foreman
Kitchen boy	Steward
Private medical practice	Clinician, Mt. Sinai Hospital
Medical interne	Resident surgeon, Bellevue Hospital
Lawyer	Municipal Civil Service Commission

Towards the close of the unemployment period of 1914, when the Seventh Avenue Subway was being constructed in New York, the National Urban League placed several hundred Negro laborers with subway contractors. In the present new subway construction there are several young Negro engineers employed in this service. As evidence of a growing opportunity for trained young colored men and women in this State, I refer to a few unusual positions held by Negroes: Draughtsmen in the building department of the Board of Education and in the Department of Docks and Bridges; special writer on a large daily newspaper; special writer for women's page of a large monthly periodical; salesman for a very large real estate firm; sub-contractor for building the forms for the concrete being poured for the foundations of the new Columbia-Presbyterian Hospital; civil engineer employed on this job, which is keeping about 125 carpenters and laborers busy; 500 public school teachers; a vice-principal; a principal retired this year; lecturers for the Board of Education; Department of Health nurses; a certified public accountant; instructors in a dental college and in an ophthalmic college. I mention a few of the important positions as they are filled almost entirely by Negroes who have migrated to New York State. And, incidentally, here we might state that three-fourths of the businesses conducted by Negroes in New York City are owned by Southern Negroes and a large part of the remainder by West Indians.

New York City has become the center of intellectual and cultural life among Negroes of America as a result of the migration. The headquarters of the leading Negro organizations working for Negro welfare, whether social or civil, are located in this city, and the most successful, influential and intellectual leaders of the race have been engaged by these organizations to conduct their national activities and propaganda from New York as a center. Thus this community has become the dynamo for generating the social energies propelling the Negro masses towards what they hope will be a better day. There are Dr. W. E. B. DuBois, the race's most fluent and influential writer, a native of Massachusetts, coming to New York from Georgia, where he had been for fourteen years, who is the Editor of the *Crisis,* the organ of the National Association for the Advancement of Colored People, and James Weldon Johnson, poet, author, secretary of the National Association for the Advancement of Colored People, a native of Florida and one of the race's most trusted and serviceable leaders; and William Pickens, one of America's great orators, uncompromising champion of Negro rights, a native of Arkansas; Harry Burleigh, musician, composer, baritone in St. George's Choir, known for his musical works, not as a Negro musician, a native of Erie, Penna.; and Paul Robeson, actor, born in New Jersey; and Charles Gilpin, of "Emperor Jones" fame, native of Richmond, Va.; and Charles S. Johnson, brilliant editor of OP-PORTUNITY—A Journal of Negro Life, native of Bristol, Va.; and Walter F. White, author and publicist, formerly of Atlanta; and Jessie Fauset, author and assistant to the *Crisis* editor, native of Philadelphia; Channing H. Tobias, Director of Colored Y. M. C. A. work, native of Augusta, Ga.; Miss Eva Bowles, holding a similar position with the Y. W. C. A., a native of Columbus, Ohio, and many other such individuals who have adopted New York as their home.

It seems to be a general impression among Negroes throughout the country that in this State they have a better chance for advancement, more rights as citizens and better prospects for the future than in other States of the Union. When the saturation point is reached for the moment in the increase of Negro population in New York and there is a dearth of jobs available to those who have migrated to the city, the backwash or surplus Negro population goes into such New Jersey communities as Plainfield, Newark, the Oranges, Jersey City, Montclair, Paterson, and into Westchester County towns such as New Rochelle, Mt. Vernon, White Plains and Yonkers and such Long Island centers as Mineola, Rockville Center, Glen Cove, Hempstead and Freeport.

Of course, with the large increase in the Negro population in this State, especially New York City, there must be attendant problems of housing and health and a decided increase in delinquency, juvenile and adult.

African American families across the South cooked on open fires and lived in houses like this one in Southern Pines, North Carolina, in 1914. *(Photo by E. C. Eddy) Courtesy of the Library of Congress*

A small tomato harvest for a family near Beaufort, South Carolina, in 1936. *(Photo by Mydans) Courtesy of the Library of Congress*

This photograph was taken in Newton County, Georgia, in 1937, but the scene had changed little from several generations before in the plantation South. *Courtesy of the Library of Congress*

A family outside their home on Lady's Island near Beaufort, South Carolina, in 1936. *Courtesy of the Library of Congress*

An African American woman carrying laundry in the same manner as her African counterparts an ocean away from this highway between Durham and Mebane, North Carolina, in 1939. *(Photo by Post) Courtesy of the Library of Congress*

Lynchings were the most dramatic form of racial terrorism that drove Black people from the South. *Courtesy of the New York Public Library, Schomburg Collection*

Inside the Mt. Gilead Colored School on the Plantation Piedmont Agricultural Demonstration Project, near Eatonton, Georgia, in 1936. *(Photo by Mydans) Courtesy of the Library of Congress*

These two men, Tom Shipp and Abe Smith, were lynched in Marion, Indiana, August 7, 1930, "by party or parties unknown"

Two men of the Fleming family (see "The Ritual of Survival"). William Fleming, my grandfather, stands proudly by his car, and Robert, my father, in his uniform. *Courtesy of Robert Fleming*

St. Nazaire, April 6, 1919. The military was a way out of the South—and a way to full citizenship for many. World War I A.T.S. Salvage Office. *Courtesy of the Library of Congress*

African Americans went where the work was. These Florida migrants left Belcroso, North Carolina, for Onley, Virginia, in 1940. *(Photo by Delano)*

The Chicago *Defender* was a major forum for exchanging information regarding the exodus and the promise of life outside the South. This is a photo engraver for the paper, at work in 1941.

Letters sent back home were the main way to let friends and family know about what awaited them in the North. Here, a woman married to a railroad worker types a letter in Chicago, Illinois, in April 1941. *(Photo by Russell Lee) Farm Security Administration/the New York Public Library, Courtesy of Schomburg Collection*

Due to the strategic move on the part of certain colored real estate men some fifteen years ago, the Negroes in New York City are occupying one of the most healthful districts of our large city—that is Harlem, where, north of 125th Street, 100,000 Negroes are now residing. Unfortunately, the houses built before their arrival were not designed to meet the needs and cope with the economic handicaps of the Negroes. Most of the inhabitants have been forced to occupy apartments with rentals beyond their income, and the lodger evil has complicated the social life of the group. In recent years an effort has been made to build houses with two, three and four-room apartments; but with the high cost of building material and labor, the average rental per room has been from $20 to $25 and the problem is still present in a little different form. Corona, Jamaica, Flushing, East New York and several other suburban sections in and around New York have furnished some relief by affording small five and six-room homes to thrifty home buyers of average income.

Although there has been very little natural increase in the Negro population, the movement of Negroes into zones of better living and working conditions is resulting in better health conditions. The death rate among Negroes is gradually on the decrease. In fact, the death rate in Northern cities is lo.ver among Negroes today than in Southern cities, despite the advanced age group comprising our Northern Negro population and the alleged difficulties that Negroes are supposed to experience in adjusting themselves to the more rigorous winters of the North. The Negro death rate in New York City was 37.5 per 1,000 in 1890; in 1910 it was 25, and in 1921 was 17.9. The Negro infant mortality in New York City is decidedly on the decline, following inversely the trend of family income of Negroes.

In 1915, when an investigation was made of infant mortality among the Negroes in New York City, it was discovered that in one section of the city where the largest percentage of mothers worked and where the families had the smallest incomes and the largest percentage of lodgers, and therefore more overcrowding, Negro infant mortality was 314 per 1,000, while for the entire city for the colored people it was 202 per 1,000 and for the whites 96 per 1,000. A campaign of improvement was organized in which social welfare agencies, the Health Department, employment placement bureaus, public schools, and, in fact, all agencies that touch the life of the family were brought into active cooperation to handle effectively this unfortunate situation. The Negro infant mortality for the city was reduced in two years from 202 per 1,000 to 173 per 1,000—a reduction of 29 points. In 1919, the infant mortality among Negroes in that district in New York City where in 1915 the rate was 314 per 1,000 had been reduced to a point lower than the infant mortality of the whites in the same district.

While there is not sufficient data for a scientific prophecy of the industrial future of the Negro group in New York State, we have sufficient information to form an opinion hopeful or otherwise. In a recent survey in Buffalo of 45 industrial plants employing 2,922 Negro workers, 32 were satisfied with their labor and 13 were not. Of the 13, estimates ranged from tolerance to such qualified expressions of satisfaction as "fair" or "greater part are satisfactory," and "in some respects 'yes' and the most part 'no.' " One interesting reply should be noted. A plant that had never employed more than one colored worker stated that because this man was found dishonest, the plant had established a policy of employing no more Negroes. One plant reported that it found them "90% efficient." This indicates a willingness to employ Negroes indefinitely. Furthermore, the variety of work engaged in by Negroes in New York City precluded a likelihood of any wholesale dismissing of Negro workers. Also there are already evidences of a demand for both skilled and unskilled workers in excess of a possible available supply from white immigration and normal increase of native white workers through the existing agencies of developing new workers. Although the growth of the union labor movements threatened Negro artisans, 1920 saw an increase in Negro carpenters from 268 to 737, chauffeurs from 490 to 2,195, workers on clothing from none to 6,000 and workers in textiles from a very few to 2,685; shoemakers from 14 to 581; stationary firemen from 249 to 1,076, and mechanics from very few or none to 467. Incidentally Negro real estate agents increased from 89 to 247. Evidently the Negro migrant is here to stay a while. It is somewhat of a paradox, however, that in those lines where the unions, workingmen's friends, are strongest, the Negro has made the scantiest progress. Ten years added but eighteen Negro brick-masons, eighty-one painters, sixteen plasterers and forty-two plumbers. But even in this direction the future is not without its encouraging prospects. In New York City an organization composed of white and colored representatives of Trade Unions has recently been formed to help increase the number of Negro members of the Trade Unions.

The most discouraging phase of the Negro migration situation is that of delinquency. A much larger proportion of Negroes are arrested and convicted of crimes and misdemeanors than they comprise of the total population. This is unquestionably due in large measure to the absence of preventive social forces in the lives of adolescent Negro youth. The much smaller juvenile delinquency rate, however, indicates that there is no racial bent toward crime and that with the further development of the agencies of social control, there will be a turn for the better. During the migration period juvenile delinquency among Negro children in New York increased from a point less than the Negro's proportion of the population to a point slightly in excess of their proportion of the population. In 1922 out of 817 cases in the Children's Court of Buffalo only four were colored—two boys and two girls—while the figures for Buffalo showed up well for the colored children, they probably indicate laxity in handling the child problem among the colored people in Buffalo, on the part of the municipal authorities. I should say before leaving this point that the Children's Aid Society in Buffalo has done some very fine work with colored cases coming under its supervision.

Negro church organizations and social service movements are developing more efficiency and better organized programs of service. The personnel employed by these organizations is increasingly of a higher intellectual standard and as a result of their work the standard of living among Negro families seems to be improving. The schools are recording great increases in pupils in the elementary and high school grades also for collegiate and professional studies. The Negro church has developed more rapidly, of course, than any other one institution among the Negro migrants of the State. Practically every group of a hundred or more Negroes in scores of towns throughout the State has its church organizations. In Buffalo fifteen Negro churches are in existence, five having edifices. The total value of the church property there is $294,200 and the membership of eleven churches was 2,789 in 1923. In Greater New York the seating capacity of Negro churches was 24,000 in 1920. In 1924 it was 21,000 in Harlem alone. The most costly Negro church edifice in Harlem—the Mt. Olivet Baptist—was purchased for $450,000. The Abyssinian Baptist Church, containing institutional features, was erected at a cost of $325,000, with only $25,000 remaining on mortgage. The St. Philip's Protestant Episcopal Church has over a million dollars of church and apartment house property. The St. Mark's Methodist Episcopal Church is erecting a new institutional church there at a cost of nearly half a million dollars. There are four Harlem churches with parish houses, four others with institutional features and several contemplating extra social service activities. In Westchester County alone there are thirty-eight established colored churches with between 7,000 and 7,500 seating capacity available to a total Negro population of 11,066. Thirty-two of these churches own or are buying property.

In Nassau and Suffolk Counties there are thirty-three colored churches, twenty-five of which are owned by the colored people and cater to a colored population in twenty towns and villages of between 8,000 and 10,000 persons, 42 per cent of whom migrated to these counties between 1910 and 1920.

All of these factors are tending to produce a group of citizens conscious of their civic and social responsibilities.

The increase in the Negro population in the State due to the migration is adding to the political strength of the group in the State. Several years ago there were a Negro assemblyman and two Negro aldermen at one time representing the Harlem Negroes in legislative bodies. During the last presidential campaign a Negro made a creditable run for Congress from this same district. This increased voting strength is sensibly divided between the various parties and is reflected in increased representation in the appointive positions accorded the race in the city and State. Some more important positions of recent years have been State Commissioner of Agriculture, Municipal Civil Service Commissioner, Collector of Internal Revenue (Federal), Deputy Federal District Attorney, Assistant District Attorney for New York County.

Not only the Negro political representatives of the Negro population, but the white politicians also who have increasing Negro constituencies are in the main making honest efforts to help in the up-building of the Negro's civic life.

If there is any concern at all in connection with Negro migration to this State, rather should it be on the attitude assumed by the white citizens of our various communities towards the newcomers. We are engaged in America in an experiment of national life which at present is an example to the rest of the world. We have made great strides forward in handling most all of the social problems we face. Probably we have made less progress in solving the problem of race contacts than in any other direction. Most people assume an air of indifference towards this question. Others are prejudiced— bitter and unreasonable. But we cannot forever ignore the problem. New York State has probably shown a fairer attitude and more open mind in handling these questions than has any other State of our country and New York City may prove to be the laboratory in which the most satisfactory local experiment will be conducted. Certainly there is no single spot of its size on the globe where so many white people and Negroes reside and where ambition and competition are so strong, and yet where there are so few points of friction.

The opportunity for statesmanship service to humanity is ours. The obligation is ours. We cannot pass on to posterity the responsibility for work which we should assume. The challenge of democracy is before us. The Negro is probably the real test of democracy in America. Shall this democracy endure? The Negro migrant to New York State may yet give the answer.

Eugene Kinckle Jones *(1885–1954) was born in Richmond, Virginia, and became an Urban League executive, devoting nearly forty years to the organization. He was recognized as "an honored elder statesman in race relations."*

JOURNAL AND GUIDE   March 14, 1917

It is difficult, if not impossible, to check the operation of an economic law, and it is perfectly natural that men should seek fields of labor in which they are promised higher wages and better conditions, but those who go and those who encourage the going of them, should get the facts of the so-called inducements and learn the truth about them before lending their influence to a movement that not only promises no permanent good to laborers, but works untold injury to the foundation of their own economic structure.

Another phase of the matter, and one that invites the condemnation of all honest persons, is the manner in which Negro labor is at present exploited to satisfy the selfish whims of a group of misguided and ill-advised agitators and fanatics on the race question. All of the nice talk about "fleeing from southern oppression," and going where "equal rights and special privileges" await them is pure buncombe. It is strange that Negro labor should stand the oppression of the South for fifty years and suddenly make up its mind to move northward as an evidence of its resentment.

The truth of the matter is that the element of Negro race in the South that feel that oppression most is not concerned in the migration movement. Nor are going to leave their homes and accumulations of half a century as a solution of their problems. They are going to remain here and fight out their problems and insist upon having their constitutional rights accorded them here in the land of their birth.

ATLANTA INDEPENDENT   May 26, 1917

Last week we discussed at length the Negro exodus. We tried to point out in plain, simple and manly language the reason and remedy for moving North. We warned our white neighbors that city ordinance and legislation could stem the tide; that humane treatment would do more to settle the Negro's industrial and economic unrest

than anything else; that the South was his natural home; that he
desired to stay here; but in order to keep him at home like the individual, he had to have contentment; he had to be assured of protection of life and property; assured of the enjoyment of public
utilities; assured of educational advantages, ample and adequate, to
prepare his children for useful and helpful citizenship; he must be
permitted to serve God unmolested and to assemble in the community where he lives, in church, in society and politics; for his own
moral, intellectual and physical benefit he must be given living wages
and reminded in his daily dealings with his white neighbor that he
is a citizen, not a Negro and that he is charged with responsibilities
like other citizens. The Negro is conscious of his racial identity, and
is not ashamed of it. He is proud of his race and his color, but he
does not like to have the word "Negro" define his relation as a citizen.

It is extremely unfortunate that the question of segregation
should be raised while the city is in the throes of a great calamity.
It is unwise and inhuman for the newspapers and politicians to raise
the race issue at the time when Atlanta's best is bending every energy to relieve the suffering and repair the loss and damages done
our citizenry.

The Negroes have no desire to live among white folk. At the
time they bought their property, they were not among the white
people; but if the progress of the community has thrown us together, the Negro has as much right to enjoy his inheritance as the
white man and the newspaper or politician, who brings up the sin
of segregation at a time when they remain at home and do not run
away to the North and paralyze our domestic industrial and social
service, is an enemy to the best interest of all the people.

REMEMORY: WHAT THERE IS FOR US

Jacqueline Joan Johnson

My story and my family's are attached like lotus leaves, interdependent yet beautiful in their own right. I arrived in my mother's life four years before her death. As a result, some of this story is the voices of my sisters and aunts. I am the only member of my immediate family that was born above the Mason-Dixon Line. The rest of my family was born in Charleston, South Carolina.

By the time I was thirteen, I had moved from Philadelphia to New York and migrated from New York to South Carolina and back to New York again. Over the years, I have looked for my mother, my geography of self in many migrations, among many people, sometimes aware and at other times not so aware of this search, this need. When I think of my migration, I also think of my migration from childhood to young adulthood and from woman to mother of self and others. In order to tell this story, I will have to tell many small stories.

About 1835, a young woman from Madagascar was sent by her father John Diana, to England. The woman was sent there to be educated. While in England, she met and married a white man from America named George Lucas. George Lucas was from Charleston, South Carolina. The woman would migrate to America bringing Malagasy customs, knowledge, and gold. Her gold would help start some of the first rice mills in Charleston, South Carolina. This woman was my great-great-great-grandmother, Henrietta Diana.

Henrietta Diana was a tall, brown-skinned woman who would live to see the Civil War and Emancipation and to participate in Reconstruction. She traveled around the country and attended such events as the Philadelphia Exposition of 1876. My grandfather, Henry O'Neil Jenkins, was born and raised in her house in Mt. Pleasant, South Carolina, in 1889. One of her legacies would be her name, which she gave to her daughter Henrietta Lucas.

Years later, my grandfather would give her name to my mother, Henrietta Jenkins. Henrietta was his spirited, rebellious, talented, middle daughter. She was a gifted orator and actress. She would travel throughout the South speaking, acting, and winning awards. She was race-conscious and involved in many clubs and community activities. She too, was brown-skinned, five feet five, and was known to be giving to a fault. My mother and her five sisters were all graduates of the famed Avery Institute; it was the first black private free school in South Carolina and produced graduates whose training made them highly sought after. Their education was the equivalent of two years of college. My mother was a daughter of promise, whom great things were expected of.

My father, Joseph Johnson was an artistic, sensitive, complicated, and rebellious young man. He was a handsome, dark-skinned man with large, sensitive brown eyes. My father started the first a capella boys choir in Charleston and had a band known as the "Kentucky Bandolers." He played guitar and sang. He too attended Avery Institute. He inherited his father "Buddy" Johnsons's awesome sense of color and design, and he excelled in electronics. My father would always work and make his living with his hands. My mother and father were childhood sweethearts. They were born in the Depression, and were of that generation of "new Negroes" who believed America would open her doors to them once they proved themselves capable. Life was to show them differently.

My parents were married on September 6, 1942, before the rituals of adulthood had been completed. Their marriage was the subject of what was to become a life-long feud between their respective families. Apparently, neither side wanted them to get married. My mother was from a high yellow family with long hair and lived downtown, and my father's family was dark-skinned and lived in what is known as uptown Charleston. What the problem really was between my family never was made clear. My parents got married anyway, though the feud lasted long after they both were dead. As a result, for a long period of time those families, which are my family, never would mix that well or that much. My mother became pregnant a year into her marriage. Not long after, my father was drafted into the navy to fight in World War II. In November of 1943, my sister Patricia Armita Johnson, was born on Armistice Day.

When my father returned from the war in 1946, my parents settled into a fairly safe and predictable southern existence. Pat, my oldest sister was so glad to see my father that she called him "Hallelujah" for weeks after he came home. My mother worked as a domestic, while my father worked at the Charleston Navy Yard. In 1947, my second sister, Gloria, was born. Time passed.

In late 1951, my mother became very ill and had to be taken to a hospital. My mother had an illness that had gone undiagnosed until she was eighteen. She was what is now known as a juvenile diabetic. For those times, she had what folks called "sugar." The nearest hospital was a segregated white hospital. At first, my pop had called the Fire Department, hoping to get a quick response. My mother was prone to diabetic reactions and comas most of her adult life. In those days, like now, a quick response meant life or death.

The Fire Department was not pleased with being called to help a black woman and a fight broke out between my father and the chief of the Fire Department. The exchange was so volatile that my father bit a hole in the Chief's neck. Ultimately, my father carried my mother in his arms to the nearest hospital, which turned out to be for whites only, though my mother was allowed in. As a result of pop's fight with the Fire Department Chief, it became known that his life was on the line.

Shortly after this incident, my father left Charleston alone, heading north towards Philadelphia. Instead, for a brief time, he lived in Flushing, Queens, in New York, then he moved to Philadelphia. For a while he lived on Vine Street, then he moved to Chestnut Street. He worked when he could find work. He also had illnesses of his own, a series of terrible colds, and a foot injury. With no medical coverage, many of his health problems went unmet. He lost weight and no doubt worried himself sick about his wife and family.

For my mother, the separation from her husband was no less traumatic. She wrote to my father every day for a year up until the day before she left to join him. She struggled to make ends meet with her two young daughters to care for. She constantly had to go to the hospital for her "sugar." My sisters caught everything and were also constantly at the doctor's. My older sister had a bad case of asthma as well. More than half of my parents' income went to pay medical costs. These medical costs would only increase over the years.

Prospects were dim for my mother in Charleston. She worked at a local restaurant and, when that job ended, did domestic work. After almost a year of trying to reconnect with her husband, she realized her only course of action was to leave Charleston. My mother decided to move to New York to stay with her father. Her plan was to get work and then move to Philly to be with her husband. My mother did not know, that like the first Henrietta, she would never see her home again. My middle sister, Gloria, was five at the time of my family's migration. What follows is Gloria's account of that migration, which changed my family forever.

We lived on Coming Street in part of a house in Charleston. I think we had two rooms. There was no inside bathroom. You went outside to the outhouse (spiders and other occupants were always present) when you took care of business. I remember bathing in a tin tub or an enamel basin. We played in the yard and climbed the fig tree for fun. Of course, we ate many green figs against Ma's advice and ended up with bad stomach aches and visits to the doctor frequently. I had the ugliest dog ever created, but he was mine. His name was Browny. Pop used to say "where is that ugly mutt." He was ug–ly!

When I learned we had to leave Charleston, I feared leaving Browny. Ma told me I had to give him away. I do remember walking to my neighbor's house who gave me Browny, trying to return him. It didn't work—Browny had a bad reputation from being so ugly. Finally the original owner relented and took him in. I cried for days. Browny and I were inseparable. I got sick with pneumonia just before we left Charleston and had to be constantly medicated. I remember Ma later told me that everyone said she would kill me going up North, since I was recuperating.

In 1953, we moved from Charleston to New York. Pop left because of threats to his life. A year prior to our move, Pop came to Philadelphia seeking work at the Navy Yard. It was in February or March that I remember hearing that Ma, Pat, and I would be going to New York to stay with Grandpa. I know we left Charleston sometime in the Spring to travel to New York. In fact, on January 20, 1953, we left Charleston by train.

Once we were on the train, Ma told me I could not stretch out my long legs, because she had bought a half-fare ticket for me. I was tall for my age and I was very uncomfortable with my legs under me. It was a long ride to New York from Charleston. Well, sleep got the best of me and I stretched out. Ma ended up paying the full fare for me.

I remember meeting my grandfather for the first time. My first and lasting impression was that he was mean and didn't like kids. Where we lived, we had to walk up a lot of steps. There was a big lady that lived in the house named Adele, who told me she didn't like a lot of crying and if I didn't listen she would spank me. I learned in a hurry how to get around Adele. Grandpa was not so easy. Now, years later, as an adult I realize he had been through a lot.

In 1928, my grandfather, Henry O'Neil Jenkins, who was a shipbuilder, became fed up with his life in Charleston. He was the first member of my family to migrate north to Harlem. What I

*know of my grandfather's migration is veiled with some mystery.
As they would say in the vernacular, the folks just ain't telling all.
I do know that his employer moved, and there must have been
some strain in his relationship with my grandmother. With $20.00
he caught the Clyde Line boat to New York from Charleston in late
1928. At the time of his migration, my mother was five years old.
He had not been in New York but half a minute when the stock
market crashed. For long months he walked holes in his shoes on
many a street in search of work. Later he got work at the Brooklyn
Navy Yard, where he stayed until his retirement in 1941. What I do
know is that he stayed in touch with my grandmother and his
Charleston family. But when I met him in 1953, grandfather was
not easy.*

*We had been in New York for the summer on into the fall and
school had started. I was not allowed to go to school because you
had to be six years old, and I had just turned five, but I had already completed the first grade in Charleston. Pat went to Catholic
school, because grandpa was Catholic. She had to study prayers
every day. Ma got a job cooking for a white minister and his family. Sometimes she would have to stay overnight and sometimes
she took us to work with her.*

*Most of my daily life was spent with grandpa. He took care of
me when Adele and Ma went to work and Pat went to school. One
thing I do remember, was inspection at the table—our faces and
hands had to be clean. Grandpa always sat at the head of the table,
and we always ate together as a family. In my case, after Ma,
Adele, and Pat left, it was just me, Grandpa and a bowl of Wheatena, or oatmeal and the razor strap. I hated hot cereal. That is all
Grandpa knew how to cook. So it was Wheatena or oatmeal for
breakfast, or if Ma didn't make a lunch, grandpa gave me Wheatena or oatmeal and fish for lunch. And if Ma was late for dinner,
it was the rest of the Wheatena and oatmeal from lunch as a snack.
I hate hot cereal to this day.*

*In our block in Harlem, there was a grocery store right down-
stairs next to our building. Grandpa and I would go for walks.
Often, we went to visit his friends, though we would always end up
at the grocery store. I took messages to the grocery store owner,
but always had to be careful if there was a police officer there.
Later, I realized, that I often took the numbers to the store owner.
I always got a piece of candy for my efforts.*

*I always felt so small. There were so many buildings and the
people were so big. I learned to hate crowds. Being little, I could*

squeeze to the front quickly. I do remember someone was always getting shot. One day, I was out with grandpa and there was a crowd. I pushed my way to the front, only to see pools of blood and a man with his face missing. This I didn't forget.

Ma loved the theater and every Sunday she took Pat and I to the Apollo Theater. I remember meeting Sammy Davis Jr., Eartha Kitt, and Pearl Bailey. We were regulars on Sunday. I never forgot the shows. Later, grandpa used to tell me stories about the ocean. He would tell me about the lighthouse and looking at the clouds to tell what kind of weather we would have. I spent time having fun sitting on the stoop or lying on a mattress and blanket on the fire escape to get away from the heat inside the apartment.

I would wait all week for Sunday dinner, when Adele would make her famous cake with the hole in the middle. Adele would always let me lick the bowl, but when the cake came out, I was told it was for a blind aunt. I cannot tell you how many tears I shed over those Sunday cakes going to Adele's blind aunt. Dumb me, there was no blind aunt. By all accounts, I remember the time spent in Harlem with fondness.

I believe we went to Philadelphia in late 1954. We lived in the Philadelphia Navy Yard projects in South Philly. This place was straight out of the "Little House on the Prairie." The stove was a wood- or coal-burning stove. Everyone had to buy their own coal or wood. We had a coalbin and woodshed outside. Our stove had no gauges, but Ma was a great cook and nothing ever failed. My job was to bring in the wood and paper to start the fire. I could even split the small pieces with the axe. Ma never saw me do this. The apartments were all attached like row houses. There were three rooms—four at best. Pat and I had bunk beds.

We had to cross a bridge to go to school, because there were railroad tracks underneath. One problem, the railroad track was safer than the bridge, which had numerous holes that looked huge to my small stature. Now, I figure they left the holes in the bridge, because they knew only blacks lived in those projects and used that bridge.

Our father was an electrician trained in the navy. We were poor, but we always had plenty to eat and ma and pop were always at the table with laughter. Friday nights was Pop's pickled pig's feet and poker night. Neighbors would come over and we all would be eating from huge glass jars of pickled pigs feet and pork skins and rinds.

We later moved to West Philly on Walnut Street, 5628 Walnut Street. By the time I graduated from elementary school, I had gone to five different elementary schools and had lived in three different states.

Some thirty years or more have passed since that migration. During the course of writing this piece, my sister found a bag of letters in her closet. Surprisingly, the bag contained letters my mother wrote to my father during the year they were separated. I was able to ascertain from the letters that my father fled the South not only because he feared for his life but because he was tired and frustrated with dead-end opportunities. The letters reveal the Charleston Navy Yard held his job open for a number of months. However, my father refused to return. Perhaps it was a combination of anger, pride, and just plain stubbornness. I don't know what my father's dreams or visions were, though he clearly found no peace in Charleston.

The letters also reveal how powerless my mother felt about her circumstances and the sudden separation from her husband. She was overwhelmed and struggled daily to make a life for herself and her daughters. Jobs were scarce, and her letters are filled with repeated requests for money for food and medical costs. Her circumstances were bleak, yet she marshaled what resources she was able to create and find "a way out of no way." For a year or more, she wrote my father letters every day. In her own way, she kept my father connected to her and his daughters. She also kept the idea of them coming back together alive in his mind and heart.

My mother, daughter of promise, bore some nine children—three girls and six boys. All of the boys died at birth or shortly thereafter. She loved my father to a fault, as the old people would say. My sisters call it the never-ending love story. She was a great believer in education and exposure to the arts. As a result, by the time I was three I could read and had my own library card. Her literary interests would later be passed on to me.

The years in Philadelphia both strengthened and disintegrated my family. My father maintained a steady job at the Philadelphia Navy Yard but depleted his pension in his efforts to provide monies for my mother's increasing medical problems. My parents' lives were not easy, they were too busy living, trying to survive. My parents' home in Philadelphia became a stopover for relatives trying to get settled and find work in the North. Lives, children, and marriages were kept together and saved there. There was always movement, drama, and change.

My mother lost her battle with her physical body and died suddenly in May of 1963, at the age of forty. At the time, my father was unemployed. Pat was in college. Gloria stayed with friends of our family in order to finish out the school year. She would eventually migrate to New York in 1964. I returned to Queens, New York, to live with my aunt. My father remained in Philadelphia, jobless and unable to keep his daughters or any remnant of his former life in place. We all missed an opportunity for growth and stability by this separation. It would be another seven years before we would all be in the same place together again. My life would go through several twists and turns.

Looking back, I remember my first move was at the age of three and a half, from Philadelphia to New York in the fall of 1962. I stayed with my Aunt Bluette, her husband, and three sons. I arrived at her house, carsick from being on the road too much. This was the first time I met my cousins, who were all sitting on a bed eating cherry vanilla ice cream. Unbeknownst to me, this was the beginning of my five-year sojourn in New York. From my Aunt Bluette I would learn piano, and how to cook and clean. I had all the privileges of a middle-class upbringing and wanted for nothing. The years passed.

In the summer of 1967, I left New York for Charleston to visit my grandmother and aunt. I left New York on a Greyhound bus line. I sat staring at my Aunt Bluette, as she shouted out last-minute instructions. I wondered if I was going to see her again. On the bus ride down to South Carolina, all I remember was my legs were too long and I got bus sick. In fact, I didn't look forward to the bus ride back at all. This visit with my grandmother was supposed to be for a summer; instead I would stay three years.

I consciously remember meeting my grandmother as she was 75 years old and I was 10. I remember standing and looking at my grandmother for a long while trying to figure out what to call her. She relieved me of my trouble and told me to call her "Hannah." I was an outspoken, loud, very active, imaginative ten year old. Little did I know it would be from this tall, sway-backed, pound-cake colored woman that I would learn my strength and, most of all, how to care for others, to give and to heal.

My grandmother, Hannah Bennett Jenkins, was born in McClellanville, South Carolina, in 1892. She had graduated from high school and wanted to become a teacher but her father would not allow it. In 1912, she married my grandfather and settled in Charleston. She would rarely travel back to McClellanville as she simply did not have the money. She was a prodigious gardener and lived true to her biblical name, "mother of mothers"; these are among the most enduring aspects of her legacy.

In 1968, my grandmother had already raised seven children of her own. Out of the nine children, there were six girls and one boy. Her first child, a boy, died in her arms because the hospital would not cater to blacks. Another child, a girl, was stillborn. Children would always be important in the life of my grandmother. At some point between the age of 55 and 65 my grandmother decided she would become a foster mother. A job which she did until the age of 87 when the city of Charleston forced her to retire. I don't know how many times children, babies, teenagers were brought to our house in the middle of the night, early morning, or just before I got home from school. Many of these children, especially the babies, were abandoned and or abused by their parents. Often they were malnourished and had severe health problems. What I learned from her over time was how to care for babies. My grandma passed her "touch" to me. Over the years, my grandmother cared for and helped to rear 27 foster children. She also had two other jobs, one as caretaker for an elderly white lady at nights and she washed and ironed linen for a local barbershop.

I spent my first summer in Charleston with grandmother and aunt enjoying the country and the wildness of play in open spaces. My Aunt Edna and I made a tour of everything from Dali exhibitions to the old slave market and James and Johns islands. The summer went by so fast that when it was time to return to New York, I opted to stay. Even then, at the age of eleven, when my Aunt Blue said, "What do you want to do? Do you want to stay in Charleston or return to New York?" I said "yes," realizing my life was changing forever.

Charleston, my new home, was a place of okra gumbo, she crab-soup, shrimp, and grits, day-old cheese rolls and little jars of flowered sachets, red, red stockings that never match anyone's complexion and lace hankies knotted in the corner with my money in it. This place of AME revivals, first menstruation, first African dance and mulberry juice on my lips and clothes. The nectar of peaches and figs my daily fruit, sewing on my grandma's 1898 Singer sewing machine in a lightning storm, preparing for Charleston Preparatory High and the preacher's son making time just for me. Countless lessons in poise, drama, and presentation.

My Aunt Edna was an elementary school teacher and a music teacher. One of our first public adventures together was my singing solo at the PTA meeting. The auditorium was filled to capacity. My Aunt started playing the piano. But no sounds came from my mouth. A lot of my new friends were sitting in the front row and were laughing their hearts out. I was to sing "What a Little Moonlight Can Do for You." Well, we got through it and to my surprise, I became a regular and requested singer at teas and other affairs.

My father's people catered to me too, and I got the best of everything. One year I had two birthday parties. Here was the primal safety, nurturing, and caring that had eluded me since my mother's death. I had so many new clothes they did not repeat for three months. I was put in the top class in school and earned my metal and stayed there for the duration of my time in South Carolina. I took piano lessons from my mother's teacher and was the first among my friends to quit. What a big to-do that was. Everyone else quit after me.

In 1970, I had discovered my desire to write and draw as an artist, and I had begun to conjure up the muse. When I traveled north that desire would travel with me too. Those three years in the land of my ancestors would mark me for life.

The more I began to move into puberty the more difficult things seemed with my grandmother. Sometimes I was accused of doing things with boys I had not even thought of yet. I was outspoken and would always speak my mind. My grandmother was trying to protect me but I was beginning to feel suffocated. I was in between girl and woman, and I saw more than I could tell. Once, my father's sister bought me two beautiful dresses with bows. When I got home and showed them to my grandmother, she stared at them and then cut the bows off. I was so hurt by her actions. At times she got mad about my parents' relationship, particularly my mother's death, and I became her whipping board. More than once I was told you're "black and ugly just like your father." This I couldn't bear, and some part of me refused to claim it. I saw what lay between my father's people and my mother's people, and knew I would become the thing that was wrestled between them. The strongest thing in me said "move, let's get out of here." And I did.

My migration to the South was easy, natural in comparison to my return to New York. I had a strong desire to see my two sisters again and I wanted to see New York and to reconnect with my old friends and family. My sisters and I had been separated for almost seven years in various ways and wanted to be family again. Somewhere we knew that without each other we would always be searching. I think my sisters thought they were rescuing me from the repressed, old ways of the South. I knew I was escaping something that threatened to close me in. We were all sheroic and naive. They were 22 and 26, barely ten years older than me, attempting to usher me into adulthood.

I left Charleston in the Summer of 1971, on National Airlines. I traveled on a student rate for $35.00—remember that? I was restless, wanting New York and all it represented. Some folks laugh, when I tell them I had the "immigrant" experience. Loaded down with Southern mores, and speech patterns, I was no longer the forward, angular little girl who had left in 1967. I returned to New York on the threshold of womanhood, shy, intelligent, aware, and acutely sensitive to everything. Often, I would speak to people on the street, telling them "good morning," only to be stared at in disbelief.

With a child's perception, I must have imagined all of my friends and acquaintances standing in a fixed point of time. I soon found out many of my friends did not want to have anything to do with me. I was sometimes laughed at, scorned, and admired among my peers. I quickly learned to keep myself to myself. I realized I didn't belong in my aunt's house any more. She had cleared away every sign that I had ever lived there. What I remembered no longer was. Many of my former friends were polite but hardly inviting or warm. In many ways, I was ahead of them and in others far behind. I would spend the years negotiating a safe distance between what was known and what I needed to know. I would spend years alone, having found no comfortable space in the niches that surrounded me. Intellectually, I was so far ahead of my classmates the school officials wanted to skip me twice. Since I had not learned a foreign language in the South, I stayed at grade level. This was the beginning of great excitement and great disappointment.

As I walked through the halls of PS 231, which was more like a zoo to me, I truly began to miss the South. I had become accustomed to living life in a certain way. I was used to having a community and having presence in that community. I was watched by my elders and peers and expected to be somebody. There was a dignity of daily life and refinement that became a part of my way of being in the world.

My daily life in New York highlighted my emotional and spiritual loss. I took freedom in not going to church, in just hanging about watching TV. I was happy to be with my sisters, but secretly I mourned the loss of a way of life as I knew it. All that hokeyness wasn't so hokey—it was foundation and a grounding for my spirit. I would fall into a depression whose only sign would be my weight gain of over 50 pounds in five months. I swallowed and ate my anger and disappointment.

I had already lived in so many places that I felt both powerless and grateful just to have a place to stay. It occurred to me back then, that no matter where I lived, geography could not save me, I was going to have a hard time. I spent most of my time looking back like Lot's wife, almost losing my life to the salt of the past. Like every immigrant, I made no real effort to return to the South.

The reuniting with my sisters thrust us all into struggle to stay alive mentally, emotionally and spiritually. Each one of us paid a different and costly price for this effort. In some ways, we are all still recovering from that. The South was a doorway, my home, the North was the road I had to travel, master in a way. I had come back to New York searching for a time that "never was, but is now."

In my journey to New York, grandmother's presence became the stuff of my dreams. It would be another ten years before I returned to Charleston and realized some essential part of me never left. Despite my painful rites of passage, the largest part of my spirit always lived in Charleston, near my grandmother and her God.

In some ways, I am still trying to settle that early nomad in me. Seventeen years in New York and I still refuse to call myself a New Yorker. I have come to think of myself as a nomad viewing "home" as any place that I happened to be in a given time. Seventeen years, I have made New York my home, knowing it is not truly my home and wondering to where do I migrate next?

Out of old letters, conversations, reconstructed memory, re-memory, and speculations comes this story of my family's migration. What there is for us, is a legacy of humor, creativity, and courage. My parents' migration started by chance, confrontation of accepted norms and a desire for change. Hope was the impetus behind all the chances they took. Theirs was hope for a better life, better opportunities, and generational progress. They dared to take the challenge of an unknown road and paid a price to travel it. No matter what the obstacles were, they kept moving. What there is for us are gifts of life stories and knowledge. Through it all, some of their dreams were sacrificed, not all were lost. They taught us while being broken, whole and able, to survive.

Jacqueline Joan Johnson *is a native of Philadelphia, Pennyslvania. She is the author of* Stokely Carmichael: The Story of Black Power *for children ages ten and up. She currently lives in Brooklyn and is working on a collection of poetry,* What Keeps Us Alive, *and a novel,* Song of Ikari.

OPPORTUNITY Magazine, February, 1925

THE PROBLEMS OF THE CITY DWELLER

Mary McLeod Bethune

It is ever the problem of living a rational, healthy life in the midst of an environment which for the masses is for the most part, unfavorable. It is the problem of fresh air, wholesome food, sunshine and freedom within limits as pitilessly circumscribed as prison walls. It is the problem of making an increased wage, a better school, an easily accessible and cheap means of transportation, electric light, motion pictures, parades and band concerts, a policeman on the corner and propinquitous neighbors, compensate for the sweep of the hill, the greeness of expansive meadows, and the lure of the endless road. It is the problem of getting a chance to live the abundant life, the door to which in our urban centers yields only to the touch of a golden key.

The problem has been greatly intensified in the past ten or twenty years by the rush from the rural districts. This rush has been neither sectional nor racial. Every section of the country has felt it. While there may be specific causes back of the "push" that has moved hundreds of thousands of Negroes from the Southern States to various points in the North-east and middle West, the migration can be truthfully considered as only another phase of the general movement of population from the rural towards the urban centers. In fact, for a long period, preceding the migrations of large bodies of Negroes northward there was a steady and perceptible increase in the Negro population of Southern cities caused by a movement of this element of the population from the country to the city.

"During the past 30 years there has been a great shift of population from the country to the town, and every class of towns, from village to great cities, has grown, whereas the country districts have actually decreased in population. The increase of the Negro urban population in the South in the decade 1910–1920 was 396,444 or 56,000 more than the increase for the same period in the number of Negroes in the North from the South—340,260. More than one-third—34% of the total Negro population is living in urban territory. The census reports show an actual decrease of 234,876 or 3.4% in the Negro rural population of the United States. In 1910 the number of Negroes reported as living in rural territory was 7,138,534. In 1920 the number thus living reported was 6,903,658."

A powerful contributory cause for recent legislation in the restriction of immigration was the alarming extent to which our future citizens were concentrating in the large seaport and manufacturing cities instead of seeking the extensive and unworked agricultural lands of the middle West and the West. It is not necessary for me to worry you with census figures, and other statistics compiled by special investigators to establish the fact that the problem of the city dweller has been greatly intensified by this almost steady and constant movement of the rural dweller to the urban centers. The causes back of this almost universal movement of population cityward are usually conceded to be economic, educational and social.

In spite of the manifold movements, plans and efforts to make Farming and other rural pursuits pay, the country lad still turns his eye towards the city as his El Dorado. He wants a shorter working day; wages that will insure him good clothes and creature comforts; an opportunity to advance in earning power as he increases his ability to be of service in his calling; a fair chance to acquire wealth and become a leader in his community. To the country lad with plenty of time to dream while he plods thru days and days of monotonous routine, this is what the city means. To many an adult, weary of the grind and isolation of wresting a living from the soil, it offers an opening for a new chance, a realized vision. And so they come— young and old—beardless youth and gnarled old age—all expecting that the road to wealth and power and influence lies down the great white way of the modern city.

The cry of the Soul to know has given another push to this modern move towards the city. Longer school terms; better-equipped school buildings; more capable teachers; the broadening influence of lectures; concerts, motion pictures, libraries, parades and festive and holiday occasions, have lured many a grizzled homesteader to abandon home and ancestral acres and move cityward. The widening out and diversification of the modern high school with its facilities for teaching the technique of skilled trades and business; home economics and agriculture as well as the arts and sciences. The extending of education at the public expense in some cities to include even a college education. The offering of night courses for underprivileged boys and girls, men and women. These are advantages which even the phonograph, the motion picture machine and the radio cannot compensate for in the country.

Then, again, in spite of automobiles, Fords, good roads and the transmission of electric light current over long distances, the country is still a lonely place for thousands and thousands of dwellers. Weary of quilting parties, barnraisings and quarterly meetings, they are impelled cityward by the age-old urge towards companionship and recreation. Happiness is usually a result of a perfect balancing of work-time, play-time and rest-time, and the normal human being is likely to continue to migrate until he arrives at a place where that balance comes nearest to being struck. The city with its socialized Churches, its civic clubs, its parks, its easily accessible amusement resorts and centers, its playgrounds, its bathhouses and skating rinks; its roof gardens, theatres and cabarets exert a pull as mighty as the social push of the rural populations toward the metropolitan centers.

Though not so often mentioned as a cause, the desire for protection has impelled many a rural dweller to move into or nearer the city. This is especially true with Negro rural dwellers in nearly every part of the South, where the lack or indifference of constabulary or police agencies make the possession of property uncertain—often hazardous and the safeguarding of life uncertain. These people turn towards the cities for protection in the exercise of the rights guaranteed them under the constitution, and a half chance to defend themselves should these rights be infringed upon. They also seek the protection from fire and ravages of disease which the superior organization and supervision of city life afford.

Because of these causes—educational—economic—social—the country has been for decades disgorging itself into the cities and the very obtaining of the advantages it has come to seek presents the biggest problem to the city dwellers. To get wealth when the cost of living keeps pace or a little in advance of increased wages; to enjoy educational advantages when creature needs require the time of all whose strength can be turned into wages; to appreciate recreations that take for toll the coin that should be spent for fuel and bread; to have better health and longer life in crowded ghettoes and sunless rooms; to have a neighbor in the man that lives next door and a friend in the thousands that pass unknowing and unknown along a hundred ways; to have children who will not grow to adult life unacquainted with a tree or afraid of a blade of grass; to have counting rooms and generous hearts; great white ways and unstained souls; apartment houses and the spirit of home; this, my friends, in homely, unscientific language, is the problem of the city dweller.

To meet this problem is the social challenge of our generation! To assist the city dweller to make the adjustments necessary to a full possession and enjoyment of the manifold blessings and privileges of urban life is the business of the Church; the mission of the trained social worker; the raison d'être of organized philanthropy and charity. To this task should be applied the earnest and intelligent aid of every group that makes up the population of our cities. It requires cooperation among racial groups widely differing in language, national customs, and color. It requires mutual racial respect and confidence. It requires tolerance and a courageous application to all sorts of unusual maladjustments, of the principle of the Golden rule. Whether the newcomer to the city is from Texas or South Carolina; whether he is from the Steppe of Russia or the sunny Plains of Italy; whether he is of Nordic hue, or wears the "shadowed livery of the burnished sun," his problem is to obtain for himself and family a living wage, and a place to invest it in cleanliness, fresh air, sanitary surroundings and wholesome recreation. Forcing individuals or groups into segregated ghettoes, with poor sanitation, unpaved streets, run-down houses, filthy alleys and surroundings conductive to depravity of both thought and action is neither a scientific nor altruistic approach to the problem of the city dweller. Agencies must be multiplied that can and will bring sufficient pressure to bear upon city governments to insure living conditions that will safeguard the well being of all the dwellers in urban centers, and the self respect of the individual. The work of Americanizing the foreigner thru easily accessible agencies for teaching him the language, customs and traditions of his adopted country, the work of protecting him in industry, educating his children, and drilling him in habits of decent living must be prosecuted with ever increasing earnestness and zeal. The breaking down of racial barriers and the conceding to every man his right to own and enjoy his property wherever his means permit him to own it; the opening up of parks and playgrounds for the enjoyment and development of all citizens alike; the firm but patient tutoring of the uninitiated newcomer in the privileges and obligations of urban life, must still be the foundation of the programme of organizations like the Urban League and other great social agencies whose militant efforts in these directions have made them national in scope and purpose.

Mary Jane McLeod Bethune *(1875–1955) was born in Mayesville, South Carolina, and went on to become a civil rights leader and adviser to presidents. She organized the National Council of Negro Women in 1935 and founded Bethune Cookman College in 1942.*

Augusta, Georgia   April 30, 1917

Dear Sir:
I will leave this city on the 10th of May for Chicago, and I would

like very much to secure a position before leaving. I am a fancy cook, I make all kinds of fancy dishes. Of course I can cook anything that southern folks have but make a specialty of fancy decoration. I can send reference if you want it.

Yours respt.

Miami, Florida   May 4 1917

Dear Sir,
Some time ago down this side it was a rumor about the great work going on in the north. But at the present time every thing is quiet there, people saying that all we have been hearing was false until I caught hold of the Chicago Defender I see where its more positions are still open. Now I am very anxious to get up there. I follows up cooking. I also was a stevedor. I used to have from 150 to 200 man under my charge. They thought I was capable in doing the work and at the meantime I am willing to do anything. I have a wife and she is a very good cook. She has lots of references from the north and south. Now dear sir if you can send me a ticket so I can come up there and after I get straightened out I will send for my wife. You will oblige me by doing so as early date as possible.

Yours truly.

CHICAGO DEFENDER   August 19, 1916

After fifty years of sound napping, depending on the white southerner and his "cotton crop," the members of the Race are migrating into northland, where every kind of labor is being thrown open to them, where decent houses are obtainable for him to house his family and better schools to educate his children.

Kissimmee, Florida   May 1, 1917

Dear sir:
I am a subscriber for the Chicago Defender have read of the good work you are doing in employing help for our large factories and how you are striving to help the better class of people to the north. I am a teacher and have been teaching five years successful, and as our school here has closed my cousin and I have decided to go north for the summer who is also a teacher of this county. I am writing you to secure for us a position that we could fit, if there be any that is vacant.

We can furnish you with the best of references. We would not like to advertise through a paper. Hoping to hear from you at an early date, I am

Yours very truly.

Atlanta, Georgia   April 11, 1917

Dear Sir
I am a reader of your paper and we are all crazy about it and take it every Saturday and we raise a great howl when we dont get it. Now since I see and feel that you are for the race and are willing to assist any one so I will ask you to please assist me in getting im-ployment and some place to stop with some good quiet people or with a family that would take some one to live with them. I will do any kind of work. I am a hair dresser but I will do any kind of work I can get to do I am a widow and have one child a little girl 6 years old I dont know any body there so if you can assist me in any way will be greatly appreciated now this letter is personal please dont print it in your paper. I hope to hear from you soon.

Respectfully.

Savannah, Georgia   April 24, 1917

Sir,
I saw an advertisement in the Chicago Ledger where you would send tickets to any one desireing to come up there. I am a married man with a wife only, and I am 38 years of age, and both of us have so far splendid health, and would like very much to come out there provided we could get good employment after getting there. So kindly write me giving full information regarding the advertise-ment. I am,

Yours respectfully.

New Orleans, Louisiana   May 5, 1917

Dear Sir:
Am applying for a position in your city if there be any work of my trade. I am a water pipe corker and has worked foreman on subser-vice drainage and sewer in this city for ten (10) years. I am now

out of work and want to leave this city. I am a man of family therefore I am very anxious for an immediate reply. Please find enclosed self addressed envelop for return answer. Hoping you will give this your immediate consideration, I am

Anxiously yours.

1944

AMERICAN HUNGER

Richard Wright

My first glimpse of the flat black stretches of Chicago depressed and dismayed me, mocked all my fantasies. Chicago seemed an unreal city whose mythical houses were built of slabs of black coal wreathed in palls of gray smoke, houses whose foundations were sinking slowly into the dank prairie. Flashes of steam showed intermittently on the wise horizon, gleaming translucently in the winter sun. The din of the city entered my consciousness, entered to remain for years to come. The year was 1927.

What would happen to me here? Would I survive? My expectations were modest. I wanted only a job. Hunger had long been my daily companion. Diversion and recreation, with the exception of reading, were unknown. In all my life—though surrounded by many people—I had not had a single satisfying, sustained relationship with another human being and, not having had any, I did not miss it. I made no demands whatever upon others.

The train rolled into the depot. Aunt Maggie and I got off and walked slowly through the crowds into the station. I looked about to see if there were signs saying: FOR WHITE—FOR COLORED. I saw none. Black people and white people moved about, each seemingly intent upon his private mission. There was no racial fear. Indeed, each person acted as though no one existed but himself. It was strange to pause before a crowded newsstand and buy a newspaper without having to wait until a white man was served. And yet, because everything was so new, I began to grow tense again, although it was a different sort of tension than I had known before. I knew that this machine-city was governed by strange laws and I wondered if I would ever learn them.

As we waited for a streetcar to take us to Aunt Cleo's home for temporary lodging, I looked northward at towering buildings of steel and stone. There were no curves here, no trees; only angles, lines, squares, bricks and copper wires. Occasionally the ground beneath my feet shook from some faraway pounding and I felt that this world, despite its massiveness, was somehow dangerously fragile. Streetcars screeched past over steel tracks. Cars honked their horns. Clipped speech sounded about me. As I stood in the icy wind, I wanted to talk to Aunt Maggie, to ask her questions, but her tight face made me hold my tongue. I was learning already from the frantic light in her eyes the strain that the city imposed upon its people. I was seized by doubt. Should I have come here? But going back was impossible. I had fled a known terror, and perhaps I could cope with this unknown terror that lay ahead.

The streetcar came. Aunt Maggie motioned for me to get on and pushed me toward a seat in which a white man sat looking blankly out the window. I sat down beside the man and looked straight ahead of me. After a moment I stole a glance at the white man out of the corners of my eyes; he was still staring out the window, his mind fastened upon some inward thought. I did not exist for him; I was as far from his mind as the stone buildings that swept past in the street. It would have been illegal for me to sit beside him in the part of the South that I had come from.

The car swept past soot-blackened buildings, stopping at each block, jerking again into motion. The conductor called street names in a tone that I could not understand. People got on and off the car, but they never glanced at one another. Each person seemed to regard the other as a part of the city landscape. The white man who sat beside me rose and I turned my knees aside to let him pass, and another white man sat beside me and buried his face in a newspaper. How could that possibly be? Was he conscious of my blackness?

We went to Aunt Cleo's address and found that she was living in a rented room. I had imagined that she lived in an apartment and I was disappointed. I rented a room from Aunt Cleo's landlady and decided to keep it until I got a job. I was baffled. Everything seemed makeshift, temporary. I caught an abiding sense of insecurity in the personalities of the people around me. I found Aunt Cleo aged beyond her years. Her husband, a product of a southern plantation, had, like my father, gone off and left her. Why had he left? My aunt could not answer. She was beaten by the life of the city, just as my mother had been beaten. Wherever my eyes turned they saw stricken, frightened black faces trying vainly to cope with a civilization that they did not understand. I felt lonely. I had fled one insecurity and had embraced another.

When I rose the next morning the temperature had dropped below zero. The house was as cold to me as the southern streets had been in winter. I dressed, doubling my clothing. I ate in a restaurant, caught a streetcar and rode south, rode until I could see no more black faces on the sidewalks. I had now crossed the boundary line of the Black Belt and had entered that territory where jobs were perhaps to be had from white folks. I walked the streets and looked

into shop windows until I saw a sign in a delicatessen: PORTER
WANTED.

I went in and a stout white woman came to me.

"Vat do you vant?" she asked.

The voice jarred me. She's Jewish, I thought, remembering with
shame the obscenities I used to shout at Jewish storekeepers in Arkansas.

"I thought maybe you needed a porter," I said.

"Meester 'Offman, he eesn't here yet," she said. "Vill you vait?"

"Yes, ma'am."

"Seet down."

"No, ma'am. I'll wait outside."

"But eet's cold out zhere," she said.

"That's all right," I said.

She shrugged. I went to the sidewalk. I waited for half an hour
in the bitter cold, regretting that I had not remained in the warm
store, but unable to go back inside. A bald, stoutish white man went
into the store and pulled off his coat. Yes, he was the boss man . . .
I went in.

"Zo you vant a job?" he asked.

"Yes, sir," I answered, guessing at the meaning of his words.

"Vhere you vork before?"

"In Memphis, Tennessee."

"My brudder-in-law vorked in Tennessee vonce," he said.

I was hired. The work was easy, but I found to my dismay that
I could not understand a third of what was said to me. My slow
southern ears were baffled by their clouded, thick accents. One
morning Mrs. Hoffman asked me to go to a neighboring store—it
was owned by a cousin of hers—and get a can of chicken à la king.
I had never heard the phrase before and I asked her to repeat it.

"Don't you know nosing?" she demanded of me.

"If you would write it down for me, I'd know what to get," I
ventured timidly.

"I can't vite!" she shouted in a sudden fury. "Vat kinda boy ees you?"

I memorized the separate sounds that she had uttered and went to the neighboring store.

"Mrs. Hoffman wants a can of Cheek Keeng Awr Lar Keeng," I said slowly, hoping that he would not think I was being offensive.

"All vite," he said, after staring at me a moment.

He put a can into a paper bag and gave it to me; outside in the street I opened the bag and read the label: Chicken à La King. I cursed, disgusted with myself. I knew those words. It had been her thick accent that had thrown me off. Yet I was not angry with her for speaking broken English; my English, too, was broken. But why could she not have taken more patience? Only one answer came to my mind. I was black and she did not care. Or so I thought . . . I was persisting in reading my present environment in the light of my old one. I reasoned thus: Though English was my native tongue and America my native land, she, an alien, could operate a store and earn a living in a neighborhood where I could not even live. I reasoned further that she was aware of this and was trying to protect her position against me.

(It was not until I had left the delicatessen job that I saw how grossly I had misread the motives and attitudes of Mr. Hoffman and his wife. I had not yet learned anything that would have helped me to thread my way through these perplexing racial relations. Accepting my environment at its face value, trapped by my own emotions, I kept asking myself what had black people done to bring this crazy world upon them?

(The fact of the separation of white and black was clear to me; it was its effect upon the personalities of people that stumped and dismayed me. I did not feel that I was a threat to anybody; yet, as soon as I had grown old enough to think I had learned that my entire personality, my aspirations had long ago been discounted; that, in a measure, the very meaning of the words I spoke could not be fully understood.

(And when I contemplated the area of No Man's Land into which the Negro mind in America had been shunted I wondered if there had ever existed in all human history a more corroding and devastating attack upon the personalities of men than the idea of racial discrimination. In order to escape the racial attack that went to the roots of my life, I would have gladly accepted any way of life but the one in which I found myself. I would have agreed to live under a system of feudal oppression, not because I preferred feudalism but because I felt that feudalism made use of a limited part of a man, defined him, his rank, his function in society. I would have consented to live under the most rigid type of dictatorship, for I felt that dictatorships, too, defined the use of men, however degrading that use might be.

(While working in Memphis I had stood aghast as Shorty had offered himself to be kicked by the white men; but now, while working in Chicago, I was learning that perhaps even a kick was better than uncertainty . . . I had elected, in my fevered search for honorable adjustment to the American scene, not to submit and in doing so I had embraced the daily horror of anxiety, of tension, of eternal disquiet. I could not sympathize with—though I could never bring myself to approve—those tortured blacks who had given up and had gone to their white tormentors and had said: "Kick me, if that's all there is for me; kick me and let me feel at home, let me have peace!"

(Color hate defined the place of black life as below that of white life; and the black man, responding to the same dreams as the white man, strove to bury within his heart his awareness of this difference because it made him lonely and afraid. Hated by whites and being an organic part of the culture that hated him, the black man grew in turn to hate in himself that which others hated in him. But pride would make him hide his self-hate, for he would not want whites to know that he was so thoroughly conquered by them that his total life was conditioned by their attitude; but in the act of hiding his self-hate, he could not help but hate those who evoked his self-hate in him. So each part of his day would be consumed in a war with himself, a good part of his energy would be spent in keeping control of his unruly emotions, emotions which he had not wished to have, but could not help having. Held at bay by the hate of others, preoccupied with his own feelings, he was continuously at war with reality. He became inefficient, less able to see and judge the objective world. And when he reached that state, the white people looked at him and laughed and said:

("Look, didn't I tell you niggers were that way?"

(To solve this tangle of balked emotion, I loaded the empty part of the ship of my personality with fantasies of ambition to keep it from toppling over into the sea of senselessness. Like any other American, I dreamed of going into business and making money; I dreamed of working for a firm that would allow me to advance until

I reached an important position; I even dreamed of organizing secret groups of blacks to fight all whites. . . . And if the blacks would
not agree to organize, then they would have to be fought. I would
end up again with self-hate, but it was now a self-hate that was
projected outward upon other blacks. Yet I knew—with that part of
my mind that the whites had given me—that none of my dreams was
possible. Then I would hate myself for allowing my mind to dwell
upon the unattainable. Thus the circle would complete itself.

(Slowly I began to forge in the depths of my mind a mechanism
that repressed all the dreams and desires that the Chicago streets,
the newspapers, the movies were evoking in me. I was going through
a second childhood; a new sense of the limit of the possible was
being born in me. What could I dream of that had the barest possibility of coming true? I could think of nothing. And, slowly, it was
upon exactly that nothingness that my mind began to dwell, that
constant sense of wanting without having, of being hated without
reason. A dim notion of what life meant to a Negro in America was
coming to consciousness in me, not in terms of external events,
lynchings, Jim Crowism, and the endless brutalities, but in terms of
crossed-up feeling, of psyche pain. I sensed that Negro life was a
sprawling land of unconscious suffering, and there were but few
Negroes who knew the meaning of their lives, who could tell their
story.)

Word reached me that an examination for postal clerk was im-
pending and at once I filed an application and waited. As the date
for the examination drew near, I was faced with another problem.
How could I get a free day without losing my job? In the South it
would have been an unwise policy for a Negro to have gone to his
white boss and asked for time to take an examination for another
job. It would have implied that the Negro did not like to work for
the white boss, that he felt he was not receiving just consideration
and, inasmuch as most jobs that Negroes held in the South involved
a personal, paternalistic relationship, he would have been risking
an argument that might have led to violence.

I now began to speculate about what kind of man Mr. Hoffman
was, and I found that I did not know him; that is, I did not know
his basic attitude toward Negroes. If I asked him, would he be sympathetic enough to allow me time off with pay? I needed the money.
Perhaps he would say: "Go home and stay home if you don't like
this job"? I was not sure of him. I decided, therefore, that I had
better not risk it. I would forfeit the money and stay away without
telling him.

The examination was scheduled to take place on a Monday; I had been working steadily and I would be too tired to do my best if I took the examination without the benefit of rest. I decided to stay away from the shop Saturday, Sunday, and Monday. But what could I tell Mr. Hoffman? Yes, I would tell him that I had been ill. No, that was too thin. I would tell him that my mother had died in Memphis and that I had gone down to bury her. That lie might work.

I took the examination and when I came to the store on Tuesday Mr. Hoffman was astonished, of course.

"I didn't sink you vould ever come back," he said.

"I'm awfully sorry, Mr. Hoffman."

"Vat happened?"

"My mother died in Memphis and I had to go down and bury her," I lied.

He looked at me, then shook his head.

"Rich, you lie," he said.

"I'm not lying," I lied stoutly.

"You vanted to do somesink, zo you zayed ervay," he said, shrugging.

"No, sir. I'm telling you the truth." I piled another lie upon the first one.

"No. You lie. You disappoint me," he said.

"Well, all I can do is tell you the truth," I lied indignantly.

"Vy didn't you use the phone?"

"I didn't think of it." I told a fresh lie.

"Rich, if your mudder die, you vould tell me," he said.

"I didn't have time. Had to catch the train." I lied yet again.

"Vhere did you get the money?"

"My aunt gave it to me," I said, disgusted that I had to lie and lie again.

"I don't vant a boy vat tells lies," he said.

"I don't lie," I lied passionately to protect my lies.

Mrs. Hoffman joined in and both of them hammered at me.

"Ve know. You come from ze Zouth. You feel you can't tell us ze truth. But ve don't bother you. Ve don't feel like people in ze Zouth. Ve treat you nice, don't ve?" they asked.

"Yes, ma'am," I mumbled.

"Zen vy lie?"

"I'm not lying," I lied with all my strength.

I became angry because I knew that they knew that I was lying. I had lied to protect myself, and then I had to lie to protect my lie. I had met so many white faces that would have violently disapproved of my taking the examination that I could not have risked telling Mr. Hoffman the truth. But how could I now tell him that I had lied because I was so unsure of myself? Lying was bad, but revealing my own sense of insecurity would have been worse. It would have been shameful, and I did not like to feel ashamed.

Their attitudes had proved utterly amazing. They were taking time out from their duties in the store to talk to me, and I had never encountered anything like that from whites before. A southern white man would have said: "Get to hell out of here!" or "All right, nigger. Get to work." But no white people had ever stood their ground and probed at me, questioned me at such length. It dawned upon me that they were trying to treat me as an equal, which made it even more impossible for me ever to tell them that I had lied, why I had lied. I felt that if I confessed I would give them a moral advantage over me that would be unbearable.

"All vight, zay and vork," Mr. Hoffman said. "I know you're lying, but I don't care, Rich."

I wanted to quit. He had insulted me. But I liked him in spite of myself. Yes, I had done wrong, but how on earth could I have known the kind of people I was working for? Perhaps Mr. Hoffman would have gladly consented for me to take the examination, but my hopes had been far weaker than my powerful fears.

Working with them from day to day and knowing that they knew I had lied from fear crushed me. I knew that they pitied me and pitied the fear in me. I resolved to quit and risk hunger rather than stay with them. I left the job that following Saturday, not telling them that I would not be back, not possessing the heart to say goodbye. I just wanted to go quickly and have them forget that I had ever worked for them.

After an idle week, I got a job as a dishwasher in a North Side café that had just opened. My boss, a white woman, directed me in unpacking barrels of dishes, setting up new tables, painting, and so on. I had charge of serving breakfast; in the late afternoons I carted trays of food to patrons in the hotel who did not want to come down to eat. My wages were fifteen dollars a week; the hours were long, but I ate my meals on the job.

The cook was an elderly Finnish woman with a sharp, bony face. There were several white waitresses. I was the only Negro in the café. The waitresses were a hard, brisk lot and I was keenly aware of how their attitudes contrasted with those of southern white girls. They had not been taught to keep a gulf between me and themselves; they were relatively free of the heritage of racial hate.

One morning as I was making coffee, Cora came forward with a tray loaded with food and squeezed against me to draw a cup of coffee.

"Pardon me, Richard," she said.

"Oh, that's all right," I said in an even tone.

But I was aware that she was a white girl and that her body was pressed closely against mine, an incident that had never happened to me before in my life, an incident charged with the memory of dread. But she was not conscious of my blackness or of what her actions would have meant in the South. And had I not been born in the South, her trivial act would have been as unnoticed by me as it was by her. As she stood close to me, I could not help thinking that if a southern white girl had wanted to draw a cup of coffee, she would have commanded me to step aside so that she might not come in contact with me. The work of the hot and busy kitchen would have had to cease for the moment so that I could have taken my tainted body far enough away to allow the southern white girl a chance to get a cup of coffee. There lay a deep, emotional safety in knowing that the white girl who was now leaning carelessly against me was not thinking of me, had no deep, vague, irrational fright that made her feel that I was a creature to be avoided at all costs.

One summer morning a white girl came late to work and rushed into the pantry where I was busy. She went into the women's room and changed her clothes; I heard the door open and a second later I was surprised to hear her voice:

"Richard, quick! Tie my apron!"

She was standing with her back to me and the strings of her apron dangled loose. There was a moment of indecision on my part, then I took the two loose strings and carried them around her body and brought them again to her back and tied them in a clumsy knot.

"Thanks a million," she said, grasping my hand for a split second, and was gone.

I continued my work, filled with all the possible meanings that that tiny, simple, human event could have meant to any Negro in the South where I had spent most of my hungry days.

I did not feel any admiration for the girls, nor any hate. My attitude was one of abiding and friendly wonder. For the most part I was silent with them, though I knew that I had a firmer grasp of life than most of them. As I worked I listened to their talk and perceived its puzzled, wandering, superficial fumbling with the problems and facts of life. There were many things they wondered about that I could have explained to them, but I never dared.

During my lunch hour, which I spent on a bench in a near-by park, the waitresses would come and sit beside me, talking at random, laughing, joking, smoking cigarettes. I learned about their tawdry dreams, their simple hopes, their home lives, their fear of feeling anything deeply, their sex problems, their husbands. They were an eager, restless, talkative, ignorant bunch, but casually kind and impersonal for all that. They knew nothing of hate and fear, and strove instinctively to avoid all passion.

I often wondered what they were trying to get out of life, but I never stumbled upon a clue, and I doubt if they themselves had any notion. They lived on the surface of their days; their smiles were surface smiles, and their tears were surface tears. Negroes lived a truer and deeper life than they, but I wished that Negroes, too, could live as thoughtlessly, serenely as they. The girls never talked of their feelings; none of them possessed the insight or the emotional equipment to understand themselves or others. How far apart in culture we stood! All my life I had done nothing but feel and cultivate my feelings; all their lives they had done nothing but strive for petty goals, the trivial material prizes of American life. We shared a common tongue, but my language was a different language from theirs.

It was in the psychological distance that separated the races that the deepest meaning of the problem of the Negro lay for me. For these poor, ignorant white girls to have understood my life would have meant nothing short of a vast revolution in theirs. And I was convinced that what they needed to make them complete and grown-up in their living was the inclusion in their personalities of a knowledge of lives such as I lived and suffered containedly.

(As I, in memory, think back now upon those girls and their lives I feel that for white America to understand the significance of the problem of the Negro will take a bigger and tougher America than any we have yet known. I feel that America's past is too shallow, her national character too superficially optimistic, her very morality too suffused with color hate for her to accomplish so vast and complex a task. Culturally the Negro represents a paradox: Though he is an organic part of the nation, he is excluded by the entire tide and direction of American culture. Frankly, it is felt to be right to exclude him, and it is felt to be wrong to admit him freely. Therefore if, within the confines of its present culture, the nation ever seeks to purge itself of its color hate, it will find itself at war with itself, convulsed by a spasm of emotional and moral confusion. If the nation ever finds itself examining its real relation to the Negro, it will find itself doing infinitely more than that; for the anti-Negro attitude of whites represents but a tiny part—though a symbolically significant one—of the moral attitude of the nation. Our too-young and too-new America, lusty because it is lonely, aggressive because it is afraid, insists upon seeing the world in terms of good and bad, the holy and the evil, the high and the low, the white and the black; our America is frightened of fact, of history, of processes, of necessity. It hugs the easy way of damning those whom it cannot understand, of excluding those who look different, and it salves its conscience with a self-draped cloak of righteousness. Am I damning my native land? No; for I, too, share these faults of character! And I really do not think that America, adolescent and cocksure, a stranger to suffering and travail, an enemy of passion and sacrifice, is ready to probe into its most fundamental beliefs.

(I know that not race alone, not color alone, but the daily values that give meaning to life stood between me and those white girls with whom I worked. Their constant outward-looking, their mania for radios, cars, and a thousand other trinkets made them dream and fix their eyes upon the trash of life, made it impossible for them to learn a language which could have taught them to speak of what was in their or others' hearts. The words of their souls were the syllables of popular songs.

(The essence of the irony of the plight of the Negro in America, to me, is that he is doomed to live in isolation while those who condemn him seek the basest of goals of any people on the face of the earth. Perhaps it would be possible for the Negro to become reconciled to his plight if he could be made to believe that his sufferings were for some remote, high, sacrificial end; but sharing the culture that condemns him, and seeing that a lust for trash is what blinds the nation to his claims, is what sets storms to rolling in his soul.)

Though I had fled the pressure of the South, my outward conduct had not changed. I had been schooled to present an unalteringly smiling face and I continued to do so despite the fact that my environment allowed more open expression. I hid my feelings and avoided all relationships with whites that might cause me to reveal them.

One afternoon the boss lady entered the kitchen and found me sitting on a box reading a copy of the *American Mercury*.

"What on earth are you reading?" she demanded.

I was at once on guard, though I knew I did not have to be.

"Oh, just a magazine," I said.

"Where did you get it?" she asked.

"Oh, I just found it," I lied; I had bought it.

"Do you understand it?" she asked.

"Yes, ma'am."

"Well," she exclaimed, "the colored dishwasher reads the *American Mercury!*"

She walked away, shaking her head. My feelings were mixed. I was glad that she had learned that I was not completely dumb, yet I felt a little angry because she seemed to think it odd for dishwashers to read magazines. Thereafter I kept my books and magazines wrapped in newspaper so that no one would see them, reading them at home and on the streetcar to and from work.

Tillie, the Finnish cook, was a tall, ageless, red-faced, rawboned woman with long, snow-white hair which she balled in a knot at the nape of her neck. She cooked expertly and was superbly efficient. One morning as I passed the sizzling stove I thought I heard Tillie cough and spit. I paused and looked carefully to see where her spittle had gone, but I saw nothing; her face, obscured by steam, was bent over a big pot. My senses told me that Tillie had coughed and spat into that pot, but my heart told me that no human being could possibly be so filthy. I decided to watch her. An hour or so later I heard Tillie clear her throat with a grunt, saw her cough, and spit into the boiling soup. I held my breath; I did not want to believe what I had seen.

Should I tell the boss lady? Would she believe me? I watched Tillie for another day to make sure that she was spitting into the food. She was; there was no doubt of it. But who would believe me if I told them what was happening? I was the only black person in the café. Perhaps they would think that I hated the cook? I stopped eating my meals there and bided my time.

The business of the café was growing rapidly and a Negro girl was hired to make salads. I went to her at once.

"Look, can I trust you?" I asked.

"What are you talking about?" she asked.

"I want you to say nothing, but watch that cook."

"For what?"

"Now, don't get scared. Just watch the cook."

She looked at me as though she thought I was crazy; and, frankly, I felt that perhaps I ought not to say anything to anybody.

"What do you mean?" she demanded.

"All right," I said. "I'll tell you. That cook spits in the food."

"What are you saying?" she asked aloud.

"Keep quiet," I said.

"Spitting?" she asked me in a whisper. "Why would she do that?"

"I don't know. But watch her."

She walked away from me with a funny look in her eyes. But half an hour later she came rushing to me, looking ill, sinking into a chair.

"Oh, God, I feel awful!"

"Did you see it?"

"She *is* spitting in the food!"

"What ought we do?" I asked.

"Tell the lady," she said.

"She wouldn't believe me," I said.

She widened her eyes as she understood. We were black and the cook was white.

"But I can't work here if she's going to do that," she said.

"Then you tell her," I said.

"She wouldn't believe me either," she said.

She rose and ran to the women's room. When she returned she stared at me. We were two Negroes and we were silently asking ourselves if the white boss lady would believe us if we told her that her expert white cook was spitting in the food all day long as it cooked upon the stove.

"I don't know," she wailed in a whisper and walked away.

I thought of telling the waitresses about the cook, but I could not get up enough nerve. Many of the girls were friendly with Tillie. Yet I could not let the cook spit in the food all day. That was wrong by any human standard of conduct. I washed dishes, thinking, wondering; I served breakfast, thinking, wondering; I served meals in the apartments of patrons upstairs, thinking, wondering. Each time I picked up a tray of food I felt like retching. Finally the Negro salad girl came to me and handed me her purse and hat.

"I'm going to tell her and quit, goddamn," she said.

"I'll quit too, if she doesn't fire her," I said.

"Oh, she won't believe me," she wailed in agony.

"You tell her. You're a woman. She might believe you."

Her eyes welled with tears and she sat for a long time; then she rose and went abruptly into the dining room. I went to the door and peered. Yes, she was at the desk, talking to the boss lady. She returned to the kitchen and went into the pantry; I followed her.

"Did you tell her?" I asked.

"Yes."

"What did she say?"

"She said I was crazy."

"Oh, God!" I said.

"She just looked at me with those gray eyes of hers," the girl said. "Why would Tillie do that?"

"I don't know," I said.

The boss lady came to the door and called the girl; both of them went into the dining room. Tillie came over to me; a hard cold look was in her eyes.

"What's happening here?" she asked.

"I don't know," I said, wanting to slap her across the mouth.

She muttered something and went back to the stove, coughed, spat into a bubbling pot. I left the kitchen and went into the back areaway to breathe. The boss lady came out.

"Richard," she said.

Her face was pale, I was smoking a cigarette and I did not look at her.

"Is this true?"

"Yes, ma'am."

"It couldn't be. Do you know what you're saying?"

"Just watch her," I said.

"I don't know," she moaned.

She looked crushed. She went back into the dining room, but I saw her watching the cook through the doors. I watched both of them, the boss lady and the cook, praying that the cook would spit again. She did. The boss lady came into the kitchen and stared at Tillie, but she did not utter a word. She burst into tears and ran back into the dining room.

"What's happening here?" Tillie demanded.

No one answered. The boss lady came out and tossed Tillie her hat, coat, and money.

"Now, get out of here, you dirty dog!" she said.

Tillie stared, then slowly picked up her hat, coat, and the money; she stood a moment, wiped sweat from her forehead with her hand, then spat, this time on the floor. She left.

Nobody was ever able to fathom why Tillie liked to spit into the food.

Brooding over Tillie, I recalled the time when the boss man in Mississippi had come to me and had tossed my wages to me and said:

"Get out, nigger! I don't like your looks."

And I wondered if a Negro who did not smile and grin was as morally loathsome to whites as a cook who spat into the food. . . .

I worked at the café all spring and in June I was called for temporary duty in the post office. My confidence soared; if I obtained an appointment as a regular clerk, I could spend at least five hours a day writing.

I reported at the post office and was sworn in as a temporary clerk. I earned seventy cents an hour and I went to bed each night now with a full stomach for the first time in my life. When I worked nights, I wrote during the day; when I worked days, I wrote during the night.

But the happiness of having a job did not keep another worry from rising to plague me. Before I could receive a permanent appointment I would have to take a physical examination. The weight requirement was one hundred and twenty-five pounds and I—with my long years of semistarvation—barely tipped the scales at a hundred and ten. Frantically I turned all of my spare money into food and ate. But my skin and flesh would not respond to the food. Perhaps I was not eating the right diet? Perhaps my chronic anxiety kept my weight down. I drank milk, ate steak, but it did not give me an extra ounce of flesh. I visited a doctor who told me that there was nothing wrong with me except malnutrition, that I must eat and sleep long hours. I did and my weight remained the same. I knew now that my job was temporary and that when the time came for my appointment I would have to resume my job hunting again.

At night I read Stein's *Three Lives,* Crane's *The Red Badge of Courage,* and Dostoevski's *The Possessed,* all of which revealed new realms of feeling. But the most important discoveries came when I veered from fiction proper into the field of psychology and sociology. I ran through volumes that bore upon the causes of my conduct and the conduct of my people. I studied tables of figures relating population density to insanity, relating housing to disease, relating school and recreational opportunities to crime, relating various forms of neurotic behavior to environment, relating racial insecurities to the conflicts between whites and blacks. . .

I still had no friends, casual or intimate, and felt the need for none. I had developed a self-sufficiency that kept me distant from others, emotionally and psychologically. Occasionally I went to house-rent parties, parties given by working-class families to raise money to pay the landlord, the admission to which was a quarter or a half dollar. At these affairs I drank home-brewed beer, ate spaghetti and chitterlings, laughed and talked with black, southern-born girls who worked as domestic servants in white middle-class homes. But with none of them did my relations rest upon my deepest feelings. I discussed what I read with no one, and to none did I confide. Emotionally, I was withdrawn from the objective world; my desires floated loosely within the walls of my consciousness, contained and controlled.

As a protective mechanism, I developed a terse, cynical mode of speech that rebuffed those who sought to get too close to me. Conversation was my way of avoiding expression; my words were reserved for those times when I sat down alone to write. My face was always a deadpan or a mask of general friendliness; no word or event could jar me into a gesture of enthusiasm or despair. A slowly, hesitantly spoken "Yeah" was my general verbal reaction to almost everything I heard. "That's pretty good," said with a slow nod of the head, was my approval. "Aw, naw," muttered with a cold smile, was my rejection. Even though I reacted deeply, my true feelings raced along underground, hidden.

I did not act in this fashion deliberately; I did not prefer this kind of relationship with people. I wanted a life in which there was a constant oneness of feeling with others, in which the basic emotions of life were shared, in which common memory formed a common past, in which collective hope reflected a national future. But I knew that no such thing was possible in my environment. The only ways in which I felt that my feelings could go outward without fear of rude rebuff or searing reprisal was in writing or reading, and to me they were ways of living.

Aunt Maggie had now rented an apartment in which I shared a rear room. My mother and brother came and all three of us slept in that one room; there was no window, just four walls and a door. My excessive reading puzzled Aunt Maggie; she sensed my fiercely indrawn nature and she did not like it. Being of an open, talkative disposition, she declared that I was going about the business of living wrongly, that reading books would not help me at all. But nothing she said had any effect. I had long ago hardened myself to criticism.

"Boy, are you reading for law?" my aunt would demand.

"No."

"Then why are you reading all the time?"

"I like to."

"But what do you get out of it?"

"I get a great deal out of it."

And I knew that my words sounded wild and foolish in my environment, where reading was almost unknown, where the highest item of value was a dime or a dollar, an apartment or a job; where, if one aspired at all, it was to be a doctor or a lawyer, a shopkeeper or a politician. The most valued pleasure of the people I knew was a car, the most cherished experience a bottle of whisky, the most sought-after prize somebody else's wife. I had no sense of being inferior or superior to the people about me; I merely felt that they had no chance to learn to live differently. I never criticized them or praised them, yet they felt in my neutrality a deeper rejection of them than if I had cursed them.

Repeatedly I took stabs at writing, but the results were so poor that I would tear up the sheets. I was striving for a level of expression that matched those of the novels I read. But I always somehow failed to get onto the page what I thought and felt. Failing at sustained narrative, I compromised by playing with single sentences and phrases. Under the influence of Stein's *Three Lives,* I spent hours and days pounding out disconnected sentences for the sheer love of words.

I would write:

"The soft melting hunk of butter trickled in gold down the stringy grooves of the split yam."

Or:

"The child's clumsy fingers fumbled in sleep, feeling vainly for the wish of its dream."

"The old man huddled in the dark doorway, his bony face lit by the burning yellow in the windows of distant skyscrapers."

My purpose was to capture a physical state or movement that carried a strong subjective impression, an accomplishment which seemed supremely worth struggling for. If I could fasten the mind of the reader upon words so firmly that he would forget words and be conscious only of his response, I felt that I would be in sight of knowing how to write narrative. I strove to master words, to make them disappear, to make them important by making them new, to make them melt into a rising spiral of emotional stimuli, each greater than the other, each feeding and reinforcing the other, and all ending in an emotional climax that would drench the reader with a sense of a new world. That was the single aim of my living.

Autumn came and I was called for my physical examination for the position of regular postal clerk. I had not told my mother or brother or aunt that I knew I would fail. On the morning of the examination I drank two quarts of buttermilk, ate six bananas, but it did not hoist the red arrow of the government scales to the required mark of one hundred and twenty-five pounds. I went home and sat disconsolately in my back room, hating myself, wondering where I could find another job. I had almost got my hands upon a decent job and had lost it, had let it slip through my fingers. Waves of self-doubt rose to haunt me. Was I always to hang on the fringes of life? What I wanted was truly modest, and yet my past, my diet, my hunger, had snatched it from before my eyes. But these self-doubts did not last long; I dulled the sense of loss through reading, reading, writing and more writing.

The loss of my job did not evoke in me any hostility toward the system of rules that had barred my first grasp at the material foundations of American life. I felt that it was unfair that my lack of a few pounds of flesh should deprive me of a chance at a good job, but I had long ago emotionally rejected the world in which I lived and my reaction was: Well, this is the system by which people want the world to run whether it helps them or not. To me, my losing was only another manifestation of that queer, material way of American living that computed everything in terms of the concrete: weight, color, race, fur coats, radios, electric refrigerators, cars, money . . . It seemed that I simply could not fit into a materialistic life.

The living arrangement of my mother, brother, and Aunt Maggie—now that I had no promise of being a postal clerk—quickly deteriorated. In Aunt Maggie's eyes I was a plainly marked failure and she feared that perhaps she would have to feed me. The emotional atmosphere in the cramped quarters became tense, ugly, petty, bickering. Fault was found with my reading and writing; it was claimed that I was swelling the electric bill. Though I had saved almost no money, I decided to rent an apartment. Aunt Cleo was living in a rented room and I invited her to share the apartment with me, my mother, and brother, and she consented. We moved into a tiny, dingy two-room den in whose kitchen a wall bed fitted snugly into a corner near the stove. The place was alive with vermin and the smell of cooking hung in the air day and night.

I asked for my job back at the café and the boss lady allowed me to return; again I served breakfast, washed dishes, carted trays of food up into the apartments. Another postal examination was scheduled for spring and to that end I made eating an obsession. I ate when I did not want to eat, drank milk when it sickened me. Slowly my starved body responded to food and overcame the lean years of Mississippi, Arkansas, and Tennessee, counteracting the flesh-sapping anxiety of fear-filled days.

I read Proust's *A Remembrance of Things Past,* admiring the lucid, subtle but strong prose, stupefied by its dazzling magic, awed by the vast, delicate, intricate, and psychological structure of the Frenchman's epic of death and decadence. But it crushed me with hopelessness, for I wanted to write of the people in my environment with an equal thoroughness, and the burning example before my eyes made me feel that I never could.

My ability to endure tension had now grown amazingly. From the accidental pain of southern years, from anxiety that I had sought to avoid, from fear that had been too painful to bear, I had learned to like my unintermittent burden of feeling, had become habituated to acting with all of my being, had learned to seek those areas of life, those situations, where I knew that events would complement my own inner mood. I was conscious of what was happening to me; I knew that my attitude of watchful wonder had usurped all other feelings, had become the meaning of my life, an integral part of my personality; that I was striving to live and measure all things by it. Having no claims upon others, I bent the way the wind blew, rendering unto my environment that which was my environment's, and rendering unto myself that which I felt was mine.

It was a dangerous way to live, far more dangerous than violating laws or ethical codes of conduct; but the danger was for me and me alone. Had I not been conscious of what I was doing, I could have easily lost my way in the fogbound regions of compelling fantasy. Even so, I floundered, staggered; but somehow I always groped my way back to that path where I felt a tinge of warmth from an unseen light.

Hungry for insight into my own life and the lives about me, knowing my fiercely indrawn nature, I sought to fulfill more than my share of all obligations and responsibilities, as though offering libations of forgiveness to my environment. Indeed, the more my emotions claimed my attention, the sharper—as though in ultimate self-defense—became my desire to measure accurately the reality of the objective world so that I might more than meet its demands. At twenty years of age the mold of my life was set, was hardening into a pattern, a pattern that was neither good nor evil, neither right nor wrong.

Richard Wright *was born in Natchez, Mississippi, in 1908. He moved to Chicago in his twenties, and his first collection of fiction,* Uncle Tom's Children, *was published in 1938. His most celebrated work is* Native Son. *He died in 1960.*

New Orleans, Louisiana   May 21, 1917

Dear Sir:
As it is my desire to leave the south for some portion of the north to make my future home I decided to write you as one who is able to furnish proper information for such a move. I am a cook of plain meals and I have knowledge of industrial training. I received such training at Tuskegee Inst. some years ago and I have a letter from Mrs. Booker T. Washington bearing out such statement and letters from other responsible corporations and individuals and since I know that I can come up to such recommendations, I want to come north where it is said such individuals are wanted. Therefore will you please furnish me with names and addresses of railroad officials to who I might write for such employment as it is my desire to work only for railroad, if possible. I have reference to officials who are over extra gangs, bridge gangs, paint gangs, and pile drivers over any boarding department which takes in plain meals. I have 25 years experience in this line of work and understand the method of saving the company money.

You will please dig into this in every way that is necessary and whatever charges you want for your trouble make your bill to me, and I will mail same to you.

Wishing you much success in your papers throughout the country, especially in the south as it is the greatest help to the southern negro that has ever been read.
Respectfully yours.

New Orleans, Louisiana   May 20, 1917

Dear Sir:
I am sure your time is precious, for being as you an editor of a newspaper such as the race has never owned and for which it must proudly bost of as being the peer in the pereoidical world. am confident that yours is a force of busy men. I also feel sure that you will spare a small amount of your time to give some needed information to one who wishes to relieve himself of the burden of the south. I indeed wish very much to come north anywhere in Ill[inois] will do since I am away from the Lynchman's noose and torchman's fire. Myself and a friend wish to come but not without

*information regarding work and general surroundings. Now hon sir
if for any reason you are not in position to furnish us with the information desired,? please do the act of kindness of placing us in
tuch with the organization who's business it is I am told to furnish
said information. We are firemen machinist helpers practical painters and general laborers. And most of all, ministers of the gospel
who are not afraid of labor for it put us where we are. Please let
me hear from you.*

Yours truly.

Lapne, Alabama   April 20, 1917

Sir
*I am writing you to let you know that there is 15 or 20 familys
wants to come up there at once but cant come on account of money
to come with and we cant phone you here we will be killed they
dont want us to leave here & say if we dont go to war and fight for
our country they are going to kill us & wants to get away if we can
if you send 20 passes there is no doubt that every one of us will
com at once. We are not doing any thing here we cant get a living
out of what we do now some of these people are farmers and som
are cooks barbers and black smiths but the greater part are farmers
& good workers & honest people & up do date the trash pile dont
want to go no where These are nice people and respectable find a
place like that & send passes & we all will come at once we all
wants to leave here out of this hard luck place if you cant use us
find some place that does need this kind of people we are called
Negroes here. I am a reader of the defender and am delighted to
know how times are there & was to glad to know if we could get
some one to pass us away from here to a better land. We work but
cant get scarely any thing for it & they dont want us to go away &
there is not much of anything here to do nothing for it Please find
some one that need this kind of a people & send at once for us. We
dont want anything but our wareing and bed clothes & have not
got no money to get away from here with & beging to get away
before we are killed and hope to here from you at once. We cant
talk to you over the phone here we are afraid to they dont want to
hear one say that he or she wants to leave here if we do we are apt
to be killed. They say if we dont go to war they are not going to let
us stay here with their folks and it is not anything that we have
done to them. We are law abiding people want to treat ever bordy
right. these people want to leave here but we cant we are here and
have nothing to go with if you will send us some way to get away
from here we will work till we pay it all if it takes that for us to go*

or get away. Now get busy for the south race. The conditions are horrible here with us. its going to be a famine just like they are treating us. they wont give us anything to do & say that we dont need anything but something to eat & wont give us anything for what we do & wants us to stay here. Write me at once what you will do for us we want & opertunity thats all we wants in to show you what we can do and will do if we can find some place. we wants to leave here for a north drive somewhere. We see starvation ahead of us here. We want to immigrate to the farmers who need our labor. We have not had no chance to have anything here thats why we plead to you for help to leave here to the North. We are humans but we are not treated such we are treated like bruts by our whites here we dont have no privlige no where in the south. We must take anything they put on us Its hard if it fair. We have not got no cotegeus diseases here. We are looking to here from you soon.

Yours truly.

Greenville, Mississippi   May 29, 1917

Dear Sir
this letter is from one of the defenders greatest frends. You will find stamp envelope for reply. will you put me in tuch with some good firm so I can get a good job in your city or in Cleveland, Ohio, or in Philadelphia, Pa. or in Detroyet, Michian in any of the above name states I would be glad to live in. I want to get my famely out of this cursed south land down here a negro man is not as good as a white man's dog. I can learn anything any other man can. Not only I want to get out of the south but there are numbers of good hard working men here that want to leave here but they do not want to pull rite up and leave here and do not know where they are going and what they are going to. Also I could get a good deal of men from here if I could get in tuch with some firms that would furnish me the money as passes. Now in conlution, I want to know what is the trubble? I cannot get anything more through the Defender. I have written to the Defender some 3 or 4 times and eather articel was never published. I recieves a free copy of the Defender every week and the peopel here are all ways after me to write some doings to the Defender and if I write anything it is never published.
Yours truly.

Greenville, Mississippi   May 20, 1917

Dear Sir:
I write to you asking you some information as I am a reader of
your paper I have been buying a paper every sunday for 5 months I
want to come to your city to live and every thing is so hard down
here every thing is so high and wages is so low until we just can
live I want to know what will it cost from St. Louis to Chicago. I
can get from Greenville to St. Louis cheap by boat. I want to come
up there the 1st of June. I ask you to asist me in getting a job I can
do most any kind of hard work and have a common education. If
you will look me up a good job it will be highly appresiated and
your kindness will never be forgotten.

Your truly.

Macon, Georgia *SOUTHERN STANDARD*   September 14, 1917

Many of us have been wondering how it is that so many conflicting
tales are told about the Negroes in the North and how they are get-
ting on and about the possibilities. In our recent visit to the West
and North, we have run-down the cause of the conflicts and we
shall attempt to explain less we bear in part the same criticism.

To illustrate, we tell the story of the blind men going to see an
elephant which is as follows:

Some blind men went to see an elephant. When they arrived on
the scene, they were placed about the big animal and asked to de-
scribe him. One stood feeling the leg and declared he was like a
tree; another grasped the trunk and declared the elephant was like
a rope; another one leaned against his side and declared that the
animal was like a wall; and still another who felt the ear said that
the elephant was like a fan.

So it has been with the colored people who have attempted to
describe the conditions in the North and West as related to colored
people. Each one has attempted to describe just so much of the city
or town to which he has gone as he has seen or come in contact. If
he got into a good place, he has declared that the whole North is
good. If he got into a bad place, he believes that the whole North is
bad. When he gets work easy, he declares that there is work for
everybody; and when he fails to find just what he wanted, he de-
clares that there is no work. When there is a riot, he declares that
the North is like the South, and those who do not see any rioting

and read but little in the papers, are not bothered about them, declare they are almost in heaven.

It takes a general visit and observation to give a correct idea of what is an average condition. But each person can easily tell what one city or town affords in the way of advantages.

We have this to say in advance,: Those that were indolent and shiftless here, those that wasted and spent all of their earnings here, and those who would not work regularly here are doing the same thing in the North, or returning to the South, where he says it is easy. The man who is willing to pay the price for success and only wants opportunity, is sticking to the job and is making goods. We assure anybody that there are great opportunities for the colored man in the North and West, but as to whether they are or have so far made good use of the advantages offered, we shall attempt to discuss under separate headings.

Fort Worth *RECORD*   July 21, 1917

The self-respecting Negro throughout the South that owns his home, his farm, his ranch, having his truck, garden growing his fruit orchard, are here and are here to stay. They are not moving; they are not thinking about going North; they are having no dreams in that direction.

It is a mistaken idea that the good Negroes of this country who are worth anything, who are willing to work and make an honest living, will ever leave their homes.

The South is our home. The southern white man is our friend. We are acquainted with him; he is acquainted with us and our interest is in the South. There never was a time that a Negro who stands for anything, should not reach the southern white man in every respect, financially and otherwise. He has made it possible here in the South for Negroes to own from fifty to ten thousand acres of land, so much so until the Negroes have accumulated wealth in Texas to establish five Negro banks, several real estate businesses, more colleges operated in the state by different Negro denominations, free orphanages and several other business interests that the Negroes themselves are very much interested in.

Any Negro is Texas, Louisiana, or Arkansas that is so ignorant and so illiterate and so no account and so insignificant that he will allow any man from the North to come through the southern states and buy his ticket and lead him on the cars and then ship him to

Pennsylvania or anywhere else in the East, is that class of Negroes that are no account when they are here, shiftless, helpless and ignorant. They should be unloaded somewhere in the North where they think there is much love for the black man, because he is black.

We must have patience, wait and trust God and work until God in His own way will unravel the great bulk of ignorance that we are so heavily burdened with. Those who want to go North without a dime, without railroad fare thinking they are so much loved, let them go.

LONG DISTANCE LIFE
"NAOMI"

Marita Golden

When I saw Washington, D.C., for the first time in 1926, I thought
I'd never seen a prettier place. Down where I come from, Spring
Hope, North Carolina, there wasn't nothing, not a single thing, to
compare with what I saw here. The big government office buildings,
the White House, the Washington Monument . . . and this is where
I saw my first streetcar. And the way some colored folks lived! Had
colored professors at Howard University and colored folks had houses
sometimes just as good as white folks. Some people called it "up
South," but it was far enough away from where I come to be North
to me.

I'd come to join my cousin Cora, who'd come up the year before
to keep house for the son of the family she'd worked for in Raleigh.
Their boy had just got a big job as a judge and they let Cora go to
come up here and work for him and his family. Cora didn't have
husband nor child and she'd lost her mama and daddy back in 1918
when that influenza killed so many people. So when her white folks
said they'd buy her ticket North and see to it that their son paid her
a few more dollars a month, she just up and went.

Soon as Cora got up here, I started getting letters all about what
a good time she was having going to the Howard Theater, how she'd
joined a penny-savers' club, and one night on U Street had seen
Bessie Smith, who she said was prettier in person than in any of her
pictures. And how there was a whole bunch of folks from North
Carolina in Washington, how it seemed like damn near every colored person in North Carolina was living in Washington, D.C. She
stayed with that judge for a little while, but got sick of "living in,"
couldn't have no freedom or do what she wanted when she wanted,
only had one day off. She wrote in one letter, "Sure they pay me a
few dollars more and I got my own room, but the running never
stops and they act like I don't never get tired. And his wife like to
almost have a stroke if she sees me sitting down. You s'posed to be
grateful for the chance to wait on them from six in the morning to
whenever at night. They think I come North to work for them. I
come North to be free." Then, sooner than you could say Jack Johnson, Cora wrote me saying she had quit her white folks and was

working two jobs—at Bergmann's laundry and doing day's work. "I'd be working a third job if I hadn't met me a real nice man from Richmond who I spends my Saturday nights with and who takes me to church on Sunday morning," she said.

Sometimes young people ask why we all left down there. Well, I think folks just got tired. Tired of saying *Yessuh* and being ground down into nothing by crackers or hard work and sometimes both at the same time. And in those days the whites'd lynch you as soon as look at you. It's a shame young folks today don't know nothing about how we were treated then. It's too bad we were so ashamed, we figured it was best to forget and our children not to know. I had a cousin lynched in Florida, a boy—just fourteen years old. He'd been playing with some little po' white trash children and one of the girls said he touched her in her private parts. The white men got together, just rode up to Jimmy's folks' cabin and took him away while his daddy was out in the fields. They lynched Jimmy that night. And his daddy had to cut him down from that tree the next day and bury him. The daddy just went crazy little bit by little bit after that and rode into town one day a coupla months later, walked into the general store and shot the man who'd lynched his boy, then shot himself before they could grab him. Oh, and if you worked hard and made something of yourself, got a little store or some land, the white folks seem like they couldn't sleep nor rest easy till they took that away from you. Maybe they'd burn your store down or run you out of town. Colored folks just got tired. That don't sound like much of a reason, but it's the best one I can think of.

Now my folks, Beatrice and Jameson Reeves, were sharecroppers. We lived in one of them shotgun houses, 'bout one room wide and three or four rooms deep. To tell the truth, it wasn't no house at all, it was a shack, but it was the first home I ever knew. We raised tobacco, 'bacca's what we called it then. All I ever saw my daddy do was work and I might have heard him speak ten words a month to us kids and my mama combined. He worked hard. But not never seeing nothing for all his labor kinda took something out of him. There was many a year my daddy never saw a dollar to hold in his hand. By the time old man Cartwright, who Daddy rented the land from, charged us for all them molasses, grits, fatback and syrup'd been sold on credit, the sale of the 'bacca almost wasn't worth it. And 'cause Daddy couldn't read or figger, Cartwright's word was law. I think my daddy was so beat down by the life he had he didn't even know *what* to say. And I watched my daddy get old before he should've.

Now my mama, you couldn't shut her up! No matter what she was doing—stripping 'bacca, cooking, washing clothes, you'd find her either talking to the Lord or singing some song or talking with herself. My daddy didn't as a rule say much, but he did say he didn't want Mama working in no white folks' homes. It was funny, they always wanted to get the colored woman up in their kitchen, or cleaning up the house, but scared to let the colored man within a mile, 'less he crawled all the way. No, Mama wasn't allowed to work in no white folks' house. So she did wash for the white families and helped on the farm.

Washing clothes meant boilin' them over a fire. Washing clothes meant using lye soap that eat up your hands like acid. Sometimes, at the end of the day, my mama would look at her hands and just sit there and cry. And she'd say, "I used to have such pretty hands, such pretty hands." And Daddy would start hollerin', "You worried 'bout your hands, I'm worried 'bout getting food for y'all to eat." And Mama'd tell him, "A woman wants to be proud of something she came in the world with, wants to think some part of her is beautiful. Even a colored woman wants that." And Daddy'd look all ashamed and confused and suck harder on his pipe and get up and go on the front porch. My mama was like all the women I ever saw down there—they worked and worked like dogs, with no thought that there was no other way to live. And we *all* worked, every one of us. There was Jackson, my older brother, then me and after me come my sister Ruby that died of TB and my youngest brother Jesse. By the time I was three I'd been trained up to bring wood for the stove, stack logs, even carry small buckets of water. When I was nine I was washing, ironing, cooking. And there wasn't no such thing as free time. Every one of your spare minutes you were finishing up that day's work or getting ready for the next day's. Humph, many's the time I walked a half a mile to a neighbor's farm to milk their cow so we could have milk. By the time I was thirteen, I was a woman.

And don't even talk about 'bacca. You never got through with it. The whole year long you were either getting ready to plant it, harvest it or cure it. My daddy was just a "hanging on" farmer with five acres and two mules. All of us helped with the 'bacca. No matter how small we was, there was something we could do. You'd start planting the seedlings in the wintertime and while the seeds were growing you'd be cutting the wood to use for curing in July and August. Whole families'd get together and cut enough wood for all of us—oak, sweetgum, poplar. In the spring Daddy'd pull out our two mules, Nat Turner and Frederick Douglass—my mama named them that 'cause they were so strong—and he'd start breaking the ground. Then you had to transplant the 'bacca. We'd use spoons to put them little baby plants in the ground. Then once it start growing you had to top it, sucker it and prime it and cure it.

With 'bacca you worked from can't see till can't see. Mama'd get up at four o'clock to fix the dinner we was gonna eat at noontime. Dew'd still be on the 'bacca when you'd go out to the fields. And if you were priming, picking off the ripe leaves, well, you could be in the fields all morning.

One time one of our barns caught on fire when Daddy was curing. All it took was one old leaf that fell into the flute, caught fire and burnt up that whole crop. Daddy liked to had a fit. When the fire was finally out, he went to town and was gone a week, come back so full of whiskey we could smell him coming home a mile away.

We were poor, but it was the kind of poor where the Lord provides just enough and surprises you now and then with some extra. Mama washed those white folks' clothes so good, the women were all the time giving her old clothes and cast-off things they didn't want no more just 'cause they wasn't new. We got a pair of shoes once a year and had to make them last, and they were mostly for Sundays. Mama dragged us to church every Sunday and we stayed all day. But there were times it seemed like the Lord forgot all about us. We was poor and so I know how it feels to be hungry. *Real* hungry. I've gone days just eating a thin slice of fatback and a hunk of bread and was so grateful that I just went on working at whatever I was doing and just put the hunger pains outta my mind.

I got me a little schooling now and then when we could spare time from the farm, so I didn't learn regular like. My daddy couldn't read at all. But Mama could and she was all the time tutoring us and teaching the ABC's and such. I wasn't never interested in no books, I'll tell you that right now. But that didn't mean I didn't have no imagination. One time I heard a carnival show was coming to town. Mama said the show was bad, had fancy women, dangerous men and city slickers. She complained so long and hard about how awful the carnival was, I knew I had to go see it. Didn't have a penny to my name, but I sneaked off from the fields one day and went on to town.

Now, we didn't usually go to town but two or three times a year. And when I got there I saw all the posters advertising the carnival. Since I didn't have no money, I stood out in front of the tent and set to wailing and crying for my life. Just boo-hooed something awful. Pretty soon a old white man come along and asked me what I was crying for. I told him I'd lost the money my daddy give me for the carnival. You know that old man reached in his pocket and gimme a dime! Tapped me on the behind and told me to get along. Well, once I got in that tent, I saw more things than I knew God had ever made—a fat lady, must've weighed three hundred pounds, a dwarf couple, a man eating fire. Even had brought a tiger and I almost fell over when the man put his head in that tiger's mouth. And looking at all those amazing things gave me a powerful appetite. I'd spent a nickel on cotton candy and needed money for some soda pop and ice cream. Don't you know I used that crying number two more times and got folks to feeling so sorry for me I had money left over.

Well, naturally, I paid for my fun. Got home that night and got beat from sundown to sunup. Mama and Daddy were so mad they took turns beating me. I couldn't sit down too good for a coupla days, but every night for a long time I sure had some powerful interesting dreams. And I entertained Jackson and Jesse and Ruby a mighty long time with stories about what I'd seen. I wouldn't have missed that carnival for nothing.

Mama and Daddy were always telling me I thought I was grown, thought I was big and how I was headed for trouble if I didn't watch out. I think they thought that would scare me, but it just made me get excited about what kind of trouble they meant and what it would be like. And I didn't see nothing wrong with wanting to be big. Hell, Spring Hope, North Carolina, was so small it didn't take much to get bigger than that.

I got married the first time when I was seventeen. And I'm gonna tell you the truth, I got married mostly to get away from home. His name was Isaiah Matthews and he was a real nice boy. His daddy was a real farmer, not a sharecropper like mine, and he had twenty-five acres of land. He grew a little bit of everything—'bacca, corn—and he even had other colored folks working for him.

Isaiah was tall and skinny and he was one of those boys that everybody's mama likes—the kind that's all *Yes, ma'ams* and *Please* and *Thank you* and tipping his hat and opening doors. To this day, I swear I don't really know what Isaiah saw in me. Mama'd tease me about my big eyes, said with eyes as big as mine I'd always find what I was looking for. We'd have these church socials in the spring and summer and he was always asking me to dance and wanting to take me for a walk. I went along with it 'cause I didn't see no reason not to and he seemed like a nice enough fella. Now, I can talk up a storm most of the time, but Isaiah couldn't get a word outta me the first times we danced or walked by ourselves. Then he commenced to coming by our place. And Mama and Daddy were always so glad to see him, I felt like I had to say something. Isaiah'd talk to me about what he knew best—his daddy's farm—and I couldn't stand hearing that, but didn't want to tell him. And the more I listened to Isaiah talk about that farm and the work he and his daddy and their hands did on it, and not just about how much they made on their crops, but the smell and feel of the soil and what having land meant, the more I got to know him. The land he and his daddy had was theirs and they was doing good enough so that it gave them a good life. So Isaiah could tell me things about farming I'd never seen or felt—what it feels like to look at land and know it's yours, how it feels to harvest your crop and know *you* can set *your* price, about how it feels to be master of the land instead of slave to it. The land never gave me and my family no real bounty, so I never saw its beauty. But Isaiah made me think about things different.

We courted for a while and then got married in the same church we'd both been christened in and met each other. We moved into a little house Isaiah had built with his daddy for us, and Isaiah started farming his own acreage. I helped out around the farm, but 'cause Isaiah had field hands, there wasn't much for me to do. Pretty soon I got tired of talking about crops and I wanted to talk about something else, but I didn't know what. Then I started wishing I'd paid attention in school 'cause at least I'd have been able to read some books better than I could. At night Isaiah'd come to bed, the smell of soil and fertilizer still on him, despite a bath, and he'd reach for me with those big old hands and get on top of me like he was mounting a horse. And Oh Lord! I'd cry all the way through it, but silent, like, so he wouldn't hear. And not never nary a kiss. That hurt more than anything, I think. I got more affection from the little boys I'd played house with in the fields. But he was happy. His daddy'd come by in the evenings sometimes, just pop in on us, and Isaiah'd hold me and slap me on my butt, playful like, and squeeze me and go on and on about what a lucky man he was.

I used to ride over to talk to Mama. She'd be in the backyard standing over a big tub of clothes, humming "Precious Lord" or some other hymn, when I'd come up on her and she'd act surprised to see me, like, now that I had my own home, I couldn't never come back to my first. And one day I went back home in this new dress Isaiah'd bought me, he'd ordered it from the Sears catalogue, and, not saying a word, I just commenced to washing clothes with Mama, stuck my

hands in that water and stood there with her, rubbing and scrub-
bing and wringing till my wrists felt like they were gonna fall off.

When we got through, I just plopped down on top of a upturned
basket and said, "Mama, I just don't feel a thing." Mama touched
my cheek with her hands, those old wrinkled-up raw hands that
made her cry, and said, "Honey, go on back to your house and your
husband. People do the best they can. Remember that. People can't
be nothin' that ain't in 'em, or do what they think is impossible.
You'd be surprised how a little love can go a long way."

I stood up and she hugged me and then told me to go on home.
I figured then, maybe if I had a baby, I'd be happy. But six months
after the baby was born, we woke up one morning and she was dead.
Just lay there in the crib Isaiah's father had gone all the way to
Charlotte for, her little face turned almost gray, no breathing, no
life. These days they got a name for what killed my baby—sudden
infant death—but back then, we didn't know what had happened or
why. And I could tell Isaiah thought somehow I'd failed Martha,
been a bad mother, neglected her somehow. He never said nothing,
not direct like, but I could feel what he was thinking, and that's all
I needed to know. And I was hurting and grieving and just tore up
inside and whenever I'd mention Martha's name he'd just walk away.

And that's when Cora started writing me. And the more letters
I got, the more I knew I had to go North. But Isaiah didn't want to
hear nothing about going North. "What I'm a go up there for?" he'd
ask me. "They ain't got no land for no niggers up there. I got family
been up there and come back, say there's no room, no space, the
crackers got you penned in, just as tight up there as down here.
What I'm a go work in a factory for when I got my own land?"

But the more letters I got from Cora, the more I realized I wanted
to go North, but mostly I wanted to get away from seeing my daddy
sharecropping with a mule and a hoe and my sister laying on the
bed on the back porch, little bit by little bit dying of tuberculosis.
And I wanted to leave the memory of my dead baby. Got so me and
Isaiah didn't have hardly nothing to say no more. Martha's ghost
was still in the house with us. And since we couldn't talk about her,
seemed like nothing else made no sense.

Then one night Isaiah told me I could leave. Said I could go on
North, since North meant more to me than him. I didn't say a word.
But that night he come to bed and held me real tight, but real gentle
like, and we made love like I'd given up hoping we ever would. And
he kissed me all over my body that night. But when he finished, he

lay next to me and said, "Naomi, you can go North, but if you do, don't look back 'cause there won't be nothin' here no more that belongs to you."

Cora had wrote me in one of her letters that soon as she got on the train to leave North Carolina she felt free. Said she felt like she was being born all over again. Sure she was sitting in the Jim Crow section, up front where all the coal, smoke and dust rose up, got in the windows and ruined your clothes. But she said the chugging of that train couldn't hardly keep up with her heart, she was so excited. I wish it'd been like that for me when I left. Pretty soon I left Isaiah and moved back home. Daddy stopped speaking to me altogether when he found out I was going North. And Mama took me out in the yard one day and we stooped down on our knees underneath of a big old juniper tree we had and she commenced to digging. Next thing I knew, she was pulling a cigar box out the ground. She rubbed the dirt off the top of it and opened the lid and inside I saw a pile of coins and paper money.

"This here is the little extra I been making over the years, setting aside for the worst times and the special times," she said. I don't think there coulda been more than thirty dollars in that box. But Mama reached in that box and gave me everything in it. She wrapped the money in a small rag and stuffed it down the front of my dress. And before I could say a word, she said, "Now, when you get settled up there, maybe Jackson can come up too. Your daddy don't want him to go, but you and Jackson's the strongest ones the Lord give us. You got to get away from here."

A few days later Mama and Jackson and Jesse rode over to the train station with me. And before I got on the train, Mama said, "Girl, you better write us every two weeks." "Mama, you know I ain't one for sitting still that long, or puttin' that many words on paper." "Well, now's the time to learn," she says. She hugged me and I thought how I'd never seen her look so pretty and sad at the same time. She had on her Sunday dress, you'd have thought she was going instead of me—she was so excited. Jackson hugged me and while I was holding on to him, I looked over his shoulder and I saw Daddy standing way off near the ticket booth, looking like he'd just come out the fields. He just stood there and held up his hand like he was waving at me, but not really waving goodbye.

Cora was living in a rooming house on Ninth and O streets. Room wasn't no bigger than a minute, but it seemed like a palace to me. She had a Victrola and had cut out pictures of Josephine Baker, Ma Rainey and Louis Armstrong and put them all over her mirror and the walls. Cora was what we used to call a good-time girl. Even down home, she was always the one knew where the fun was and if there was no fun happening she could make some.

First thing I wanted to do was get a job so I could start sending money back home. But Cora wouldn't even let me talk about a job that first week. And all we did was party. The woman that run the rooming house was a big old Black woman named Blue. All you had to do was look at her and you'd know how she got that name. And seemed like the downstairs where Blue lived was always filled with folks coming in all hours of the day and night. And it was always liquor flowing and cardplaying.

We'd go over to the O Street Market and you could get pigs' feet and chitlins and fresh greens as good as down home. And Cora seemed to never run outta money. I figured that had to do with her never running outta men.

We were having a good time, then one night when we were getting ready to go to a party, I noticed Cora putting this cream all over herself. I asked her what it was and she showed it to me. It was bleaching cream. Now, Cora's about the color of half-done toast, so I was confused. "What you using this stuff for?" I asked.

"Everybody uses it, men and women," she told me, snapping her stocking tops into her garter. "Girl, there ain't no such thing as a brown beauty in this here town. You either yellow or you ain't mellow." Cora was just rubbing the cream in her skin, all over her face and arms, as she told me this, like she was trying to get it down into her bones.

"Well, I'm gonna take my chances," I told her. "I sure ain't gonna use no mess like this. Besides ain't you heard 'the blacker the berry, the sweeter the juice'?"

But Cora had to have the last word, saying "Naomi, I ain't heard *nobody* say that since I come up here and I'll bet money you won't neither."

Finally I started working. I lived in with a Jewish family for a while, but living in didn't suit my style. The madam worried me to death, all day long talking and complaining 'bout her husband, scared he didn't love her, scared he was running around with somebody else, scared she was getting old. That was 'bout the loneliest woman I ever knew. I could hardly do my work for her bending my ear. But the worst thing was I couldn't go when and where I wanted. Nighttime I'd be so tired, all I wanted to do was go to bed. And so then I started doing day's work, had three or four families I cleaned up for and I got my own room in Blue's house and started sending money home regular like.

Now, day's work wasn't no celebration either. And I had every kinda woman for a madam you could think of—the kind that went behind you checking corners for dust and dirt, the kind that run her fingers over the furniture you just got through dusting, the kind that just got a thrill outta giving orders, the kind that asked more questions 'bout my personal business than anybody got a right to, the kind that tried to cheat me outta some of my pay. But in those days there wasn't much else a colored woman could do. Hell, even some of the college girls—the dinkty, saditty ones—cleaned up for white folks in the summertime.

For the longest time I just worked and saved and worked and saved. Then one evening I come in and Blue was sitting in the dining room. For a change, she was by herself. Seemed like Blue wasn't happy unless there was a crowd of people around her. But this night she was by herself. I'd been having this same dream over and over about somebody named Macon and I figured I might bet a few pennies on the dream's number. So I asked her to look up Macon in her dream book. She looked it up and said the number was 301. "I think I'll put fifteen cents on it," I told her, reaching into my pocketbook. I thought Blue was gonna laugh me right outta that room. "Fifteen cents?" she hollered. "Fifteen cents?" And she commenced to laughing so hard she was shaking all over and tears came into her eyes and start to rolling down her fat old Black cheeks. She wiped her face with a handkerchief and says, "Girl, what you waiting for? I been watching you going out here day after day, cleaning up the white folks' houses. That all you want to do with yourself?"

Now nobody'd ever asked that—what I wanted to do—the whole time I'd been North. Cora was so busy partying and I was so busy struggling I hadn't had time to think further than the day I was in. So I didn't quite know what to say at first. "Well," Blue said, folding her arms in front of her, looking at me like the schoolmarm in that one-room schoolhouse I went to did, when she knew I wasn't ready to give the right answer. And that look in Blue's eyes and her laughing at me made me pull up something I'd been carrying around since I moved in her house. And I just said it all of a sudden. "I want what you got. I want a house. And I want plenty money." And just saying it like that set me trembling so hard I dropped my pocketbook on the floor and my feet kicked over the bag of clothes one of my madams had give me that day instead of my regular pay.

"Well, tell me how you aim to get it? Lessen you got some book education or your folks gonna *leave* you some money, there ain't no legal way for you to get either one. You gonna have to start gambling with everything you got."

"But I ain't got nothing," I cried.

"You got more than you think. You got dreams, like the one you come to me with just now, and, honey, they worth more than you think. They sho 'nuff worth more than fifteen cents. You got sense and deep-down feelings. Listen to 'em. They'll tell you what to do. You think the Rockefellers got to be Rockefellers playing it straight? And if all you gonna put on 301 is fifteen cents, I won't even write it up."

I put a quarter on 301 and it come out the next day. I give Blue a cut and that was how it started.

I got to playing the numbers pretty regular then and soon I was playing every day. To be honest about the thing, though, most folks never won nothing. But seemed like I had some kinda gift. Numbers were about the only thing I paid attention to in that one-room schoolhouse in Spring Hope. That first year I hit two times for small change. Then I played a number that come to me the night one of my madams accused me of stealing. I played that number and hit for enough to start me on the way to saving for a house.

My first house was over on R Street. I rented out the top two floors to decent folks, respectable people who'd come up from the South like me. But where Blue'd let anybody live in her house, I'd only let families or married couples or single folks I thought wouldn't give me no trouble live in my place. Folks who went to church on Sunday and went to bed at night 'cause they had to work the next day. Now, that don't mean I was a saint, but I sure didn't want to live amongst a whole buncha sinners.

I found out I couldn't live in a whole house like I lived in one room. Cora took me downtown and bought me the kinda clothes that said I was a lady and just putting those clothes on made me feel different, made me feel *big* like Mama and Daddy'd always said I wanted to be. Then Cora told me I couldn't have a house without a car and her and her boyfriend took me to this place where I bought a big black Chevrolet.

When I got settled good in the house, I sent for Mama and Daddy and Jackson and Jesse to come up and spend some time with me. Mama had a time getting Daddy to come, even after I sent them all train fare. But finally they came. And seeing that house through Mama's eyes was like seeing it for the first time. I'd planted a Carolina garden out in the backyard of squash, tomatoes and peas, just like I'd have done back home and Mama sat on the back porch when she saw it, shaking her head and smiling. I'd put a big mirror with gilt framing over the fireplace and seemed like every time I looked up Mama was staring at herself in that mirror, almost like she'd never seen herself before. She took off her shoes in the house and walked barefoot on the carpeting I'd put all on the first floor. And she had me take a bunch of pictures of her sitting in my car. And the big bathtub with running hot water, humph, I thought Mama was gonna live in it, she found a excuse to take a bath three times a day.

But Daddy, seemed like the house just made him mad. Mama was all the time pointing something out to him and he'd just go on out on my porch like he did on the porch back home, and sit there sucking on his pipe and not saying a thing. Daddy and one of my roomers, Mr. Chavis, would sit out there talking about down home. He talked to Mr. Chavis more than he talked to me. And so one night I just went outside and butt into their conversation, told Mr. Chavis I wanted to talk to my daddy. "Now, you ain't said hardly nothin' to me since y'all got here," I told him. "Not even *Congratulations* or *Good job*. I worked hard for what I got, Daddy, and I want you to be proud."

He took the pipe outta his mouth and said, "I am proud of you, Naomi. Real proud. But you got to understand. I've worked another man's land for over twenty years and just barely kept my family from starvin'. My daughter comes North and gets so much it puts me to shame. Tell me how I'm s'posed to feel about me. Sure I'm proud of you. So proud I'm damn near ready to bust. But I look at all you done and feel like all my life's been a waste. You a landlord. I'm your daddy and I'm still a tenant."

"Why don't y'all stay on up here? You don't have to go back."

"I got to go back 'cause of the land. That farm, little as it is, is all I know. I ain't got much longer. I'm too old to learn a new way of living. 'Sides, they can't run us all out. That land's got more of our blood in it than theirs. Not all us s'posed to leave. Some of us got to stay, so y'all have a place to come back to."

Well, ended up Jackson stayed on and I gave him a room in the house and he got a job as janitor at the post office.

Now, in all this, I hadn't really had me no romancing. There'd been one or two men, but if they'd been worth remembering, I woulda told you about them. And most times I was working so hard to get something, make some money, I didn't have time to be courtin' nobody. The truth is, I didn't make no time. So when Mama and Daddy went back home, I went with them and filed my papers and got my divorce from Isaiah.

Well, with Cora's help, I finally found me a sweetheart. It was 1929. Now, whenever you say 1929 to folks, first thing they think of is the Depression. Well, I think white folks were hurt most by those bad times. Colored folks were born in a Depression, everything just about that they knowed was Depression. Yeah, times got tough. But then, they'd always been tough for us, weren't no big thing, so we knew how to get through it.

Folks down home were hit real hard. I was sending home not just money but clothes and food. And going down three or four times a year just to check for good measure. But lots of folks just gave up and that made it easier for folks like me who wanted to get going!

I was renting out my second house by then, over on P Street, and Cora was living in it, collecting rents for me. One night we had a fish fry. I was hitting numbers pretty good and was even a bag lady now and then, what they call a courier, taking folks' numbers and their money and delivering it to a old Italian guy downtown. The coloreds was the front men, but it was the whites that really controlled the numbers game. I was figuring to get outta that end of things 'cause that old Italian couldn't take the money without putting his hands on me, no matter what I said.

So we had this fish fry and the house was packed. I can't remember now the exact reason we had that party, but in those days didn't always *need* a reason. That night me and Cora was frying up the fish when her boyfriend Harold walked in with the handsomest man I'd ever seen. Now, I don't mean handsome in the way he looked so much, but the way he stood and carried himself. It was just something kinglike about him. He stood up so tall and straight and looked at you like you'd be a fool not to like him. And when him and Harold come in the kitchen out there in the living room somebody had put a Alberta Hunter record on. The song was "Gimme All the Love You Got."

I was standing at the table, my hands covered in cornmeal, dipping porgies in batter, and Rayford Johnson looked at me like he didn't plan to never look nowhere else. He was half bald and the top of his head was real shiny. And he had a mustache and the Lord knows I'm a fool for a man with hair on his face.

Harold introduced Rayford to me and Cora and since I couldn't shake his hand I gave Rayford Johnson the biggest, brightest smile I could muster. Then him and Harold went on into the parlor, where folks were dancing and laughing and Alberta was singing, "I want all your loving 'cause I can stand a lot." Dipping some fish in a frying pan of oil, Cora says, "Harold told me Rayford's a teacher over at Dunbar."

"Well, I wouldn't mind studying with him sometimes." I laughed.

Well, all the while we were cooking those fish, Rayford was hanging around near the kitchen, peeking in now and then, like what we were doing was the most interesting thing. I had a houseful of liquor, music, fast and pretty women and he wanted to watch us cook fish, so I told him to come on in and pull up a chair. He had a bottle of beer, looked like he hadn't took a single sip from it. Soon as he got settled in a chair, though, Cora took off her apron and said, "I'm going to dance."

He watched Cora leave us alone, like he was glad to see her gone, and I went on frying the fish, just like he wasn't even there. "So all this belongs to you?" he asked me.

"What you mean?"

"This house."

"Yessir, I guess it does," I said, kinda cold and suspiciouslike, wondering if he was after my money.

"You should be proud of what you've achieved."

"I am."

"I can look at you and if you don't mind my saying, I can tell you believe in dreams *and* hard work."

I didn't know what to say. Hadn't too many folks been able to read me so fast and especially not saying it like he did.

"Our race needs women like you if we're ever to progress. Our men do too."

I had gone to the sink and was washing my hands and his words just felt like a warm welcome cloak all around me. I'd gone to the sink 'cause he was looking at me so open like and yet so friendly and trusting I could hardly stand it.

"Miss Naomi, I can look at you and tell you're a good woman, somebody I'd like to know."

And you know, all those words didn't sound like jive to me. He had the sincerest way of saying things. Rayford made you feel like he wasn't the kind of man who'd lie to you.

So with all that noise going on in the living room and fish frying on the stove, Rayford Johnson acted like he didn't care about neither. And I sat down at the table with a plate of porgies in front of me and I asked him, "You sound like one of those race men."

"And proud to be," he said, real serious. He kept looking at me like he was trying to figure me out. He looked just like a schoolteacher. But I knew I could make him crack a smile if I wanted to. He took a big swiggle from his beer and then he says, "What do you think the Negro's got to do to progress in this country?"

Now, I'll tell you, I wasn't expecting no question like that right then. I was thinking he'd tell me how good I looked or ask me to go out and dance. Politics and all that—well, the folks I run with, we didn't get too concerned about all that. But after I got over being surprised I felt kind of special. He must've thought I could answer the question or he wouldn't have asked it. So I said, clearing my throat real good before I started to speak, "Well, I think the colored, I mean the Negro, has got to depend on himself and develop something of his own before anybody will respect him."

"You're a very astute observer," he said, smiling at me like I was one of his students who'd done him proud.

"Well, I don't know about all that." I said, getting up to turn over the fish. "But I do know we won't make no progress unless we all make it together."

"So you don't subscribe to Du Bois's Talented Tenth theory?"

Now, I hadn't heard nothing about this man Du Bois or his theory, but I asked Rayford, just guessing, "What happens to the other ninety percent?" And don't you know he smiled and then laughed and I could see the part of him he tried to hide. He took a swig of his beer and just said, "Miss Naomi, you got real good sense, real good."

When I sat down I asked him, "You don't sound like you from the South, where you from original?"

"Oklahoma. An all-Negro town called Langston. My folks were some of the first Negroes to go to the West in the 1880s. They left Tennessee, looking for land and a better life than they had in the South."

"Did they find it?"

"Took them some time, but they did. My daddy's a undertaker and my mother teaches music."

Now, with all that behind him, coming from those kinda folks, I'd have figured Rayford to be stuck on himself, but all he was telling me didn't seem to phase him one bit.

"How come you left Oklahoma?"

"Well, I'd been teaching school and then I heard about Marcus Garvey."

"You mean that little old Black man from the West Indies? The one always talking about Black this and Black that?"

"Well, I wouldn't describe him quite that way. He was and is a prophet. A man ahead of his times."

"Ain't he in jail now?"

"Unfortunately, yes. But that's where most prophets end up at some point in their career. He was a Moses, a *Black* Moses for his people."

"What did you do with him?"

"I was business manager of the *Negro World,* the paper of the Universal Negro Improvement Association. Worked for him three years. That was the best time of my life."

"Why you say that?"

"The man's vision, his accomplishments. And for a period of my life I was part of it all, helping to make a difference in the lot of the Negro." Rayford got real sad when he said that, like he was remembering something so special he didn't know how to put a value on it. "I mean, do you know what the man and the organization did?" he asked me. "The UNIA set up groccery stores, had a chain of laundries in cities all over the country, a publishing company. We had members in the Caribbean and Africa. And, of course, the Black Star Line."

"I heard that ship almost sunk," I said, sucking in my jaws.

"The white men that sold it to us took advantage of our inexperience, sold us a piece of junk, a ship that wasn't seaworthy. But had there ever been a shipping line owned by the Black man in America before?"

I felt ashamed for saying what I did. Then Rayford reached in his pocket and pulled out his wallet and in a little side compartment he pulled out a cigar ring and shows it to me and it's got Garvey's picture on it. As he handed the paper ring to me he says, "The best years of my life, bar none."

Well, by the time Rayford got through talking about Garvey, I didn't feel like eating no fish. But me and Cora set everything out. I didn't feel like dancing neither. I just felt like sitting there, looking at Rayford Johnson.

We sat in the kitchen till two o'clock in the morning, just telling each other stories about what we'd done. Until I met Rayford, I didn't think I had much to tell that anybody'd be interested in. When I told him about my parents sharecropping, he talked about all the poor Black folks down South, when I told him how bad I felt for my daddy and what he'd said about my house, Rayford talked about all Negro men, and when I told him how Jackson had settled into his job cleaning over at the post office, he wondered if the North was really gonna be much better. When Rayford Johnson left my house that night, I knew I had found me a sweetheart.

Now, imagine that, me, who hated the thought of the inside of a schoolhouse, courting a teacher!

Well, me and Rayford became a pretty hot item. And 'cause of the kind of man he was, I kinda cut back on so much partying and almost turned into a homebody. In the summertime, we'd go over to Griffith Stadium and see one of the Negro League teams play and one time Rayford took me to the Jungle Inn to see Jelly Roll Morton. But Rayford could turn a evening just having dinner and listening to the radio into something special. But he was the seriousest man I ever met. He was renting a room and all in the corners and under the bed he had stacks and stacks of those "race" magazines, *The Crisis* and *Opportunity*. It was 'cause of Rayford that I started reading more than the comics and the obituaries in the paper. I had to keep up with him so I started reading the news too.

One day I went over to Dunbar and watched Rayford teach a class. He had those kids eating out of the palm of his hand. He lectured them about everybody from Hannibal to Herbert Hoover and Mrs. Bethune. The thing I liked was, he talked about folks living right then and slowed the kids how they were making history. I'd grown up thinking education was studying folks that were dead. Rayford let me know education was just about everything you did or thought, no matter when it happened.

I felt pretty good. Had a sweetheart and no more empty bed blues. And serious as he was, Rayford Johnson knew how to please a woman. Some mornings I'd get outta bed when we'd been together and feel like I could tear up the house and put it back together again. He wasn't making no whole lotta money as a teacher but he never asked me for a dime. He had a old Ford somebody gave him and when we went out we went in his car, not mine. He had pride and I think that's what won my heart more than anything else.

Well, we'd been going together almost a year and I knew what I wanted. So one night he came to see me. I'd fixed pork chops, rice, gravy, collard greens and biscuits. He coulda took one look at that meal and knew I meant business. We listened to some Louis Armstrong records he'd brought over and then we got in the bed. Oh, he fixed me real good that night! And afterwards, we're laying there, him smoking them Chesterfield cigarettes he'd been smoking, he told me once, since he was sixteen, and I'm feeling all soft and warm and happy and I just asked him, just like that, to marry me. I hadn't never seen a man blush before, but Rayford laid there, looking like what I'd said had made his day.

When he got himself composed, he says, "You don't leave nothing to chance, do you, *Miss* Naomi Reeves?"

And I told him, "Only way I'm gonna get what I want is to ask for it. I always figure on hearing yes. And no don't scare me 'cause I heard no all my life and it ain't never stopped me yet. But smart as you are, I knew you'd have sense enough to say yes."

Now, once I become Mrs. Rayford Johnson, I was happy as a fox in a henhouse. I turned over the running of my two houses to Rayford, let him collect all the rents, cut him in on everything. I've heard women talk about *Never let the left hand know what the right hand is doing* and you know who the left hand is. But you can't keep secrets in a marriage. Not a real marriage anyway. And I'd waited too long to share my blessings with a man to play hide-and-seek once I got him.

I was twenty-four when me and Rayford got married. And I felt like I had already lived a lifetime. In those days wasn't no such thing as waiting till you grew up, life just come along and dragged you into it. Yeah, I was young, but had already had one husband, lost a child, been divorced, been dirt-poor, left home, worked like a dog, cleaned up other folks' homes, played the numbers, got a house and decided I could have the kind of life I wanted. I was young, but only in age. And where I had come from, age didn't mean nothing no way.

When I got pregnant, then I had everything I'd always wanted. I went back home to Spring Hope to have my baby. Back then, no matter where you lived—in New York, Chicago, Philadelphia, wherever—*home* was where you come from, and it was just natural to go home to do something as important as having your child.

Mama and Daddy was still inching along on the farm, but the money I was sending made a difference. They'd bought some new furniture and Daddy'd bought a car, but it sat in the yard half the time, 'cause he ran out of money for tags or repairs. I went home in April to have Esther and maybe 'cause I was gonna give birth, or 'cause I was so happy—whatever—seemed like home was the most beautiful place. I just took it easy till my time come, sitting on the porch in the day, doing little chores around the house, going for a walk with Mama sometimes in the afternoon, staring at the stars at night. No place else smells like the South in springtime—the azaleas, the flowering dogwood just bust out and you can't hardly smell nothing else. And waiting for Esther to come, I realized that it was the beauty and the feel of the South that I missed, living in the North.

Well, Esther start coming about two o'clock one morning. They say a child that comes early in the morning won't have trouble finding their way through life. Mama told Daddy to go on over and get the midwife, Aunt Gin, but when he went out to start that old car, the engine was dead. So Jesse got on the old mule, Nat Turner, to ride the two miles to Aunt Gin's. Daddy's out in the yard in his long johns, cussing at the car and kicking it. And my water's broke and the pains are coming so fast I can't hardly breathe. Well, don't you know, Mama's just holding my hand and praying real hard, trying to drown out Daddy's cussing and telling me to push, to push real hard, and I'm moaning and screaming for God and Rayford and by the time Aunt Gin gets there Esthers' come on out.

About the only thing Aunt Gin was good for by the time she got there was to give me some of that special root tea they give to women after they give birth. I'd lost one baby in Spring Hope and now I had come home and had another one and I'd decided that this child was gonna live.

About a week after Esther was born, I'm still taking it easy and waiting for Rayford to come and drive us back to Washington and Mama comes in the bedroom while I'm nursing Esther and tells me Isaiah had come to see me. Now, you know how it is when somebody is on your mind and you just can't shake them and next thing you know, there they are, well, there was Isaiah.

I finished nursing Esther and put her down to sleep and I combed my hair and put on a pretty dress Rayford had bought me and then Isaiah comes in the room.

"Howdy, Naomi," he says, fumbling with his hat. He's dressed in a suit and I could smell he'd just shaved before he come.

"Howdy, Isaiah." He'd filled out some and looked like a man, not the boy I married. He sits down in a chair beside the bed and says, "I see the North's been good to you."

"You could say that."

"That's a pretty little baby you got there. What you name her?"

"Esther."

"I got two boys, Gregory and William," he says. Then he takes out a picture of them and shows me. And they look just like him.

"Mama told me you and Vera Robinson had got married. She's a good woman," I said.

"Sure is. Don't take a lot to satisfy her."

"You satisfied me, Isaiah, as far as you could. I was just s'posed to leave, that's all."

"And I was s'posed to stay."

We sat there talking a pretty good time, about crops and the land, some of the things we used to talk about and about some new things. I told him about Rayford and then he told me all about Vera. Just felt like I was talking to a friend, not somebody who I'd hurt real bad one time. Then Mama comes in and invites Isaiah to stay to dinner, but he says no, he's late getting home already. And then he tells me to bring Rayford to the house when he comes and not to be a stranger. And I feel real good when he leaves 'cause I know Isaiah just like I'd never left him and I know he meant every word he said.

Being a daddy don't change Rayford much, except he spoiled Esther and got even more serious than ever, worried about the world and the Negro's place in it. Then those nine boys down in Scottsboro got accused of raping two white women on a train and the white folks tried them in lickety-split time and wanted to send them to the electric chair. I felt pretty bad about those boys. All you had to do was read the story and know the women made the whole thing up. And one of the boys wasn't but twelve years old, still a child. Rayford got involved with a bunch of folks raising money for their defense. Although he didn't cotton much to the NAACP, he attended their rallies and even wrote a couple of articles for the *Chicago Defender* about the case. Then in '33, he took me and Esther down to a big protest in front of the White House to try to get Roosevelt to get the Scottsboro boys out of jail. Now, I've never been one for raising Cain in the streets and I'll tell you I didn't want to go, but Rayford said I had to bear witness, had to put myself on the line. Said if all those white folks, the Communists and the socialists, if they could come from all over and march for nine Negro men, why couldn't I? Well, I did and carried Esther too, although Mama woulda had a fit if she had known that. Roosevelt not in office a good three months and us knocking on his door about the Scottsboro Boys.

That demonstration didn't set them free, but I did feel good being part of it. And to this day, one of my favorite pictures is one Rayford took of me standing in front of the White House gate, holding Esther, and she's got a sign in her hand that reads:
ROOSEVELT ENFORCE FULL RIGHTS FOR NEGROES.
When it come to Esther, Rayford told her everything he knew, and I give her everything I never had. She had her daddy's walk, come into a room just like a queen coming into a court, and she had my spirit. I wanted her to have everything I never did, so I gave her tap dance and piano lessons. And Esther had the prettiest room in the house. But she was my daughter so I couldn't raise her to be useless. I trained her to help me around the house and in the summertime she'd go to Spring Hope for a few weeks and help Mama and Daddy on the farm, same way I did.

Rayford was all the time reading to her. He didn't believe in fairy tales and such and at bedtime he'd tell Esther stories about folks like Harriet Tubman and Sojourner Truth. I asked him once why he was always pounding all that stuff in Esther's head all the time, why he couldn't just let her be a little girl. "She'll find out she's a Negro soon enough," I told him. And he just said, "But we got to let her know what it means."

Those were good years. Roosevelt had set up a whole bunch of agencies—the NRA, the "ABC" and the this-that-and-the-other—to turn the Depression around and we were doing OK. I felt like my life was set—you know how it is when you finally get everything in place, just the way you want it and everything you touch, near 'bout, turns to gold. Well, we had a coupla years like that. Then, the same year that fool Hitler got the white folks to killing themselves in every country they lived in, my world turned upside down too.

Rayford had been feeling poorly for some time, had been coughing a lot and having trouble breathing. Finally he got to feeling so bad he went to the doctor. Turned out he had a cancer of the lungs. Now, back then, if you had cancer they just wrote you off and started digging your grave. Folks didn't even like to say the word in public, that's how much it scared them. The doctor gave Rayford six months to live, but he held on for two years.

Rayford fought that cancer the way he fought everything, like he couldn't think of not winning. Mostly, he just decided not to give up, and he threw away those Chesterfields and never smoked another one. We found a doctor that put him on a special diet and we thought we had it licked, but it come back and come back strong. He started losing weight and got so sick he had to be put in Freedmen's Hospital. The doctors there said it'd be a waste of time to operate. Well, I just about moved in the hospital with him. Slept on the floor beside him every night and I'd hear him wheezing and rasping and his breath coming so hard and slow it sounded like every breath was his last one. He couldn't breathe good and he couldn't sleep. He was too proud to let them shoot him full of morphine, so the pain was always there. He'd lost so much weight he was down to damn near nothing, cheeks all sunk, and his hair had got gray.

And I'd get up from the pallet on the floor and let him know I was there for him. Help him struggle to get a sip of water and just hold his hand. And he'd whisper sometimes, when he could muster a breath, "Tell me a story, Naomi. Tell me a story." And I'd tell him about Spring Hope or the time I ran away to the carnival or how Blue shamed me into playing the numbers. I'd tell him, real slow like, to make the time last and it wouldn't be until I was finished with the story that I'd feel the tears on my face.

One night Rayford opened his eyes while I was talking to him and he saw me crying and he says, "Dying is the most frightening thing I ever had to do and, Naomi, I'm so scared." And then we both started crying and somehow us crying together like that gave me strength.

Rayford died in his sleep one night with my laying there on the floor beside his bed. I woke up the next morning and loved Rayford Johnson so much I was glad his misery was finally over. Then I saw a piece of paper on the bedstand next to his medicine. He'd scribbled on the paper in a handwriting that looked like something Esther would write: "I had all the time that belonged to me and I found you."

Esther didn't speak a word for a year after Rayford died. And I wore black so long my friends had to talk me out of it. I wish'd I'd been a child so I could've just shut out everybody and closed in on myself. I birthed Esther, so I knew she hadn't gone crazy or got retarded like folks was saying, telling me to take her to the doctors. Hell, my baby missed her daddy and she just didn't have the words to say how bad she felt. And when she did start talking, the first thing Esther says over dinner one night is, "Mama, he's coming back. He told me." And I said to her, "Baby, he didn't go nowhere. I got him right here in my heart."

Marita Golden *has published three novels, including* And Do Remember Me, *and one autobiography,* Migrations of the Heart. *She lives in Washington, D.C.*

OPPORTUNITY Magazine   October 1929

A NORTHERNER'S VIEW
OF THE NEGRO PROBLEM

Arthur C. Holden

Some one asked me once if I were not interested in the Negro Problem. Let me make it clear at the outset that I'm not particularly interested in the Negro problem. As a human being, however, I am vitally interested in the social problem. I recognize that the continued improvement of the well-being of the human race is necessary for both individual progress and individual happiness.

The Negro is a part of the human race. Originally he didn't live among white men. He had a home of his own principally in Africa or the "Dark Continent," as Europeans like to call it. The needs of civilization caused Negroes to be brought to America, mostly against their will and caused white men to penetrate the jungles of Africa, mostly aginst the will of the black men. Certainly the responsibility for mixing up the races rests with the white men.

I don't mean to blame us white men who are living today. We had no more to say about that than the Negro. Perhaps our ancestors made a frightful mistake in thinking that the Negro was worth bringing to America. Our forefathers acted as it served them best at the time and they rest in their graves safe from blame.

The Negro is here. It does no good today to point a fault-finding finger. He is a part of our national life whether we like it or not. He requires food, he requires shelter, he requires clothes, he has other human needs. On the other hand, he has earning power.

It is not necessary to discuss whether the Negro's earning power is as great as the white man's. Certainly it isn't at the present time. Maybe it will never be. Personally I am not interested in the discussion about equality. As an average man what I want to know is, has the Negro enough earning power to keep himself from being a drag on me. If I were a manufacturer and wide awake, I'd be interested too to know whether or not the Negro has enough earning power to buy the goods I am eager to sell him. Our manufacturers have learned a great lesson in the last ten years. Expressed in plain everyday words it is just this: "High wages mean workers with power to buy." Buying power means prosperity. I remember the talk we used to hear ten and twenty years ago about the evils of high wages. "Dear me;

what was the world coming to with the laboring man getting a talk-ing machine and finally an automobile." You don't hear the regrets you used to hear about that. There are too many people who have gotten rich or who have had their conditions bettered because so many laboring men were buying automobiles.

Now I've never lived in the South except to do service on the Texas border and I don't pretend to understand Southern condi-tions, but I sometimes wonder whether the Southern white man has made the most of his opportunity to develop the buying power of the Southern Negro. Certainly if the Southern Negro can earn more than he does now he is going to be able to buy more. Then it seems self evident that the community in which a man with buying power lives is going to reap the first benefits.

But, as I said, I am a Northerner. I don't know the Southern point of view. But, I do know one thing. I want the people who live near to me to have buying power. Especially I want them to have enough buying power so they can get the necessities for decent and healthful living. I don't want people who live in my community to be a drag on me, or on the community in which I live.

Now in recent years, beginning especially in 1919, a great many Negroes have migrated from the south and settled in northern cities. They have become a part of our urban problem. There are some-where near 200,000 Negroes living in the upper part of the Borough of Manhattan alone. A community big enough to form a fair sized city of itself. But as things stand this community isn't self-sustain-ing. In many ways it's a drag rather than a help to the large cos-mopolitan community of which it is a part. By that I don't mean that every Negro in Harlem is a drag upon the City of New York. It isn't true when you pick the individual at all. But when you con-sider the group, Harlem as a community is a drag rather than a help to the economic and social life of the city. Let me illustrate this by giving a few examples of what I mean:

First, the health standards of Harlem were found to be lower than the health standards for the city as a whole. Something had to be done about it. The city itself and the public health organizations had to spend money to investigate, to educate, to eliminate and lessen disease. You can't build a Chinese wall around a part of a modern city and keep disease and bad health standards shut off from the rest of the city. If the city is to be healthy all the city has to be healthy. Hence the rest of the city has to pay to improve health standards in the backward section.

Second, twenty to thirty per cent of the cases in our criminal courts were found to be Negroes. This is all out of proportion, because something less than 4 per cent of New York City's population is Negro. You can't build a Chinese wall around a part of an American city and expect to lessen crime. You would be more likely to make that section a breeding place for criminals. Our modern public welfare organizations have been pointing out that the greatest incentive to crime is bad living conditions. The whole city has to pay for law enforcement and for trying to stamp out crime at its source.

Third, the living standards in Harlem are decidedly worse than in other parts of the town. Bad living conditions mean rapid depreciation of property values. With the influx of the Negroes into Harlem property values fell and while they have risen somewhat since, principally due to overcrowding, they are low when compared to most other parts of the city. Lagging property values mean that taxes for administration purposes fall more heavily elsewhere. You can't build a Chinese wall around a backward section of the city and forget about it. From the point of view of the administration of taxes alone, a backward section soon becomes a drag upon the whole city.

Most of us don't feel directly this drag upon us caused by backward groups among us, but most of us feel that it is a great deal harder than it ought to be for us to get some of the simplest things done and for us to satisfy our most essential human needs. We are constantly told that we must put up with congested streets and conditions of bad light and air because the city hasn't the money to remedy the situation. Our cities constantly face serious social and economic problems.

When a situation gets particularly acute a call goes out for somebody to take a hand and help. I happen to be one of those who was called upon for help by the New York Urban League. We found that the Negro is likely to become a drag when he settles in our northern cities just as we found that the European immigrant, was likely to be a drag when he first reached America. At the root of the trouble seems to be the underlying fact that the Negro has had even more difficulty than the European in developing his earning power. Here is something very fundamental. Some people think that this is simply because the Negro is the Negro. With that they shrug their shoulders and dismiss the subject. I can't understand the philosophy of such an attitude. Such people don't realize that if the case of the Negro is really hopeless it is their own shoulders that must bear the burden. The drag of their backward neighbors will be upon them even though they do not know it.

A hundred years ago when the ordinary man's earning power was crippled by this sudden coming of the machine, whole sections of the community became a drag upon society. Amidst a great hue and cry about wickedness, a band of reformers went out with rules and moral precepts to set things right. Now in a hundred years we have learned one thing. You may teach, you may set rules, you may suppress, but if the passions of men have not a proper and sufficient outlet, they burst their bonds. Today we are studying how to apply our human passions, through work, through recreation, through our sense of the joy of life. Help a man to develop his own earning power and he will work out his own salvation. We have had enough of philanthropy and prisons. They may have their uses for extreme cases but they will not do for a whole group in the community or a whole race. It is "not alms but opportunity that men crave." It's easier to give alms; its harder to study and seek out opportunities. The alms do not go far, the opportunity does. Help the Negro to gain earning power and he will not be a drag upon you. As a self respecting and self supportint member of the community he will in addition help you yourself along. Think for a moment of all the poor people in our nation, of those who do not earn and think for a moment upon the increased buying power. I'm not saying this in a material sense alone. Think also of the vast increase in spiritual capacity and consumption. Look at it anyway you will, neglected humanity is neglected opportunity.

I'm a northerner and I don't understand the southern point of view. I don't pretend to, but I don't want any groups living in the community in which I live to be a drag upon me and upon my community. I think we northerners are shrewd enough and have enough brain power to look ahead a bit. Perhaps Yankee shrewdness and foresight has had something to do with buildings up the greatness and the prosperity of our nation. At any rate we are going to use our brains to prevent the race problem from becoming a millstone around our necks.

Arthur C. Holden, *Chairman of the New York Urban League, is the author of a "Primer on Housing," and also "The Settlement Idea." This article is taken from a speech which he delivered over the radio station WNYC during the summer of 1929.*

OPPORTUNITY Magazine   August 1932

Migration Again

T. Arnold Hill

For several years during the war and post-war periods the chief topic of discussion concerning Negroes was the migration. From 1923 to 1930 there has been little mention of the movement of southern Negroes to the North, not because they were not moving northward, but because a steady flow was scarcely noticeable during the period of prosperity. The past three years have experienced a migration approaching in size that of the war period. The occasion for the two movements was the same in each instance—namely, employment; but their reception was vastly different. There was work during the war period: there has been none for the better part of the past three years.

As a result of this latest migration the percentage of Negroes receiving relief from both public and private agencies is greatly in excess of their population and work ratios. This is particularly true in Cincinnati, Chicago, New York, Philadelphia and Detroit. Consequently dispatches have been released warning them not to come to almost every industrial community in the North. A year ago Newark, New Jersey, with a Negro population of 38,880, which is one-twelfth of the city's total, was caring for 6,500 unemployed Negroes which consisted of one-third of the total relief cases. Today it is thought that fully one-third of the employable heads of families are out of work, and the City Fathers see[s] no other solution to the situation than that of returning them to their former places of residence.

No solution is offered Negroes in the North by forcing them upon their poor relatives in the South. The South wanted the Negro back after the war because work was plentiful. The South does not want him back today for it has thousands of unemployed people already there for whose care adequate funds are not available. In the list of states scheduled to collect money from the Federal Government for relief purposes, are southern states as well as northern states. It is conceivable that a city might relieve itself of the burden of caring for idle families by such a process, but it is inconceivable that the welfare of the dispossessed family would be improved thereby.

DALLAS EXPRESS   July 21, 1917

Being a member of the race, I feel it a duty to make mention of the race. I feel it my duty to make mention of the present labor situation among our people.

Negro labor has become a severe problem; one that is arousing the thoughts of the entire nation.

The Negro race is taking advantage of the offer extended him by northern industries and to-day we find our people leaving by the hundreds for northern fields.

All of this is caused by poor wages, disfranchisement, discrimination and general mistreatment.

All of these things have caused a continual unrest among our race, and to-day we are seeking better fields of labor, better wages and more liberty; and on the contrary I venture to say that none of these adventures will be gained successfully unless some stand is taken to prevent calamaties, such occurrences as the East St. Louis riot and other conflicts that will follow this recent occurrence.

The thing that hinders us as a race is incompetent leadership. We have hundreds of educational leaders at the head of the institutions of learning who are silent on this public issue that is of so vital importance to the people whom they represent.

We need to perfect an organization to deal with our present race conditions, supported by the entire race and all of its organizations and institutions combined.

I would suggest a conference of our educators, ministers and professional men from every state and district to confer upon the present situation and to consider the best methods to solve the problems before us.

Our labor must be organized, not for the purpose of bringing about strife or walk-outs, but to protect the laborer against unfairness and to make him more efficient and reliable, so as to demand more for what he does, to make appeals to the government against lawlessness that has begun to spring up to prevent the Negro labor rising.

We note an occurrence at Shreveport, La., Tuesday of this week. An incident which was a violation of the fourteenth Amendment, when sheriff of that city prohibited two hundred members of our race from leaving that state of Pittsburg, Pa. to enter service of the Pennsylvania Railway system, which had offered better wages than they could receive in their home state. Now for any state to pass a law to prohibit any of its citizens from exercising their rights as American citizens, that state is using state rights which is strict violation of the law between the states. I am for an organization that will make continuous appeals to the administration for the enforcement of the laws of this government that the Negro might receive a square deal in the South as well as in the North.

I believe that the white South has now awakened to the fact that northern industries can use Negro labor at a better wage than he has been receiving in the past, and now he will be willing to pay the price to maintain Negro labor in the future and when the South makes it worth while the Negro will find it as pleasant to stay in the South as to go elsewhere.

Let us come together and organize.

I make this earnest appeal to the men of our race for the betterment of our own conditoins.

(Signed) Frank D. Dixon, 4007 Avent St.

GOING EAST

Cynthia Simmons

Papa's back was perfectly straight as he carried Sister's bags down the aisle of the train. Gone was the almost imperceptible roundness she'd noticed three weeks ago when he bounded from the sofa to call her siblings to the dinner table. Until then she'd never seen anything bow her Papa and the thought that a perfectly coiffed white matron—whose most taxing accomplishment had probably been organizing a dinner party—had caused her Papa's shoulders to sag even a little bit filled Sister with a rage greater than any she'd ever experienced. That woman wasn't fit to wipe her Papa's boots. Her Papa who, just one generation out of slavery, was providing college for his children. Something ninety percent of the state of Georgia didn't have colored or white, rich or poor. Her blood had been boiling for three weeks. Papa's straight back let her relax. Tension oozed from her body like steam from a pressure cooker.

Papa put her bags in the luggage racks above the seats. There were only two. Since she did not know for sure she'd be staying, hadn't made no sense to drag all her stuff home. She'd left most of her things at Dr. Gilcrest's house in Richmond.

Papa hugged her warmly. "I want you to know I'm mighty proud of you cutie, might proud. I know you'll make me proud in New York too. Just watch out for Sally. She's been known to help people forget their manners." The tears welling up in his eyes were about to spill over, quickly he left the train.

Sister put the food basket Mu'd prepared snugly under her seat and settled in as the train began to move. Her family followed it a few feet, tears flowing as they waved to her through the window. Then the train picked up speed and Sister quickly lost sight of them, she closed her eyes to press this family picture into her memory bank. But for the umpteenth time her memory turned her back to the afternoon she spent with Mrs. Taylor.

People stared. A woman was watching her from the picture window of the house directly across the street. She started walking toward town thinking maybe she'd get less attention if she were waiting at a bus stop just as Emory, Mrs. Taylor's driver, drove up.

"Sorry little lady," he'd said with a smile, reaching across the seat to open the door of the pick-up. "When the missus heard I was coming to town to pick up the flowers, she made a list of things for me to get at the pharmacy."

Earlier that afternoon when he'd driven her out to the Taylor house they'd talked easily. Now they rode back in silence. Her afternoon with Mrs. Taylor curbed the easy conversation they'd shared. He didn't speak again till he dropped her at the corner to catch her bus.

"Took a lot for you to stand up to Miz Taylor like you did. You tell your Papa Emory said he raised a mighty fine girl, mighty fine."

Sister shook his hand warmly smiling her thanks. People were starting to go home from work so the buses downtown were packed. Choosing not to be indecently pressed against some stranger today, Sister let a couple that were too full pass.

Dinner was fixed and Mu was watching at the dining room window when Sister came up the driveway. Sister was on foot, Mu thought, something must have happened. The Taylor's had picked Sister up downtown for the drive out but they were supposed to bring her back to her door. "Byrd," she'd called, her voice going up to her high register. "Sister's back. Come to the front room now."

Just as Mu reached the front door Sister was stepping onto the porch. Feeling like a little girl, she threw her arms round her Mama's neck but the tears still didn't come. Arms to waists mother and daughter went to the living room to talk with Papa.

The vein under Papa's left eye was pulsing when she finished her story.

"Lemme make sure I've got this right. This woman asked you to take a test for syphilis before coming to work at her house?" he asked slowly, trying to keep a lid on his anger.

"Yes, sir," Sister said quietly.

"Dead bobbitt," Papa said bounding up from his seat.

It was then, when he got up from the sofa that Sister'd noticed the slump. Just a little rounding, just enough so anybody who really knew him would notice. He bellowed for Brother and Mozelle to come to the table as he went down the hall to the bathroom.

All the children were seated when he came to the dinner table. They ate silently except Louise, the youngest, who insisted on talking. Brother and Mozelle, being older, followed Mu and Sister's lead. Soon as Papa finished his last forkful of mashed potatoes he pushed his chair back from the table. He didn't ask for seconds or tell Louise about the number of starving children the leavings on her plate could nourish or wait for Mu to dish up the blueberry cobbler that had perfumed the house all afternoon long. He was not himself.

"Idella," he'd said scraping his chair across the tile floor, "find Sally's address for me. I'm gonna go write out a telegram to her. I'll need you to take it to town and send it off for me tomorrow."

Abruptly the train stopped jarring Sister's eyes open. "Ain't no use going over that afternoon again," she said out loud, causing the man in front of her to turn round. Embarrassed, she reached into her oversized pocketbook and retrieved the magazine and book she brought. Mindlessly she flipped through the pages of the now six-month-old issue of "Opportunity" Susie had sent her. Susie, her best friend from Freedman who was working at Seaview, had been sending little things all year trying to convince her to come to Seaview.

Why did she feel so guilty? Not even Mu, who generally went along with Papa's notions, shared his dream of them living together on a family farm. Her leaving didn't really destroy that dream, she told herself trying to stop this feeling she couldn't shake off. It was doomed already. This mess with Mrs. Taylor had been unpleasant but it had gotten her what she wanted, the chance to work in a real hospital. Till her afternoon at the Taylor house Papa had ignored everything she tried to tell him about this job at Seaview. That afternoon had caused him a lot of pain but he seemed fine now, she thought, as she turned to Alain Locke's article "The Year of Grace" and settled in to read it again. Colored people in New York were doing some of everything. If colored actors could work on Broadway in "Green Pastures" and colored writers like Langston Hughes could get their books printed there in New York, in time surely she would get a job working as a nurse working in an operating room. Her family's faces through the window of the train flashed in Sister's mind. She sighed as the train moved forward. They'd probably never live together as a family again. As happy as she was about going to Seaview she couldn't help but feel sad about that.

The taxi driver wanted $8.00 to carry Sister out to Staten Island. Said it should have been ten because of the trunk Dr. Gilcrest had sent from Richmond to meet her at the train station there in New York. $8.00 seemed a fortune. Sister wasn't about to start off her stay in New York by letting some slickster overcharge her. She haggled with him and got the ride down to $6.50.

Staten Island was nothing like New York City. The City had too many people in it, too many people and too many buildings. Staten Island looked more like home. Peace settled over her when the taxi turned into a long driveway where a small plaque announced "Seaview Hospital." It looked like a college campus, so it felt familiar. Wasn't that she hadn't trusted Susie's description of the place, she just needed to see for herself. The buildings were set back off the road, separating the grounds some from the main street. Grass, trees, and shrubs made Seaview feel even more familiar. This doesn't seem a bad place to live, Sister thought, as the taxi headed for what seemed to be the main building.

Susie, Mable, Elsie, Stell and Sister—known to them as Evie—all gathered in Stell's room after supper though they all had duty the next day. The Freedman girls, class of '29—the largest class Freedman ever had and the first class of nurses to go out with the doctors in the daytime. All, except Sister, had come to Seaview at Dr. Long's suggestion right after graduating Freedman. Though they were full trained nurses, they had to work as aides since Freedman had lost its New York accreditation. It riled them some to work for one-third less than the colored nurses here who trained at New York's two schools, Harlem and Lincoln. But every one of them knew the best-trained colored nurses working at Seaview were in this room. New York accreditation or not, all those Lincoln and Harlem girls would've given their eye teeth to come to Freedman cause it had the best basic training program of all the schools teaching colored nurses.

"All in?" Stell asked, stretching her tall slender frame before sitting down to shuffle the cards.

"Girl you sure you didn't grow some more while I was off at Peeks?" Sister asked.

"Girl, ain't none of us grown an inch since high school."

"Except out," Mabel said patting her now rounding hips.

"Y'all just shrimp," Stell added dealing the cards.

"Watch who you calling a shrimp," Mabel said teasingly, "you may have a full foot on the rest of 'em but you only got six inches on me."

"And me and Evie got at least two inches on Elsie so you can't be talking to us."

The five women were as different in color as they were in height, Elsie being the lightest of them. She and Stell usually partied together and always got attention when they came into a place. Elsie was just a little under five feet and the lightest shade of beige. Dark chocolate Stell was almost a foot taller. Susie and Sister, the other twosome in the group, could pass as sisters. They were about the same height, though Sister was rounder, both the same shade of tan. Mable was dead center of all of them. She was half a foot taller than Elsie and the color of maple syrup.

"Old Stone Face will probably get Richardson to show you the ropes tomorrow," Susie said arranging the cards in her hand.

"I don't know why she puts so much store by Richardson," Mable chimed in. "Don't nobody like her. Even the Lincoln girls act like they can't stand her and they trained with her."

Picking her last card up from the table Stell added, "That's probably a star in her crown with that old stoolpigeon. Got to watch what you say round Nurse Bessie Lee."

They were silent for a moment while everyone arranged their cards. Elsie pulled a card and spread—five, six, seven of hearts—then discarded the ten of clubs.

Sister pulled from the deck and discarded. "Y'all heard anything about our accreditation?"

"Evie, ain't nobody saying a word about that. I don't think anything's gonna happen till after this depression."

"I think Mable's right about that cause they not even giving the nursing test. Say they don't need no more nurses right now."

"Stell what they need with more nurses when they got us?" Susie said, pulling a card from the deck and discarding another. "We do the same work as the girls from Lincoln and Harlem and get aide's pay. It's not fair but Dr. Long warned all of us this might take a little time. One thing for sure, it beats being nurse to some white baby."

"That depends on who you talk to."

"Mable's sure right about that. Me and my Mama had a terrible fight when I took this job. 'Stell,' she said, 'you ain't nothing but a damn fool. The only reason they letting y'all nurse in that hospital is cause it's full of TB patients.' She was sure right about that cause most all the nurses here are colored."

"Big Lena, my mama's sister, had it," Sister said. "Papa had a fit when he found out I was stopping by after school every day to help her. They had to have a family meeting to convince him it was safe for me to go. If you know someone's got it and you're careful, it's not much chance you'll catch it but people don't know that."

By this time the hand had gone around again and it was Susie's turn. She picked up three cards from the discard pile and spread everything that was in her hand.

Stell threw down her hand revealing three aces, "Damn you, Susie!"

"Should have spread them aces when you had the chance. You got anything to eat around here?"

"Susie, I'm not sure I wanna share this maple walnut cake my aunt made for me with all of us."

"Girl you better stop being such a bad sport and cut me a piece of that cake."

Still miffed, Stell got a knife and some napkins from her desk, the cake tin from the windowsill, and brought them back to their makeshift card table. "Girl, soon as you get a Sunday off you got to go to the Small's Paradise Saturday night. They play some good music up there and got a nice-sized dance floor. And the men! Lord have mercy. They sure do make a pretty picture."

"They let you smoke in there?" Sister asked.

"Course they let you smoke in there Evie, it's a nightclub."

"You know I don't like to go no place where people do a lot of smoking. That smell gets all in your clothes. I'm gonna have to hang these things I got on outside after sitting in here with y'all smoking and a-puffing."

"Well, the music and the men in that place's worth sending them to the dry cleaners, far as I'm concerned. Last time Elsie and I went up there, we had three tantalizing tan visions join us at our table."

"Sharp as a tacks with big wads of money in their pockets, which me and Stell helped them spend. All of 'em got to stuttering when you asked what they did for a living. Real New York slicksters."

Stell and Elsie busted out laughing.

"The taxi driver tried to slick me. Told me it cost $10 to come out here."

"Did you have a trunk?" Mable asked.

"What does my trunk have to do with the cost of the taxi ride Mable?"

"They charge extra up here for a trunk. $8.00 for the ride and an extra two for the trunk. He wasn't trying to cheat you, things up here just high."

"How come he let me talk him down to $6.50 then?"

"The depression," they all said practically in unison.

"It's that bad up here?" Sister asked. "We read about it, but wasn't no difference I could see back home."

"Well, let's just say we're lucky," Susie continued on alone. "Everybody we know's got a job. But the soup lines in Harlem are mighty long. There's plenty of grown men can't find no kind of job who used to working, and their women are out there doing day work for pennies trying to hold the family together. Lots of them that's working are getting half of what they usta get 'cause white folk ain't got no money to spend."

"Girl, if I'd have known all that I'd have given the man the $8.00"

Susie was right. The next morning Nurse Lee did have Richardson show her around. Richardson was siddity, just like Susie'd said, kept her nose in the air like she was always smelling something. Sister didn't much like her either but managed to get along with her anyway, just nodded and smiled while she continually emphasized the things aides couldn't do without a real nurse.

Things at Seaview suited Sister. Mostly she worked the early shift. The New York nurses with families asked for the overnight so they could be home when children came from school and give them their dinner and get them to bed. Each morning she got her list of assigned patients. After getting them washed and dressed it was her job to see they kept their schedule for the day. Wasn't no medicine for TB, just rest and sunshine till your X-rays cleared so patients stayed a good while, at least three months. Sister thought she'd especially like that 'cause she'd have to time to get to know them.

Her first day off she'd gone to the pictures with some of the other nurses. She felt guilty as the dickens about not spending this day with family, so made her way up to Aunt Sally's that second week. By that time her hair was a mess. She started to let Miss

Hattie, a woman in Staten Island who the other nurses used, to do it, but decided to wait. None of the nurses were as particular about their hair as Sister was. Aunt Sally kept her hair just so and Sister was sure her hairdresser would do her hair just like she wanted it. Two days before she left for Harlem she called the shoe shop where Sally's man, Louis, worked. She got the hairdresser's name and address from him and asked him to tell Aunt Sally she'd be stopping by Wednesday afternoon. She'd go to the hairdresser first 'cause usually they were less busy in the morning.

Early that morning Sister left Seaview. It was a long trip to Harlem, first a bus, then the ferry and a train. It was almost ten when she got to 135th Street. Miss Lula, the hairdresser, was just a three block walk from the train. Louis had given her good directions so she found the building easily. She didn't like Harlem any more than she did on her first visit with Mu. There were too many people, even more than before, too many men just hanging around idle like they had nothing to do. She was feeling like a stranger till she got to Miss Lula's apartment.

"You must be Sally's niece," Miss Lula said when she came to the door.

"How'd you know that?" Sister asked, "we don't look a thing alike."

"Sally stopped by this morning and told me you'd be coming. Described you to a tee. Girl, come on in here and sit down. I'll be with you in a few minutes, just got to put a few more curls in my customer's hair. Pauline this is Sally's niece, Evelyn."

"Pleased to meet you. Me and Sally have had us some good times together."

Miss Lula didn't have a shop but did hair in her kitchen like the women at home. She had put in a special shampoo sink and had a little gas burner for her hot comb and curling iron. Pauline was in the middle of telling Lula about some trouble she was having with family back home.

"I told them it didn't make no sense to come running to New York in the middle of a depression. He come telling me, weren't no jobs at home. 'Ain't no jobs here either,' I said. 'Least at home you got food and a roof, which is more than plenty got here right now.' Folks up here wish they had them a little piece of dirt so they could plant a garden. The only time I have some real good eating is when I go home."

"My Papa always says that," Sister added, "ain't no good eating in the city, according to him."

Instantly the three women started a lively conversation. It felt, almost, like being back home.

Looking like new money, Sister stepped out into the June sunshine. She walked to St. Nicholas Avenue and caught the bus. She peered out the window as she rode up to Sugar Hill. Everything was like she remembered from her trip four years ago with Mu. All the buildings were taller than at home, though the townhouses weren't as big as the others. All were connected to each other with no yards. At least when she passed 150th Street she saw more boxes with flowers in the windows. And some of the buildings had shrubs and roses growing in big cement boxes in the front. She got off the bus at 155th Street and walked down the hill one block to St. Nicholas Place.

Sister smelled the fried chicken soon as Sally opened the door. She hadn't changed a bit. There wasn't one wrinkle on her red-brown, high-cheekboned face. She didn't seem like she'd added one ounce of flesh to her large frame. She reached down and hugged Sister to her ample bosom.

"We'll catch up while we eat," Aunt Sally said ushering her into the kitchen. "I've been cooking all morning and am powerful hungry now." Looking her up and down she added, "You look like you enjoy a good meal too, you ain't no string bean." She dished up two heaping platefuls of chicken, hopping john, stewed okra and tomatoes and some sweet corn, which Sister carried to the table. Sally brought two large slabs of cornbread with butter dripping from the sides and a big pitcher of lemonade.

Of all her aunts Sister liked Sally best. She had more backbone. She was the only one who'd had the nerve to buck Papa's wishes and straighten Sister's hair that Easter.

"Sylvester," Sally told him when he came in from work, "I didn't see nothing wrong in straightening the child's hair like she wanted for Easter Sunday. Ain't nothing sinful or womanish in a girl her age caring about how she looks."

And she gave you a straight answer if you asked her a question, like the last time Sister visited. Sister had been surprised to find Ursula there. Ursula was her cousin who'd mysteriously moved away. Sister, like her other cousins, had thought Ursula was Grandma's child, just much younger than Grandma's other children. The cousins felt sorry for Ursula. She didn't get to go and do near as much as they did, what with Grandma being so strict. The cousins didn't see Ursula near as much as they saw each other. Then, close to adolescence, Ursula moved away. One Saturday morning Mama spent the hind part of the morning and most of the afternoon at Grandma's. When she came home, she told the family at dinner that Ursula had gone to stay with some kinfolk up North and said it in a way that the children knew not to ask any questions. Sister didn't see Ursula again till she and Mu came to visit Aunt Sally. She could tell by Mu's face she wasn't surprised to find Ursula there. Sister was dying to know what Ursula was doing there and waited till she and Aunt Sally were alone to say anything.

"Aunt Sally, why did Grandma send Ursula here to live with you?"

"Cause she's my child."

"I thought she was Grandma's."

"No, Mama was just keeping her for me till I got settled."

"It sure took a long time."

"What, honey?"

"To get settled. We were out of grade school before Ursula left."

Sally'd thrown her head back and laughed. "Everything don't happen quick, honey. I wasn't making much money, and since me and Ursula's daddy weren't married I had only myself to depend on."

Sister was dumbfounded. She didn't know what startled her most, Aunt Sally having a love child or the nerve to say it. Every Byrd female knew wasn't no sin greater than having a child out of wedlock. It was a miracle, Sister thought, that Grandma had kept Ursula. She had a high regard for Aunt Sally from that moment.

After stuffing themselves, Sister and Sally moved to the living room and were on their second glass of lemonade when Ursula came home from work. Ursula seemed even shyer now than she'd been as a child. On her last visit Ursula seemed to be coming out some, but now seemed almost completely hidden in Sally's shadow. She pulled in even further, if that was possible, about an hour later, when Louis came home.

Louis was a fine-looking sporting man. He and Sally were a matched set. He was about the same color as Papa but taller—maybe even six feet—medium build and muscular. Like most of the fellas Sister'd seen up in Harlem he was well groomed—creased pants, shined shoes, manicured nails. He asked Sally for a drink as soon as he got in. Louis had his bourbon and Sister had another quick glass of lemonade then headed back to Staten Island. She had the early shift again in the morning.

The next morning Sister added the ribbons and barrettes she'd bought at the dime store in Harlem to her tray and offered them to her women patients when she helped them fix their hair. She saved a special piece of ribbon for Mrs. Hopkins, who didn't seem to have anything nice. Sister believed that part of being a nurse was doing what she could to keep her patient's spirits high. She knew that living away so long from the people they loved had to make them lonely. Deep down everyone of them had to be scared. She did whatever she could to help them, was never too busy to answer their questions or take care of any reasonable request.

The first year at Seaview passed quickly. By winter, when the grounds were blanketed in a shrinelike whiteness, her ribbons and barrettes had made her a favorite with the women patients. On winter Sunday mornings, if she wasn't working, she'd sit on her bed and look at her pictures.

She'd been dying to have a camera since she worked at Peeks but had resisted the impulse since it seemed such an awful extravagance. Then one day—on the spur of the moment as she was walking from Miss Lula's apartment to catch the bus to Aunt Sally's—she went in the camera shop and paid down on one. She soon had a wonderful picture collection. She took her camera everywhere—up on the roof, where the patients went to catch the sun, to Miss Lula to photograph her customers followed by afternoons at St. Nicholas Place with Aunt Sally, and everywhere the Freedman girls went.

Coming up on her first anniversary at Seaview the Freedman girls got their invitations to their alma mater's 1931 Graduation Exercises. Soon as Sister read hers she made up her mind to go. She had the first shift the next day and handed nurse Lee her vacation letter when she got to work.

"I sure hope nobody else's asked for that week off. My old school's having their graduation that week and I sure want to be there."

Nurse Lee liked Sister. She was direct, told you what she wanted and why. "Nobody else's asked about vacation yet so there shouldn't be a problem."

Sister got her vacation and Stell and Susie found someone to cover their shifts so the three of them set out for D.C. just after three. It was a Friday late in May. They arrived too late to see Washington in its springtime glory but the last burst of pink and white blossoms perfumed the night air.

By the time they checked in, the hotel dining room had closed. Susie had planned for this. She'd packed an extra tin with late-night snacks. They were grateful for the food but turned in as soon as they finished.

They'd arranged to meet their friends at breakfast. Sybil and Jean were already in the dining room when they came down. Isabel, the last to join them, came a half hour later. Together they set out for graduation. Handkerchiefs dabbed at tears in the corners of their eyes as they walked around the reservoir on Freedman's campus trying to contain their feelings. Freedman had taken them away from their families into a bigger world and had been like a second home for them the three years they lived there.

Tears flowed freely as they watched the class of '31 march in. It had been two years since Sister walked down that aisle. Two good years, but she wasn't working as a registered nurse and seeing the new graduates made that painfully clear. How long would it take for them to be full nurses at Seaview? Someone here at the school must have some kind of clue, she thought. Dr. Long would be the best person to ask. He might not know himself but could get an answer and owed it to them to try. He was the one who convinced the others to go to Seaview. She made up her mind to seek him out before she left.

She saw him at the reception standing with two of the new graduates while she was in the buffet line. After she got her food she joined them offering her congratulations. The two girls soon sashayed off to other well-wishers.

Soon as they were out of earshot Sister said, "Dr. Long, are any hospitals hiring colored nurses?"

"Things aren't working out well for you there at Seaview?" he asked.

"No, things are just fine. I like the work there. I just don't like working as an aide. We got the same training as the New York girls who work as nurses for almost double the pay. It's just not fair."

"You always were one for fair play and never did have much patience," he chuckled. "This is not gonna last forever. Nurse Burse forgot to file some papers one year, that's how all this trouble started, but Nurse Stanley's in charge now and she'll straighten things out. Jobs are hard to come by now—give Seaview a little time."

Give Seaview a little time. Sister repeated this over and over to herself the next four years. It took that long to straighten things out. Time and again she had to remind herself that it was Dr. Long's work in heart surgery that had made her want to work in an operating room. He'd been her favorite teacher and she trusted his judgment. That trust didn't stop her from calling him twice every year to ask the same question, "How long would it be before Freedman got back it's accreditation?"

The beginning of the second year the waiting got easier when she started dating Eddie Varlack, Aunt Sally's boarder from the Caribbean. She hadn't liked him when they first met, seemed hinckty as the dickens to her then. But months later she changed her opinion of him when he drove out to Seaview with a friend who was visiting another nurse.

Sister'd noticed him standing outside the dormitory and, needing a little sport, had gone over to tease with him. One of the first things out of his mouth was how he couldn't see himself coming that far to visit a girl.

Coyly she smiled to him and asked, "You wouldn't come that far to visit me?"

He'd been coming every Sunday since, rain or shine, snow or sleet, he and Mr. Powell were the only two men to never miss a Sunday. Eddie Varlack had made Sister's waiting easier.

And it was worth the wait. Soon as she moved up to registered nurse she was assigned to the operating room. Dr. Long was like a proud father when she called to tell him, went on about how she was one of his favorite students. She wasn't sure she'd learned patience, but her time at Seaview taught her that things worth having were worth waiting for.

Cynthia Simmons *was born in New York City in 1950, raised in Atlanta, Georgia, and is now a playwright and actress. She is most known for her one-woman play* Sally of Monticello. *She currently lives in New York City and is working on a collection of short stories,* Granpa's Mama Usta Tie Him in the Yard.

OPPORTUNITY Magazine   June 1924

THE MIGRATION: A SOUTHERN VIEW

George J. Baldwin

(From an address delivered before the Atlanta Chamber of Commerce)

We have recently seen a considerable migration of our Negro citizens to other parts of the country, partly due to economic causes and partly to a condition of lawlessness which has led the Negroes to fear for the safety of their homes and lives.

I ask you whether we wish to encourage this migration until the last Negro leaves us, or shall we remove its causes and keep them with us? I unhesitatingly assert that the prosperity of Georgia depends upon our keeping the Negro here. Our only alternative is to let them go and replace them by immigration from Central and Eastern Europe, bringing with it the Bolshevist and the Anarchist into the purest Anglo-Saxon state in the Union, where ninety-seven percent of our white population is American born of unmixed parentage and American bred in American ideas.

The economic question will settle itself. We can afford to pay the Negro as good wages as any other section of the country, measured by the quality of the services he renders. When this is known and acted upon the economic question will settle itself. Many of the migrants are returning South, evidently having found out that this section offers them equal industrial opportunity.

The question of social equality long ago settled itself and the false hopes held out in other sections, having been found fallacious, are today not considered seriously by the better class of our Negroes.

The other principal cause of the migration is the Negroes' fear for the safety of their lives and property and the injustice often done them by our courts because their interests are not safeguarded by competent counsel, and it is to these two latter points that the Interracial Committee, composed of the leaders of both races in Georgia, is giving its attention. A fund has been raised which provides payment for good legal advice and help in the trial of any Negro in Georgia when it seems needed to secure that equal justice to which he is entitled. In addition, this committee is endeavoring by suitable publicity to bring about a public opinion in Georgia which will never again permit the execution of any man, white or black, save after due and fair trial in the courts we have set up to insure justice to every citizen. We need freedom from lynch law in Georgia.

The economic question will adjust itself, the social question is a dead issue, but that of equal justice and protection is a living one and when that is settled, there will no longer be a "Negro Question."

The Episcopal Bishop of Georgia is the president of our local committee in Savannah. We need the influence of the church, not any particular sect but of the church as a whole, not only on this question but for its influence on the family, for its help in building up an unselfish community spirit, thus aiding in what I believe to be the most needed and most materially profitable part of the work of our Chamber of Commerce—the building up of the spirit of the community. Once this is done, the material things will follow as naturally as the waters flow from our mountains to the sea.

Black vendors serve hot lunches to white construction workers who are building government offices, 1941. *(Photo by J. Collier) Courtesy of the Library of Congress*

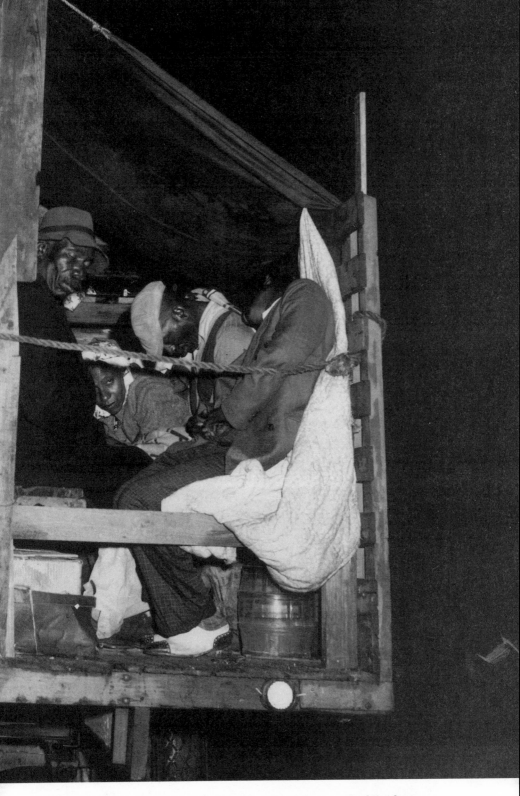

A woman on this truck developed pleurisy before they reached Bridgetown, New Jersey, in 1942. They started on the road in Florida and traveled three days and nights for eight dollars per person. *(Photo by J. Collier) Courtesy of the Library of Congress*

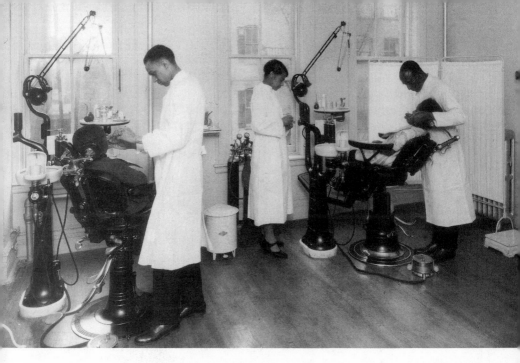

Black dentists and a female hygienist treat young patients in the New York Tuberculosis and Health Association, Inc., in 1926. *(Photo by A. Tennyson Beale) Courtesy of the Library of Congress*

The North did not offer prosperity for every migrant. This elder smokes a clay pipe at a poorhouse in Washington, D.C., in 1930. *Courtesy of the Library of Congress*

Cooking in a Missouri shack in 1938. *Courtesy of the Library of Congress*

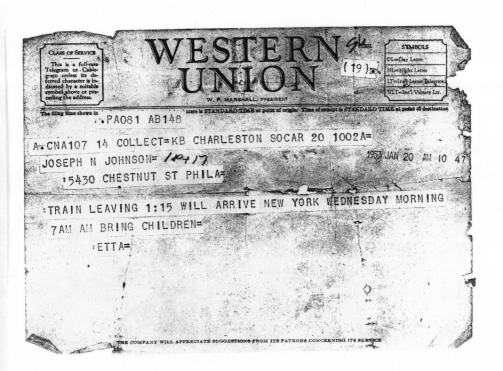

A member of Jacqueline Johnson's family sent this telegram announcing her arrival from Charleston, South Carolina, to join her family in Philadelphia in 1953.

A family headed North in 1940. *Courtesy of the Library of Congress*

Migrants on the road from Florida to New Jersey attend to car trouble near
Shawboro, North Carolina, in July 1940. *(Photo by Delano) Courtesy of the
Library of Congress*

The makeshift stairway of a rooming house in a Black Chicago neighborhood in 1941. *(Photo by Russell Lee) Farm Security Administration/Courtesy of the Library of Congress*

A family crowded into a living space in Chicago 1941. *(Photo by Russell Lee) Farm Security Administration/Courtesy of the Library of Congress*

Children of a family on relief learning music in Chicago in 1941. *(Photo by Russell Lee) Farm Security Administration/Courtesy of the Library of Congress*

A multiple-family dwelling rented to Blacks in Chicago, 1941 *(Photo by Russell Lee) Farm Security Administration/Courtesy of the Library of Congress*

In a storefront Baptist church in Chicago, 1941. *(Photo by Russell Lee) Farm Security Administration/Courtesy of the Library of Congress*

Easter Sunday in front of Pilgrim Baptist Church Chicago, 1941. *(Photo by Russell Lee) Farm Security Administration/Courtesy of the Library of Congress*

Easter Sunday. A northern Black man on his way to church service. (*Photo by Russell Lee*) *Farm Security Administration/Courtesy of the Library of Congress*

Chicago, Illinois, 1941. Black women took in laundry as one source of income so they could work at home.

The office of a Chicago insurance company that employed and insured Blacks, 1941. *Farm Security Administration/Courtesy of the Library of Congress*

Among the benefits of living in northern cities earlier in the century were moviehouses, nightclubs, music, theater—a taste of the good life—to balance out the hard work. 1941 *(Photo by Russell Lee) Farm Security Administration/Courtesy of the Library of Congress*

Black employees of the Works Progress Administration project in Chicago, 1941. *(Photo by Russell Lee) Farm Security Administration/Courtesy of the Library of Congress*

An independent Black business man and his candystand on Chicago's south side, 1941. *(Photo by Russell Lee) Farm Security Administration/Courtesy of the Library of Congress*

INVISIBLE MAN

"Chapter 8"

Ralph Ellison

It was a clean little room with a dark orange bedspread. The chair and dresser were maple and there was a Gideon Bible lying upon a small table. I dropped my bags and sat on the bed. From the street below came the sound of traffic, the larger sound of the subway, the smaller, more varied sounds of voices. Alone in the room, I could hardly believe that I was so far away from home, yet there was nothing familiar in my surroundings. Except the Bible; I picked it up and sat back on the bed, allowing its blood-red-edged pages to ripple beneath my thumb. I remembered how Dr. Bledsoe could quote from the Book during his speeches to the student body on Sunday nights. I turned to the book of Genesis, but could not read. I thought of home and the attempts my father had made to institute family prayer, the gathering around the stove at mealtime and kneeling with heads bowed over the seats of our chairs, and his voice quavering and full of church-house rhetoric and verbal humility. But this made me homesick and I put the Bible aside. This was New York. I had to get a job and earn money.

I took off my coat and hat and took my packet of letters and lay back upon the bed, drawing a feeling of importance from reading the important names. What was inside, and how could I open them undetected? They were tightly sealed. I had read that letters were sometimes steamed open, but I had no steam. I gave it up, I really didn't need to know their contents and it would not be honorable or safe to tamper with Dr. Bledsoe. I knew already that they concerned me and were addressed to some of the most important men in the whole country.

That was enough. I caught myself wishing for someone to show the letters to, someone who could give me a proper reflection of my importance. Finally, I went to the mirror and gave myself an admiring smile as I spread the letters upon the dresser like a hand of high trump cards.

Then I began to map my campaign for the next day. First, I would have a shower, then get breakfast. All this very early. I'd have to move fast. With important men like that you had to be on time. If you made an appointment with one of them, you couldn't bring them any slow c.p. (colored people's) time. Yes, and I would have to get a watch. I would do everything to schedule. I recalled the heavy gold chain that hung between Dr. Bledsoe's vest pockets and the air with which he snapped his watch open to consult the time, his lips pursed, chin pulled in so that it multiplied, his forehead wrinkled. Then he'd clear his throat and give a deeply intoned order, as though each syllable were pregnant with nuances of profoundly important meaning. I recalled my expulsion, feeling quick anger and attempting to suppress it immediately; but now I was not quite successful, my resentment stuck out at the edges, making me uncomfortable. Maybe it was best, I thought hastily. Maybe if it hadn't happened I would never have received an opportunity to meet such important men face to face. In my mind's eye I continued to see him gazing into his watch, but now he was joined by another figure; a younger figure, myself; become shrewd, suave and dressed not in somber garments (like his old-fashioned ones) but in a dapper suit of rich material, cut fashionably, like those of the men you saw in magazine ads, the junior executive types in *Esquire*. I imagined myself making a speech and caught in striking poses by flashing cameras, snapped at the end of some period of dazzling eloquence. A younger version of the doctor, less crude, indeed polished. I would hardly ever speak above a whisper and I would always be—yes, there was no other word, I would be *charming*. Like Ronald Colman. What a voice! Of course you couldn't speak that way in the South, the white folks wouldn't like it, and the Negroes would say that you were "putting on." But here in the North I would slough off my southern ways of speech. Indeed, I would have one way of speaking in the North and another in the South. Give them what they wanted down South, that was the way. If Dr. Bledsoe could do it, so could I. Before going to bed that night I wiped off my brief case with a clean towel and placed the letters carefully inside.

The next morning I took an early subway into the Wall Street district, selecting an address that carried me almost to the end of the island. It was dark with the tallness of the buildings and the narrow streets. Armored cars with alert guards went past as I looked for the number. The streets were full of hurrying people who walked as though they had been wound up and were directed by some unseen control. Many of the men carried dispatch cases and brief cases and I gripped mine with a sense of importance. And here and there I saw Negroes who hurried along with leather pouches strapped to their wrists. They reminded me fleetingly of prisoners carrying their leg irons as they escaped from a chain gang. Yet they seemed aware of some self-importance, and I wished to stop one and ask him why he was chained to his pouch. Maybe they got paid well for this, maybe they were chained to money. Perhaps the man with rundown heels ahead of me was chained to a million dollars!

I looked to see if there were policemen or detectives with drawn guns following, but there was no one. Or if so, they were hidden in the hurrying crowd. I wanted to follow one of the men to see where he was going. Why did they trust him with all that money? And what would happen if he should disappear with it? But of course no one would be that foolish. This was Wall Street. Perhaps it was guarded, as I had been told post offices were guarded, by men who looked down at you through peepholes in the ceiling and walls, watching you constantly, silently waiting for a wrong move. Perhaps even now an eye had picked me up and watched my every movement. Maybe the face of that clock set in the gray building across the street hid a pair of searching eyes. I hurried to my address and was challenged by the sheer height of the white stone with its sculptured bronze façade. Men and women hurried inside, and after staring for a moment I followed, taking the elevator and being pushed to the back of the car. It rose like a rocket, creating a sensation in my crotch as though an important part of myself had been left below in the lobby.

At the last stop I left the car and went down a stretch of marble hallway until I found the door marked with the trustee's name. But starting to enter I lost my nerve and backed away. I looked down the hall. It was empty. White folks were funny; Mr. Bates might not wish to see a Negro the first thing in the morning. I turned and walked down the hall and looked out of the window. I would wait awhile.

Below me lay South Ferry, and a ship and two barges were passing out into the river, and far out and to the right I could make out the Statue of Liberty, her torch almost lost in the fog. Back along the shore, gulls soared through the mist above the docks, and down, so far below that it made me dizzy, crowds were moving. I looked back to a ferry passing the Statue of Liberty now, its backwash a curving line upon the bay and three gulls swooping down behind it.

Behind me the elevator was letting off passengers, and I heard the cheery voices of women going chattering down the hall. Soon I would have to go in. My uncertainty grew. My appearance worried me. Mr. Bates might not like my suit, or the cut of my hair, and my chance of a job would be lost. I looked at his name typed neatly cross the envelope and wondered how he earned his money. He was a millionaire, I knew. Maybe he had always been; maybe he was born a millionaire. Never before had I been so curious about money as now that I believed I was surrounded by it. Perhaps I would get a job here and after a few years would be sent up and down the streets with millions strapped to my arms, a trusted messenger. Then I'd be sent South again to head the college—just as the mayor's cook had been made principal of the school after she'd become too lame to stand before her stove. Only I wouldn't stay North that long; they'd need me before that . . . But now for the interview.

Entering the office I found myself face to face with a young woman who looked up from her desk as I glanced swiftly over the large light room, over the comfortable chairs, the ceiling-high bookcases with gold and leather bindings, past a series of portraits and back again, to meet her questioning eyes. She was alone and I thought, Well, at least I'm not too early. . .

"Good morning," she said, betraying none of the antagonism I had expected.

"Good morning," I said, advancing. How should I begin?

"Yes?"

"Is this Mr. Bates' office?" I said.

"Why, yes, it is," she said. "Have you an appointment?"

"No, ma'm," I said, and quickly hated myself for saying "ma'm" to so young a white woman, and in the North too. I removed the letter from my brief case, but before I could explain, she said,

"May I see it, please?"

I hesitated. I did not wish to surrender the letter except to Mr. Bates, but there was a command in the extended hand, and I obeyed. I surrendered it, expecting her to open it, but instead, after looking at the envelope she rose and disappeared behind a paneled door without a word.

Back across the expanse of carpet to the door which I had entered I noticed several chairs but was undecided to go there. I stood, my hat in my hand, looking around me. One wall caught my eyes. It was hung with three portraits of dignified old gentlemen in winged collars who looked down from their frames with an assurance and arrogance that I had never seen in any except white men and a few bad, razor-scarred Negroes. Not even Dr. Bledsoe, who had but to look around him without speaking to set the teachers to trembling, had such assurance. So these were the kind of men who stood behind him. How did they fit in with the southern white folks, with the men who gave me my scholarship? I was still staring, caught in the spell of power and mystery, when the secretary returned.

She looked at me oddly and smiled, "I'm very sorry," she said, "but Mr. Bates is just too busy to see you this morning and asks that you leave your name and address. You'll hear from him by mail."

I stood silent with disappointment. "Write it, here," she said, giving me a card.

"I'm sorry," she said again as I scribbled my address and prepared to leave.

"I can be reached here at any time," I said.

"Very good," she said. "You should hear very soon."

She seemed very kind and interested, and I left in good spirits. My fears were groundless, there was nothing to it. This was New York.

I succeeded in reaching several trustees' secretaries during the days that followed, and all were friendly and encouraging. Some looked at me strangely, but I dismissed it since it didn't appear to be antagonism. Perhaps they're surprised to see someone like me with introductions to such important men, I thought. Well, there were unseen lines that ran from North to South, and Mr. Norton had called me his destiny . . . I swung my brief case with confidence.

With things going so well I distributed my letters in the mornings, and saw the city during the afternoons. Walking about the streets, sitting on subways beside whites, eating with them in the same cafeterias (although I avoided their tables) gave me the eerie, out-of-focus sensation of a dream. My clothes felt ill-fitting; and for all my letters to men of power, I was unsure of how I should act. For the first time, as I swung along the streets, I thought consciously of how I had conducted myself at home. I hadn't worried too much about whites as people. Some were friendly and some were not, and you tried not to offend either. But here they all seemed impersonal; and yet when most impersonal they startled me by being polite, by begging my pardon after brushing against me in a crowd. Still I felt that even when they were polite they hardly saw me, that they would have begged the pardon of Jack the Bear, never glancing his way if the bear happened to be walking along minding his business. It was confusing. I did not know if it was desirable or undesirable. . .

But my main concern was seeing the trustees and after more than a week of seeing the city and being vaguely encouraged by secretaries, I became impatient. I had distributed all but the letter to a Mr. Emerson, who I knew from the papers was away from the city. Several times I started down to see what had happened but changed my mind. I did not wish to seem too impatient. But time was becoming short. Unless I found work soon I would never earn enough to enter school by fall. I had already written home that I was working for a member of the trustee board, and the only letter I had received so far was one telling me how wonderful they thought it was and warning me against the ways of the *wicked* city. Now I couldn't write them for money without revealing that I had been lying about the job.

Finally I tried to reach the important men by telephone, only to receive polite refusals by their secretaries. But fortunately I still had the letter to Mr. Emerson. I decided to use it, but instead of handing it over to a secretary, I wrote a letter explaining that I had a message from Dr. Bledsoe and requesting an appointment. Maybe I've been wrong about the secretaries, I thought; maybe they destroyed the letters. I should have been more careful.

I thought of Mr. Norton. If only the last letter had been addressed to him. If only he lived in New York so that I could make a personal appeal! Somehow I felt closer to Mr. Norton, and felt that if he should see me, he would remember that it was I whom he connected so closely to his fate. Now it seemed ages ago and in a different season and a distant land. Actually, it was less than a month. I became energetic and wrote him a letter, expressing my belief that my future would be immeasurably different if only I could work for him; that he would be benefited as well as I. I was especially careful to allow some indication of my ability to come through the appeal. I spent several hours on the typing, destroying copy after copy until I had completed one that was immaculate, carefully phrased and most respectful. I hurried down and posted it before the final mail collection, suddenly seized with the dizzy conviction that it would bring results. I remained about the building for three days awaiting an answer. But the letter brought no reply. Nor, any more than a prayer unanswered by God, was it returned.

My doubts grew. Perhaps all was not well. I remained in my room all the next day. I grew conscious that I was afraid; more afraid here in my room than I had ever been in the South. And all the more, because here there was nothing concrete to lay it to. All the secretaries had been encouraging. In the evening I went out to a movie, a picture of frontier life with heroic Indian fighting and struggles against flood, storm and forest fire, with the out-numbered settlers winning each engagement; an epic of wagon trains rolling ever westward. I forgot myself (although there was no one like me taking part in the adventures) and left the dark room in a lighter mood. But that night I dreamed of my grandfather and awoke depressed. I walked out of the building with a queer feeling that I was playing a part in some scheme which I did not understand. Somehow I felt that Bledsoe and Norton were behind it, and all day I was inhibited in both speech and conduct, for fear that I might say or do something scandalous. But this was all fantastic, I told myself. I was being too impatient. I could wait for the trustees to make a move. Perhaps I was being subjected to a test of some kind. They hadn't told me the rules, I knew, but the feeling persisted. Perhaps my exile would end suddenly and I would be given a scholarship to return to the campus. But when? How long?

Something had to happen soon. I would have to find a job to tide me over. My money was almost gone and anything might happen. I had been so confident that I had failed to put aside the price of train fare home. I was miserable and I dared not talk to anyone about my problems; not even the officials at Men's House, for since they had learned that I was to be assigned to an important job, they treated me with a certain deference; therefore I was careful to hide my growing doubts. After all, I thought, I might have to ask for credit and I'll have to appear a good risk. No, the thing to do was to keep faith. I'd start out once more in the morning. Something was certain to happen tomorrow. And it did. I received a letter from Mr. Emerson.

Ralph Ellison, *born in Oklahoma City, Oklahoma, in 1914, attended the Tuskegee Institute from 1933 to 1936. He won the 1953 National Book Award for* Invisible Man. *His second book, a collection of short articles and essays,* Shadow and Act, *was published in 1964.*

THE ALLEY

Peggy Dye

They would catch me, I saw, half turning round to see my rear but still kicking my heels forward. "Nigger! nigger—catch a nigger by the toe, eeny meeny miney mo!" The one in the lead of the pack sneered at me, his black forelock whipping his pale forehead and horse face. In spite of my fear, I almost giggled. He was panting like a big old workhorse Uncle Evans kept in Michigan to teach kids and old ladies how to ride. "Nicaragua" was the horse's name. Evans said the animal had walked all the way from that country to Michigan and that was why he was always so wore out and wouldn't buck nothing no matter if you beat him with a broom or a flyswatter.

"He's just old, that all," my mother had said, "Don't mind Evans's tall tales."

"Where'd he get them?" I asked, wanting some of my own.

"I get them places nobody else goes." Evans overheard me.

"Huh?"

"Don't frown up so, Peggy Anne," said my mother. "It'll give you a prune face before you're 20. And don't think about going where Evans goes. Evans is a country negro."

Before I could ask what that was, Evans piped in, "I am a country Negro for sure. I don't have no time for these Evanston Negroes with they big cars and fancy lives. What I like is peace and quiet. The only place quiet here is the alley. Sugar, that's the place. I get my stories in the alley. Fine stories there. Everything happens worth seeing in the alley."

I smiled through my racing body. If I could make it to the alley the pack of Italians chasing me would get lost. It would be safe in the alley, I told myself.

My body speeded. It could outrun old workhorse white boys.

"You little brat. We'll get you. No business coming over our side of town. You want to play with white boys. We'll play you something!" The voices yelled. I heard five different ones. Ring leader was Maggio. He'd been gunning for me. All week. At that school.

My feet pounded on the cracks of the cracked sidewalks. We had just cleared Sherman Avenue and the black side of town lay ahead.

I was going to be safe. Five more blocks and I'd be at Dodge and Church and the alley leading to my house. Maybe Madelyn and Roland would be waiting there for me. It was Friday afternoon. They often waited then for the stories we could tell each other about the whole week.

"What's the white kids doing now, Peggy? Are they really nose pickers? Charlie Johnson says they eat buggers and that's why they faces so pasty."

"Roland you know Charlie gets that from his daddy. Charlie don't even know how to talk like that with words like 'buggers.' " said Madelyn. "Tell us, Peggy, what south Evanston is like. That's what we want to know. Is it got more ice cream places than we? Are they classrooms bigger? My mamma said yours says you have a library in that school that is as big as Foster School's auditorium and that you went home with a German girl for lunch. Is she looking like Hitler? Huh?"

"Marjorie Huber wasn't no Hitler German. She's too little. She's like us. She ain't never seen a colored girl before though," I said. "She asked to touch my skin. Wanted to know if the brown came off."

"She did?" Madelyn laughed. "Did you put some brown on her, too?" We laughed and then I told them that the white kids were all upset about me because I wasn't black enough for them. They thought Negroes should be cold-black and violent.

Now I glanced behind but didn't need to. The hot wind coming on my back was the breath of Jimmy. He was hardly three feet behind me now, and his face was beet red. He was kicking and trying to trip me. White boys were violent and thought we were, too.

I saw myself as a race horse the way Uncle Evans had taught me to pretend in the summer when we ran races in the Michigan fields, an hour's drive away. I spurted ahead and even whinnied a little.

"Get away from me!" I panted as I pumped on my eighteen-inch legs. "Please!" and I felt the tears in my eyes. I was running and trying so hard to not fight, choking down the anger. I was resisting. I felt a big pain in the stomach. Was it anger? It was a rock and it rolled inside my ribs and hurt as I breathed. I was carrying this. I had been carrying it three weeks. Against the questions of the white kids. It was three weeks into the school year and I had stood quietly—not cried or jumped up or fell over even once—at all the things the white kids had done these three weeks.

"It's a war, baby, a war, and don't you forget it. Don't you let them get you down. See, your daddy will go over there and whip anybody that bothers you. But don't you get yourself in the middle of no fights. Alright? The school will be looking for a way to say you're trouble. You're only one of a few of us there, remember that, OK? So don't you make trouble. Resist anything that tries to make you make trouble. Come on home and tell me. OK?" My father had made me swear I'd be patient and on my best behavior. No matter what.

And I had been. I'd listened to the white kids ask me if my skin hurt, and if I had a tail, and if the Negro part of me was stupid. "Sure it is," said David Ogelby, "but Peggy's white part is so smart it cancels it out." He nodded his red head and freckled nose up at me.

"You look like a red cocker spaniel my Aunt Izzy has. He has the same freckles." I had sniffed at him. His eyes bugged out and he said, "Are you picking on me? Hey David! She said something. Is she picking. . . ?" David Smart, his bigger buddy in second grade, stared at me. "You're more white than colored, my mother said. She saw you. And you know what? My dad's a plastic surgeon. Maybe we could get you an operation and get all the colored colored over, and then you'd be just like me."

I'd flinched at that. And then looked at my skin and the white kids. For three weeks I'd been learning—in these first weeks of school at first grade I'd been learning how to see myself in the eyes of these foreigners. My mother told me that at first. When I came home the first day and said, "Mother, the kids say there's something about me that's not as good as them. They say Negroes are not as good as white people."

My mother had looked at my father over the dinner table, and then before he stabbed his pork chop with his knife like he'd do he said when he was killing Japs in the jungles in the South Pacific— he just stuck that knife out and jammed it into the chop and made the plate go, 'ping, 'ping, and I jumped a little. My mother eyed my father and he didn't say anything but he stabbed that pork chop, and then my mother said, her face turning pale itself under the olive of her cheeks. "The kids are just ignorant foreigners, that's all, baby.

Some of them are immigrants. you know, Germans and Polish," she swallowed. "And they come from families that can hardly speak English. In this country, you do get people who are white and not of a good class who want to look down on Negroes. But don't you listen. Resist their comments."

"It hurts. I want to show them." I started to cry but swallowed down the rock.

"Yes, well you can. You just love them. Forgive them. And keep going. Look above them."

I nodded, practicing looking over the top of my mother's and then father's heads for the next day at school. At school, looking above the white kids worked for a half day the next day. Then I saw the eye of Bobby Perdue and he was studying me and mashing ants in the cracks of the sidewalk at recess at the same time, and the ants were black and big and juicy and he was screwing up his face and watching me. I squirmed. "Bobby Perdue! You are mean." I said.

"You're a 'fraidy cat." He giggled. He'd put my pigtail in the ink well already and winked at me. "I hate girls," he whispered in my ear. "But your hair is a good rope. I'm a pirate. Let's go in the alley and climb a fence." We were going to do it. Down in the white folks section of town. Behind Central School, where my parents had sent me, bussed me a whole hour, hadn't they, to get me to school? So I could get a "good" education.

Me and Bobby were going to go explore the alley down there at recess. And I was excited. "The alley is the best place." My Uncle Evans had said. "The whole world is there."

"It may be the safest place, he's right, in this world of war and crazy folks," my father had said. My father went up and down the alley to the store in our neighborhood, the same way me and Roland and Madelyn went. Said it reminded him of the South Pacific. "Jungles. Full of holes and ditches and little squirrels and the smell of garbage and flowers too, hedges in the back and you can go and not see anybody but a hound dog or you kids—you can go all over the world and see ahead of you without having to run into white folks—in the alley." My father had said. White people didn't use the alleys in Evanston the way my father and Evans and we kids did. "An endless road to adventure, these alleys go, where the Italians and the Poles and them crackers don't want us to go. It's another way to get somewhere, ain't it?" My father told my mother.

"It's dirty." My mother sniffed. "You just don't want to confront those crackers. We have to face them, Will. Peggy Anne is learning how. Learning their language. She's going to learn, get their education, and she'll have the chances we didn't."

"She don't need their education! I don't want her going cross town to that immigrants school, lying about our address and far from where it's safe. It's like being in Mississippi again down there with them Poles." My father had tapped his pipe on the ashtray. "I'll have to get my gun out and go down there like old Japan," he snorted. "Is a war, Alice, to send the baby to the school in South Evanston. We come all the way up here from Mississippi to get away from the fighting and the having to bow to those folks. Now, we got schools over here on this side of town. Why can't she go?"

" 'Cause she's got to learn to be for the best in herself. Like the white folks do. I want her to have everything they do. Not be like us—getting second best, and hand-me-down books. I want her to know their culture and be at home in it, so she can do everything they do, and better!"

So I was running now and praying to do it better than Maggio. Maggio had been gunning for me for a whole week when he found me and Bobby Perdue climbing a fence in the South Evanston that led to his aunt's pork store. Said we were trying to break in. And "that little nigger is going to get Bobby in trouble! You dumb Polack!" He had smacked Bobby in the face and Bobby cried and was afraid to tell his mother who worked in a factory and didn't come home till after 5. Bobby and me had tried to climb the fence after school to use up time. I didn't want to go straight back to my side of town. The bus took an hour and Bobby had nothing to do. I had told him the truth. I didn't live at the address I gave the school. To get in my parents had lied. He promised not to tell. I liked him for a boy. I watched him too. To see if he picked his nose. He didn't.

We'd gone half way up the fence when Maggio caught us.

After slapping Bobby, he tried to grab me, but I did a Jap maneuver My father had showed me. To duck and slide on my belly like a snake. "Them Japs are slick as snakes," he had showed me. And I got away. My father told me all the time about the war now. He'd been home and it was over. But there were still hard feelings about the war. "Only thing lower than a Negro in America now is a Jap," said Evans. "I don't know. This country is hateful place."

"It's white folks that's hateful." My mother said. "You have to resist their hate."

She was telling me to resist and telling me every day, and when Maggio tried to grab me and I slinked away, I resisted kicking him in the knee. I could have. I had on my Buster Brown shoes and I was in the right position to just knock him one. But I didn't. I was trying to act Christian like I was taught.

But it hurt me. I saw Maggio's face looking down at me and the red in his eyes and the fire and I knew he was pressing me into the dirt with his eye. And I couldn't see how to resist and feel good. My stomach hurt and a rock started to grow there. I felt littler and littler. As the days wore on. And that moment, I ran from Maggio, and he didn't chase me. He laughed, Bobby was sniveling and I ditched Bobby. "Scarey cat! Nigger!" Maggio had called. Maggio was big. Must have been fifth grade and lean like a big dirt-dobber insect. All legs and fast.

I ran now. He was almost on me. "Maggio, Maggio, leave me alone." I had tried so hard all week for the two weeks to avoid him and he had picked on me. Ever since.

Bobby had looked at me warily from then on, and then one day, David Ogleby spurted out. "I know you don't live around here. Bobby told us. You better get an operation and get white. You're so smart. We like you. You shouldn't be a Negro."

"I—I'm—a Negro and it's fine." I stuttered. First time I ever did stutter. And then, I saw Bobby's face and he was defeated, and for the first time, I was ashamed of who I was.

How could I tell Madelyn and Roland? What adventure was this? I'd gone to get a good education and lost Bobby. "You go to that school like we go down the alley and it's going to be an endless adventure. If you can go down the alley and to all the places we go, all the secret places," Roland had pointed at the latest undergrowth we'd found behind Old Man Granston's greens field. We'd found that under the clump of bushes he used for hedges to shade the end of the field in the hot part of the day was a tunnel, and it really was a water pipe—enormous enough to crawl into—and we'd climbed down and crawled, it felt like a block, before we hit a snake and got scared and scrambled back. "It wasn't nothing but a garter snake," Roland said as me and Madelyn hollered. But Uncle Evans had taught me, it was better to "not resist fate, if that was safer," as he said when we watched his rowboat float away from the dock in Michigan the summer when I was in kindergarten and he swum after it until he hit the deep water and he wasn't a strong swimmer, so he let her go. "It was it or me," he told Aunt Nora when she started to cry about the cost of the boat and how it was only a season old and oak and someone on the other side of the lake would get it and never return it. "I'm worth it, Nora, don't fret. You'd rather have me or a boat at the breakfast table, hmn?" All this was flowing in my mind, now as I kept running, and trying to make sense of how I had gotten into this predicament where I needed to be running. My feet seemed to pound out that going after the adventure got me into more trouble than I could escape. Maggio had legs twice as long as mine and every time he yelled "nigger" I felt my legs turn concrete, it was like being shot. Uncle Evans had once shot a man for calling him that, he said. But that's another story. I felt dirty not being able to do anything but run. Finally. The running had come at the end of the two weeks that seemed to drag us all at the school into a moment where I would have to be chased. Or the others would. Somebody was going to have to back down.

At first the white kids stopped talking to me in recess. And the bigger pack of Italians had started tripping me. I was scared.

Then today Maggio came after me.

I had tried to give him the slip and get on my bus after school and come home fast, and I actually managed a seat near the front. It was a public bus and you could sit anywhere, except kids usually sat with their parents in side seats. I took the seat by the door where the old ladies like to sit. But I didn't care. I just wanted to get where I'd be safe and seen.

Mr. Bundy was driving and he said, "You are in a hurry, aren't you?" And eyed me like I might have swiped something. I made a mental note that when I got bigger, I would never suspect kids of doing anything wrong. The way Mr. Bundy looked at me shrunk me a good inch, I felt so low. And yet, I held my ground. Maggio was a worse danger than an adult's opinion.

Just as the bus was pulling out of the stop in front of Central School, Maggio ran up with four of his gang, pounded on the door and Mr. Bundy opened it as the wind drained out of my lungs.

We rode in silence for the hour it takes to cross from the white immigrant section of the suburb where I was raised, Evanston, to the black part where I lived. I calculated as only someone under ten can do what tactics would work to escape the bully boys. In truth I didn't think so much as see. I saw my self duck off the bus like a butterfly, scarcely touching ground and flitting as if on wind the half block between the stop and Church and Dodge—heart of the black community—and the crooked, gravel path overhung with green vines and trees of the alley. If I could get to the alley, the white boys wouldn't dare come after me. White folks feared black folks' alleys. For good reason, since black people's dogs tended to hang out in the alley and without leashes. Black people in my home town, unlike white people, didn't leash their animals. And the dogs walked around and investigated life and came home for sleep. That's true even today in Harlem. Dogs will be going for a walk in Harlem all by themselves, and even the police don't stop them. Dogs obey the stop lights, don't soil the streets but know where the vacant lots are to do their business and everybody is happy. But a loose dog knowing the neighborhood people is one thing. Sort of like a guard dog. When a stranger comes, that dog will eat the bird alive, sometimes. Especially if the bird looks exotic and not like the folks the dog knows. A dog used to living around black folks will just go after a piece of the meat when it sees white flesh. And the alleys of Evanston were full, in the 1940s, of dogs from the black migrating folks new in Evanston and these animals were virgins in seeing a white face. So a lot of white folks got bit. They stayed out of black alleys.

So, when the bus stopped, I did fly off like a butterfly, as I saw myself. But Maggio and his gang were killer bees and they lit out as fast as me. I was whirring towards that alley. God! I just wanted to get there. The sun flickered down onto the canopy of green and you could see shade speckle the gravel path into the deeper road. I smiled at the sense of a curtain falling that would just cover my back as I slipped in. This was a stop on the railroad to freedom, it felt like. I had escaped the slave hunter and was about to go underground. I looked at my skin and olive as it was. I saw the blackness under the pale. The alley was my passage south, down to Mississippi and Georgia. I was running, running at seven, and it was Illinois but it was Mississippi too—my mother's home—and Maggio was calling me the name of the southland's saint: nigger! I was trying to resist Maggio, I kept trying to resist him getting me. I was almost there.

Then, I made it to the alley and breathed easier. Safe. I sprang ahead.

Turned to the side and had made half a block in before I realized that I was seeing Maggio, not slow down and back off, but following me fast. He wasn't giving up.

Sweat poured off me. I trembled yet with a coldness. The Italian was not giving up. I resisted and resisted and tried to keep him back and the nigger voice callings and I heard then they were going to catch me. My legs couldn't go the three more blocks home. I didn't have the heart anymore. I saw those white boys' faces and didn't have the heart. I was a block of shame. I could smell Maggio's breath—garlic and spices—behind me and I braced myself for the attack. They would beat me up and maybe worse. I felt myself want to start crying already. "Resist getting them too serious," my mother had said. "Resist."

I held on to the resistance and felt it slipping from me, scared, and slippery and sick to my stomach now. It looked like. Evans's boat, sliding away from the shore. I suddenly saw it in my mind's eye, all my efforts to not engage in the name-calling and the race-calling, and my running and my struggling to fit in. The boat they made was sliding away from me and leaving me in deeper water than I knew. And then, I felt myself in the deep and saw Maggio right on top of me. At the same minute I heard my Uncle Evans's voice, saying "me or it—that was the thing and I'm worth it, I kicked that water up and hightailed it back to shore. The boat ain't worth my life."

And I whirled, hearing the words, and raised my Buster Brown right shoe and kicked with all my might into Maggio. Something soft and boney, too, thunked into the shoe tip, and Maggio screamed, and I kicked again, this time higher, and he doubled up and started to fall over. The other boy's eyes widened like I had shot them and I kicked out with my Buster Browns and gave the Indian whoop like I saw in the Saturday movie at the Varsity Theater where my parents sent me every weekend so they could rest.

I screeched and danced my war dance, and while the boys looked scared I was screaming for bloody love. I was kicking finally, because all I had left was a desire to take care of myself. I'd lost being a good token, lost covering my feelings, all of that had failed.

I loved me.

I was no longer a nigger.

Peggy Dye *was born in Ft. Huachuca, Arizona, in 1943 and raised in Evanston, Illinois. She is a journalist and a community organizer. Her work has appeared in the* Village Voice, New York Newsday, The New York Times, *and* Essence *magazine, and it has earned her an award from the New York Foundation for the Arts in 1990. She lives in New York City.*

Birmingham *WEEKLY VOICE*   December 2, 1916

If the Negro feels that he can better himself in the steps he is taking, why should we not grasp him by the hands and bid him God-speed instead of prognosticating an ill will toward him? Is he not free to go where he will or may? Has not his freedom been dearly bought and paid for my many gallons of blood freely spilled in the strife of the Civil War? There are many Negroes who will do about as well away from the South as they do here, and there are many who won't do well any place; so take it all in all, it's just about as broad as it is wide, so you men who claim to be leading the race, look well into it and remember that cowardice among the Negroes must fade away and die, that we may stretch forth our hands and cry: "Ethiopis! from out of thy destiny came virility with which I and my people have gained the recognition well worthy of our being."

THE EXODUS TRAIN

Arna Bontemps and Jack Conroy

Two lanky Negro youths, their overalls powdered with the red dust of a Georgia road, paused at a street corner to listen to their friends and neighbors discussing Kaiser Bill, the Battle of the Marne, the boll weevil, "doodlum," and other matters interesting to a Saturday-afternoon street-corner crowd in a small town of the Georgia farming country.

"Why'n't y'all get outa this whole mess?" one of the youths inquired. "Go North where you can make big money and live like a man besides?"

"How you gonna go?" one of the elder share croppers inquired mockingly. "Ride shanks' mare?"

"Don't have to. Don't even have to ride a freight. A Chicago labor agent's gonna be in town today. Carry all the hands he can get up there free and on the cushions. Stockyards in Chicago's crying for fifty thousand men to take the place of them foreigners they used to hire. Listen to this, what I got out of a Chicago paper for colored folks called the *Defender*."

He fished a creased newspaper clipping from his pocket and began to read:

> *"Some are coming on the passenger,*
> *Some are coming on the freight,*
> *Others will be found walking,*
> *For none will have time to wait."*

A deputy pushed through the crowd and laid his hand on the boy's shoulder.

"Reckon you'd better come with me, son," he said. "The sheriff wants to see you."

"What for? Ain't done nothing but read a little old poem."

"That's just it! Got orders to arrest all you colored boys I catch reading poetry out of that Chicago *Defender*. Been a lot of that stuff read and it's raising hell all over the South. Hands leaving the plow right in the field and running away from their honest debts to traipse North. You'll likely be charged with 'inciting to riot in the city, county, and throughout the state of Georgia.' Yes sir, son, looks like you're bound for the prison farm."

The boll weevil, an insect migrant from Mexico, invaded Texas in 1892. Armed with its sharp proboscis for puncturing tender young cotton bolls, it ranged northward and eastward at a speed reaching one hundred and sixty miles annually, leaving behind it thousands of wilted and devastated cotton fields. In 1915 and 1916 the boll weevil was particularly destructive, while unprecedented storms and floods added to the desolation of Southern agriculture. The credit system enslaved the lord of the porticoed mansion as inexorably as it did the share cropper in his ramshackle cabin. The share cropper or field hand, living on a hand-to-mouth basis and depending on the credit which the landlord was no longer able to willing to give, could not afford to wait for better times. He had to do something and do it fast. Inevitably, the paralysis spread to the cities.

Consequently, World War I, which cut off the supply of European immigrant labor, was at first considered an indirect blessing by impoverished planters who could no longer command credit with which to operate. Northern factories needed laborers, and the Southern Negroes needed work.

The Nashville *Banner* expressed the opinion that the migration might serve . . . "to relieve the South of the entire burden and all the brunt of the race problem, and make room for and create greater inducements for white immigration that the South so much needs." The Vicksburg *Herald* concurred, and added: "Then, too, a more equitable distribution of the sons of Ham will teach the Caucasians of the Northern states that wherever there is a Negro infusion, there will be a race problem—a white man's burden—which they are destined to share."

But Southerners who had professed to see in the Negro a liability rather than an asset to the economy of the region, took alarm as the migration assumed tidal proportions. This movement was more or less leaderless, and spontaneous; there was no "Moses" comparable to "Pap" Singleton directing it. Nevertheless, as in Singleton's time, it looked as though nobody would be left to till the fields and do the hard work. The Birmingham *Age-Herald* pointed out that

It is not the riffraff of the race, the worthless Negroes, who are leaving in such large numbers. There are, to be sure, many poor Negroes among them who have little more than the clothes on their backs, but others have property and good positions which they are sacrificing in order to get away at the first opportunity. The entire Negro population of the South seems to be deeply affected. The fact that many Negroes who went North without sufficient funds and without clothing to keep them warm have suffered severely and have died in large numbers has not checked the tide leaving the South. It was expected that the Negroes would come back sorry that they ever left, but comparatively few have returned.

The fact that Southern planters and manufacturers sought to hamper the activities of labor agents sent South to recruit workers served only to convince the skeptical that there must be something to the reports of high wages and better living conditions. Clubs of migrants secured special rates from the railroads, or traveled free on passes supplied by agents. The Illinois Central Railroad alone is credited with having transported tens of thousands of colored plantation hands to Illinois, principally to Chicago. Chicago was known to all. It was the big town by the lake from which the mail-order catalogues came, and thus vaguely associated in the minds of hinterland folks with everything desirable but hitherto unattainable.

Securely established Negro citizens were perturbed by the avalanche of their rustic brethren whose manners and personal appearance were not always so prepossessing as they might be. Feet used to a plowed field found it hard to steady themselves on a lurching streetcar, so that migrants stepped on toes and jostled their fellow passengers. A great many of the new arrivals found employment at the stockyards and boarded public conveyances without changing from their malodorous work clothes. Others were still glowering with resentment over their treatment down South, and were inclined to vouchsafe their new freedom a bit too aggressively—a little beyond the limits of common courtesy. Unfortunately, the whites of the New Canaan were not without their prejudices, for the virus of racial hate has never been confined below Mason and Dixon's line. The awkwardness of the migrant—his unfamiliarity with city mores— was given all sorts of unfavorable interpretations. Some behavior traits common to certain individuals of all races often were indicated as manifestations peculiar to or inherent in the Negro character. For example, hostile white Chicagoans frequently complained that Negro factory hands always boarded elevated trains by way of the window. Impartial observers noted that fully as many whites as Negroes used this means of entrance when doors were congested.

The migrants kept coming to Chicago. The Chicago *Defender* received thousands of letters out of the Deep South, as did the Chicago Urban League, the organization to which the paper usually referred prospective migrants inquiring about employment.

The legend of the Great Northern Drive, as the reported mass movement was popularly called, spread rapidly months before the appointed date, May 15, 1917. The Birmingham staff correspondent noted on March 10:

> The Great Northern Drive spoken of by the Chicago *Defender* is taking place long before the time set by the paper. They are leaving here by the thousands. The Birmingham *Age-Herald* is trying to make light of so many leaving but they seem to have the *Defender* tonic in their system and are heading North.

A month earlier a Savannah correspondent had said:

> The word has been passed along from father to son, from mother to daughter, brother to brother and sister to sister, prepare for the day is coming. This spring a general movement will be started northward by millions of members of the Race from all over the South. It is expected before that time, however, that thousands will have left despite the fact that many educated men of the Race who have hid behind the cloak of schoolteachers and ministers of the gospel, aided by the publicity to their acts given them by the white press, have tried to scare them with the cold-weather gag. Not only this but some of the more trifling kind took advantage of free transportation given by railroads and other industries, went North without desiring to work, and found out that there was no white man in that section of the country who would give him money to tattle on Jim or John, has come back with some excuse. These fellows are "good niggers" and find their names in print the day following their arrival back home.

The exodus was helped along by such poems as William Crosse's "The Land of Hope," which appeared in the Chicago *Defender.*

> *I've watched the trains as they disappeared*
> *Behind the clouds of smoke,*
> *Carrying the crowds of working men*
> *To the land of hope,*
> *Working hard on southern soil,*
> *Someone softly spoke;*
> *"Toil and toil and toil and toil,*
> *And yet I'm always broke."*
>
> *On the farms I've labored hard,*
> *And never missed a day;*
> *With wife and children by my side*
> *We journeyed on our way.*
> *But now the year is passed and gone,*
> *And every penny spent,*
> *And all my little food supplies*
> *Were taken 'way for rent.*
>
> *Yes, we are going to the north!*
> *I don't care to what state,*
> *Just so I cross the Dixon Line,*
> *From this southern land of hate,*
> *Lynched and burned and shot and hung,*

And not a word is said.
No law whatever to protect—
It's just a "nigger" dead.
Go on, dear brother; you'll ne'er regret;
Just trust in God; pray for the best,
And at the end you're sure to find
"Happiness will be thine."

"Farewell—We're Good and Gone," "Bound for the Promised Land," and "Bound to the Land of Hope" were slogans often chalked on the sides of special trains carrying exodusters. In many instances local authorities tried to divert or halt the emigrants. The *Defender*, after reporting the addition in Memphis of two eighty-foot steel coaches to the Chicago train in order to accommodate exodusters, printed the text of a telegram just dispatched:

THIS IS TO NOTIFY BRAVE CHIEF OF POLICE PERRY THAT THE CHICAGO DEFENDER HAS MORE THAN 10,000 SUBSCRIBERS IN THE CITY OF MEMPHIS WHO GET THEIR PAPERS DIRECT THROUGH THE UNITED STATES MAIL, AND TO ACCOMPLISH HIS PURPOSE OF PREVENTING RACE MEN AND WOMEN FROM READING THE DEFENDER, WE WOULD SUGGEST THAT HE HAVE HIS ENTIRE POLICE FORCE ARREST EVERY MAIL CARRIER LEAVING THE MEMPHIS POST OFFICE ON THE MORNING OF JUNE 1, 1917.

Even those labor agents who had succeeded in getting their charges aboard an exodus train sometimes encountered the opposition of Southern industrial and agricultural interests as expressed through the law-enforcing agencies. The following letter from Brookhaven, Mississippi, indicates that such expedients were but puny obstacles to the mighty torrent of the Great Northern Drive. The will to quit the South was irresistible.

Following a continual exodus of members of the Race from this section of the country by labor agents, the police, spurred by the continual wail from the lumber mills of their losing all the help, arrested a white man by the name of Kelly on the arrival of a North-bound train. At the time of his arrest Kelly was in charge of two carloads of laborers on their way to Bloomington, Illinois. After the arrest of Kelly the police made the trainmen switch the two cars on a sidetrack and there the occupants spent the night. An account of the men in the coaches shows there were 125 in all. The word having passed around, some 100 more crowded the station seeking to go North. The police used more brutal force to disperse them. The sawmills, railroads, and other concerns are badly in need of laborers. Every member of the Race that can leave for the North has gone. One section gang left their tools on the spot, not stopping to get their pay. The treatment of the Race in general, coupled with the open way some of the women members of the Race live with white men and with no thought of marriage, the seducing of the daughter, the Jim Crowing and other cases including lynching, has set the members of the Race to a pitch of unrest, and nothing will be left undone until the Southern sections of the country have been cleared of every soul with a bit of black blood in their veins will remain in the South unless the whites put the Negro Race back on their statute book as a man with all the equality accorded to the law and constitution of the United States.

This letter came from Rome, Georgia:

I've just read your ad in the *Defender* on getting employment. So I will now ask you to do the best for me. Now Mr. ——— I am not a tramp by any means I am high class churchman and businessman. I am the Daddy of the Transfer Business in this city, and carried it for ten years. Seven years ago I sold out to a white concern. I prefer a job in a Retail Furniture store if I can be placed, I'll now name a few things that I can do. Viz. I can reparing and Finish furniture I am an expert packer and Crater of furniture I pack China cut glass and silver war. I can enamel grain and paint furniture, and repair violins guitar and mandolins, and I am a first class Umbrella-man. I can do anything that can be done to a Umbrella and parasol. I can manage a Transfer business. I know all about shipping H. H. Goods & Furniture, and can make out bills of Lading and Write Tags for the same.

If you can place me in any one of these trades it will be O.K.

The desire for better educational facilities, either for themselves or for their children, actuated the writers of many letters. One from West Palm Beach, Florida, read:

While reading the *Defender* I saw where you needed laborers in Chicago. I have children and I lost my wife a few years ago. I would like to properly educate them. I am a barber by trade, and have been barbering for twenty years. I have saved enough for our fare. If I could make more money in Chicago, I will come there where they can get a good education. I am a church man and don't drink whisky.

A resident of the same city wrote:

I saw your advertisement in the *Defender* for laborers. I am a young man and want to finish school. I want to look out for me a job working mornings or evenings. I would like to get a job in a private family so I could continue taking piano lessons. I can do everything around the house, but drive and can learn that quick. Send me the name of the best high school in Chicago. How is the Wendell Phillips College. I have finished grammar school. I can not come before the middle of June.

The letter came from Alexandria, Louisiana:

I am planning on leaving this place about May 11, for Chicago and wants to know everything about the town. My job for the past eight years was with the Armour Packing Co., of this place. I know all about the office and what goes on in a packing company. I am doing the smoking in this company now. I am thirty-six years old and have a wife and two children. I have been here all my life and would like to go somewhere I could educate my children so they could be of service to themselves when they gets older, and I can't do it here. I will pay you for your trouble if you can get me a job with any of the big packing companies there, if not I will accept any job you can get.

Professional and businessmen often followed or accompanied their departing clients. Many preachers led their entire flocks North and established their churches anew, usually in vacant storerooms. A *Defender* reporter interviewed Rev. R. H. Harmon, who had arrived with his wife and twenty-eight members of his congregation in a carload of exodusters from Harrisburg, Mississippi, and other Southern points. Rev. Harmon said:

I am working at my trade. I have saved enough to bring my wife and four children and some of my congregation. We are here for keeps. They say that we are fools to leave the warm country, and how our people are dying in the East. Well, I for one am glad that they had the privilege of dying a natural death there. That is much better than the rope and torch. I will take my chance with the Northern winter.

Most of the preachers toiled each weekday at some other job, putting aside their work clothes to occupy the pulpit on Sundays or for "prayer meetings" and other occasions, such as protracted "revival" services held nightly.

A great number of less daring preachers nevertheless were perturbed at the course of events. One of these wrote from Newborn, Alabama:

> We desire to know if you are in a position to put us in touch with a reliable firm or private family that desires to employ two young women; one is a schoolteacher in the public schools of this country and the other is a high school pupil. The teacher has a mother and sisters to care for and she is forced to seek employment, because wages are so low. The high school pupil is able to work in a private family. Wages are terrible here a grown man is forced to work for 50 cents a day. Sometimes he may earn 75 cents for all kinds of work. Here a man is only able to get a peck of meal and from three to four pounds of bacon a week, and he is treated as a slave. As leaders we are powerless for we dare not to resent such or even show disapproval. Only a few days ago over a 1,000 men and women left here for the North and the West. The white man says that we all can't go but he doesn't raise our pay. As a minister of the Methodist Episcopal Church I am on the verge of starvation simply because of the above conditions. I shall be glad to know if I could be of any real service to you as director of your society. Thanking you in advance for an early reply, and for any suggestions that you may have and be able to do for us.

From Greenville, Mississippi, came this letter:

> Please inform me as to whether there is employment for colored insurance agents by company as industrial writers, sick and accident and death in a company that handles colored agents, in Chicago or surburban towns. Please see whether the supt. of a company could use a live reliable agent. I am planning on moving to Illinois. This is confidential. I have been working for 15 years as agent in an insurance company.

There were similar appeals from barbers, automobile mechanics, schoolteachers, and others who had been left stranded by the exodus.

The *Defender* maintained its role as the friend and adviser of the exodusters after they had settled in the city. However, the columnist "Wise Old Owl" early in March 1917 saw fit to add a word or two of advice. After discussing desirable objects and outlining the civil rights to be demanded in the North, "Wise Old Owl" concluded:

> But it must be remembered that these rights are not to be abused and the rules governing them are the same for white and members of the Race alike. Be clean, ladies and gentlemen; water is cheap and deportment should be at a discount; avoid loud talking, and boisterous laughter on streetcars and in public places; keep away from the buffet flats like you duck a smallpox sign; help starve out the gypsy fortuneteller—they are conducting an illegal practice and there is a gang of them every day in the police courts for thieving; and don't show your ignorance by entrusting your money with anybody without a proper receipt for same, and then only with responsible people. In thinking all this over and while praising the Lord for your deliverance from the bloody zone in the South where the lynch-billies are supreme,

remember and deal only with your own race and shop where A MEMBER OF THE RACE IS EMPLOYED. If you do these things you will be doing yourself and your people an inestimable good and at the same time you will be pleasing the WISE OLD OWL as he deserves for the worrying he is doing about your welfare.

The *Defender* did not relax its vigilance. An item published a few weeks later struck a grim note:

The Chicago *Defender* wishes to impress firmly upon the minds of the newcomers to carry an identification card in their pockets all the time. If you are a newcomer and your family are still in the South, carry their name and address and your nearest relative's name on you at all times. In case of accident we may be able to notify them. Twenty deaths and accidents occurred last month and the bodies of these persons are still at the County Morgue, unidentified.

In May the paper found it necessary to repeat some of the advice offered by "Wise Old Owl."

Laboring men who have been placed at shops and factories are urged to appear on the streetcars and in public places in clean decent clothes. They can leave their working clothes where they work, and put on better ones when they leave. In the North a man is usually judged by the clothes he wears, how clean they are, and they have cars and elevated roads to keep themselves clean going to and from work. It is different here in the North. In the South they don't care how they dress; here they make it a practice to look as well in the week as they do on Sunday. We have seen a number of Southern women wearing boudoir caps. They don't seem to know when to wear them. Don't wear them on the street and on the cars. They are to be worn in the house with a kimono. . . . Also wear your kimonos in the house.

The *Defender* warned against "scheming preachers and labor agents getting rich off newcomers," the latter "charging them a dollar a month for the entire year." That fee, the paper said, was "outrageous," and asserted that "half of those sent do not know anything about the work or what they are going for, and consequently there is a breach between labor and the employer, who is dissatisfied with his new laborers and gets a grudge against all members of the Race." The *Defender* also condemned "scheming preachers through this section of the country and the East, who for fifty cents and a dollar find one a job. You go to the place and they want no labor, but your money is gone." Censure was directed at twenty men who had declined "to leave the 'bright lights' of the city and 'State Street' " to accept out-of-town jobs procured for them by the Urban League. Though it stoutly championed the cause of "the hard-working man, the steady fellow with a family, who has come North to be able to associate with the whites on an equal basis," the paper was not inclined to coddle idlers. In one issue it complained:

With conditions more promising than at any time in the history of the city, A *Defender* reporter found many loafers hanging around the poolrooms near Thirty-first and Thirty-fifth on State Street. When asked if they wanted work, they shook their heads in the negative. The bright lights are attracting them strongly. They care not how they live or where they stay. It is only a question of time before these people, poorly clad, without proper food, will succumb to the white plague. In addition to the foregoing there is another class that depends on gambling for a living, and they imbibe too freely of whisky. The police are gradually cleaning up this sort, and the judges are getting severe. This class we do not want here, and the better element of the city will do all they can to see that those who do not behave themselves will be handled by the proper authorities.

Though the *Defender* urged courtesy and respect for the rights of others, it did not advocate servility. Workingmen were admonished:

Quit calling the foreman "boss." Leave that word dropped in the Ohio River. Also captain, general, and major. We call people up here Mister This and Mister That. When your pay day comes, take it home. Depend on your work to keep you in a job and not the dollar or two you have been used to slipping the foreman. Cut that out. If you are working for $18 keep it.

Your employer pays the foreman much more than you, and if he has got to graft let him go to the employer. If you can't stay because you don't pay, quit and go somewhere else, or go in person to your employer and complain.

When you get among white workmen, treat them as you want them to treat you— AS A MAN—not as his inferior. Keep your hand off your hat when you pass men in and around the shop or plant. There is no law that requires you to tip your hat to a man because he is white.

The South sought to restrain the exodusters first by blandishments and minor concessions, and then, if necessary, by force. The perpetual debt under which most Southern Negroes (particularly those in the rural sections) struggled was a convenient weapon, as were unpaid fines for minor offenses. Moving to the North, perforce, was construed as evasion of such obligations and consequently a criminal offense. Even in the North, the refugees were not always safe, for Dixie employers and planters honing for the services of fleeing bondsmen were quick to take advantage of the extradition laws. The *Defender* reported a typical case:

Southern kidnapers made a bold and successful raid on Chicago citizenship Saturday when in broad daylight a sheriff from Mississippi went to the railroad yards at Eighteenth Street and with the help of Chicago police "captured" a man named James Halley, and in less than two hours had this man handcuffed and on a train bound for Holly Springs, Mississippi, to stand trial for selling a pint of whisky, made a penitentiary offense for the purpose of establishing a new form of slavery in the South and setting forth a complicated condition of affairs in the state which the Race has started to fight in order to protect its own citizens from illegal kidnaping.

Attorney Ferdinand L. Barnett interested himself in these kidnapings, ordinarily effected with the assistance of Chicago police. Another exoduster was saved from extradition on the charge of having "insulted a white woman in Memphis" when his wife summoned Barnett in time for the attorney to procure a writ of habeas corpus. The Southern officers prudently refrained from pressing their charges in court, and departed without their intended victim. One hard-working migrant was astonished when a detective from Atlanta approached him and informed him that he was wanted back home for "spitting on the sidewalk."

The *Defender* ran this notice:

ATTENTION NEWCOMERS

IF THE POLICE ATTEMPT TO MOLEST YOU AND YOU ARE NOT GUILTY, OR IF YOU GET IN TROUBLE, SEND FOR ONE OF THE FOLLOWING LAWYERS.

F. L. BARNETT—184 W. WASHINGTON STREET
ELLIS AND WESTBROOKE—300 SOUTH STATE STREET

Enterprising advertisers sometimes profited from the *Defender's* insistent warnings to gullible exodusters who might fall prey to city slickers. The State Theatre offered a motion picture entitled *Beware of Strangers,* exposing "methods of blackmailing and facts about clairvoyants," and "endorsed by the United States Department of Justice." Directed to the "Attention Newcomers from Southland," the advertisement read:

Little did Hinton Clabaugh think when he brought to justice a blackmailing syndicate preying on the unsuspecting public that he was laying the network of a moving picture. An eight-reel play exposing the organizations of crooks and showing how they operate. It is not the proper food for juvenile minds so children must stay at home. The subject is of paramount interest and is worth seeing. Selig made this a worth-while picture and not one of those fly-by-night things. Its moral is "beware of strangers."

No matter how suave, sweet, or smiling Mr. Stranger may be do not entrust in him either yourself or your money. If you do you are liable to get blackmailed or go to jail. This and the reason why are pointed out in this film. The cast includes Fritzi Brunette, Thomas Santschi, Jack Richardson, Bessie Eyeton.

Whatever might befall them, few of the exodusters even contemplated a return to the South. Sparrell Scott wrote for the *Defender:*

WHEN I RETURN TO THE SOUTHLAND IT WILL BE

When lions eat grass like oxen
And an angleworm swallows a whale,
And a terrapin knits a woolen sock,
And a hare is outrun by a snail.

When serpents walk like men,
And doodle-bugs leap like frogs,
When grasshoppers feed on hens,
And feathers grow on hogs.

When Tom cats swim in the air,
And elephants roost in the trees,

When insects in summer are rare,
And snuff can't make you sneeze.

When fish live on dry land,
When mules on velocipedes ride,
And foxes lay eggs in the sand
And women in dress take no pride.

When a German drinks no beer,
And girls deck in plumes for a dime,
When billy goats butt from the rear,
And treason is no longer a crime.

When the mockingbird brays like an ass,
And limburger smells like cologne,
When plowshares are made of glass,
And the hearts of true lovers are stone.

When ideas grow on trees,
And wool on cast-iron rams,
I then may return to the South,
But I'll travel then in a box.

Though they had been glad to escape from oppression, nostalgia for the more pleasant associations of the homeland assailed the exiles. Homesick for familiar speech, faces, and scenes, they banded themselves into social and fraternal clubs named for the states and localities from which they had emigrated. There were the Alabama Club, the Mississippi Club, the Vicksburg Club, the Louisiana Club, the Arkansas Club, et cetera.

An establishment on State Street bore the cumbersome but expressive name of the "Florida East Coast Shine Parlor," while the "Carolina Sea Island Candy Store" opened its doors for business on Wabash Avenue.

Store-front churches, too, helped in the readjustment process. These sprang to life in abandoned or condemned buildings formerly housing retail shops such as grocery and dry-goods stores. The established places of worship maintained their formalities of dress and conduct, but no such rules circumscribed the store-front congregation. The preacher usually worked somewhere during the day, and sometimes lived in the rear of the long room furnished with crude benches and a goods crate altar. Front windows were rudely painted in imitation of the stained-glass windows of more pretentious edifices.

But the most important thing about the storefront was that everybody participated. Untrained but powerful voices joined in hymns sung in such an unorthodox manner that they gave rise to a whole new body of gospel music. The preacher might be illiterate, but he spoke a homely, straight-from-the-shoulder language understood by all. The names of the store-front churches were as picturesque as their services—Willing Workers' Spiritualist, Israel of God, Canaan's Pilgrims, Spiritual Love Circle, Blessed St. Martin, Peter's Rock Baptist, Prophetic Spiritual, Purple Rose Mystical Temple, Crossroads to Happiness, Followers of Exodus, Church of Lost Souls.

A churchwoman who had heeded the call of the "Promised Land" sent back this report to her church sisters:

> My dear Sisters: I was agreeably surprised to hear from you and to hear from home. I am well and thankful to be in a city with no lynching and no beating. The weather was a great surprise to me. I got here just in time for one of the greatest revivals in the history of my life—over 500 joined the church. We had a holy-ghost shower. You know I like to run wild at the services—it snows here and even the churches are crowded and we had to stand up last night. The people are rushing here by the thousands, and I know that if you come here and rent a big house you can get all the roomers you want. I am not keeping house yet, I am living with my brother. I can get you a nice place to live until you get your own house. The houses are so pretty, we has a nice place. I am very busy I work in the Swift Packing Co., in the sausage department. My daughter and I work at the same place. We get $1.50 a day, and the hours are not so long, before you know it, it is time to go home. I am so thankful the Lord has been so good to me. Work is plenty here, and we don't loaf we are glad to work. Remember me to Mrs. C. and T. and tell all the children I am praying for them. Hurry up and come to Chicago it is wonderful. I hope I see your face before I die.
>
> Pray for me I am heaven bound. Let me know if you are coming soon as I will meet you at the railroad and bring you to my house, and what a good time we will have thanking God and going to church.

And enclosed was this special greeting and request:

> DEAR ———: How are you. I am fine the family is well to. I am working and have been since I left. I make $90 a month with ease. Hello to all the people of my home town. I am saving money, and have joined the K of P up here. Send me five gallons of country syrup. Love to all yours in Christ.

Arna Bontemps *was born in Alexandria, Louisiana, and grew up in California. An author, librarian, and educator, he won the Alexander Pushkin Award in 1926 for* Golgotha Is a Mountain *and the* Crisis *poetry prize a year later.*

from ONE-WAY TICKET

I am fed up
With Jim Crow laws
People who are cruel
And afraid,
Who lynch and run,
Who are scared of me

And me of them
I pick up my life
And take it away
On a one-way ticket—
Gone up North
Gone out West
Gone!

Langston Hughes

BIBLIOGRAPHY

James P. Comer, *Maggie's American Dream*. New York: New American Library, 1988.

Harold Cruse, *The Crisis of the Negro Intellectual* (1967). New York: Quill, 1984.

David R. Goldfield, *Black, White, and Southern*. Baton Rouge: Louisiana State University Press, 1990.

James R. Grossman, *Land of Hope: Chicago, Black Southerners, and the Great Migration*. Chicago: University of Chicago Press, 1989.

Herbert G. Gutman, *The Black Family in Slavery and Freedom, 1750–1925*. New York: Vintage, 1976.

Florette Henri, *Black Migration: Movement North 1900–1920*. New York: Anchor Press, 1975.

Leroi Jones, *Blues People*. New York: Quill, 1963.

Jacqueline Jones, *Labor of Love, Labor of Sorrow*. New York: Basic Books, 1985.

John Oliver Killens and Jerry W. Ward Jr., eds., *Black Southern Voices*. New York: Meridian, 1992.

Nicholas Lemann, *The Promised Land*. New York: Knopf, 1991.

Stanley Lieberson, *A Piece of the Pie: Blacks and White Immigrants Since 1880*. Berkeley: University of California Press, 1980.

Elmer P. Martin and Joanne Mitchell Martin, *The Black Extended Family*. Chicago: University of Chicago Press, 1978.

Benjamin Quarles, *The Negro in the Making of America*. New York: Collier, 1987.

Frank A. Ross and Louise V. Kennedy, *A Bibliography of Negro Migration*. New York: Columbia University Press, 1934.

Emmett J. Scott, *Negro Migration during the War* (1920). New York: Arno Press, 1969.

Donald P. Stone, *Fallen Prince: William James Edward, Black Education and the Quest for Afro-American Nationality*. Snow Hill, Alabama: Snow Hill Press, 1989.

Clifton Taulbert, *The Last Train North*. Tulsa, Oklahoma: Council Oaks Books, 1992.

About the Author

Malaika Adero *was born in Knoxville, Tennessee. She earned a B.A. from Clark College and M.L.S from Atlanta University. She received the Tony Godwin Award for Young Editors in 1988, while an editor at Simon and Schuster. Her writings have been published in* Essence *magazine and in* Black Southern Voices, *edited by John Oliver Killens and Jerry W. Ward, Jr.*